RENEWALS 458-4574
DATE DUE

GAYLORD			PRINTED IN U.S.A.

To Robert Davidson

Mary Garden

Michael T.R.B. Turnbull

AMADEUS PRESS
Reinhard G. Pauly, General Editor
Portland, Oregon

First published in North America in 1997 by
Amadeus Press (an imprint of Timber Press, Inc.)
The Haseltine Building
133 S.W. Second Avenue, Suite 450
Portland, Oregon 97204, U.S.A.

A catalog record for this book is available from the Library of Congress.

Publication was made possible by the generous financial support of the Scottish Arts Council, the Winston Churchill Memorial Trust and Shell UK Exploration and Production.

ISBN 1-57467-017-4

Typeset in Sabon by Raven Typesetters, Chester and printed in Great Britain.

Contents

List of Plates   vii

Foreword by Neville Garden   ix

Acknowledgements   xi

1   Discovery of a Talent: 1874–1896   1

2   Studying in Paris: 1896–1900   9

3   Debuts and Debussy: 1900–1903   24

4   Wider Horizons: 1903–1907   39

5   The Creation of a Legend: 1907–1908   55

6   *Salome* and Scandal: 1908–1910   66

7   *Salome* in Paris and On Tour in America:
1910–1911   79

8   Praise and Criticism: 1912   97

9   American Tours and War in Europe: 1913–1914   107

10 The War Years: 1915–1919   122

11 Directa: 1920–1922   140

12 Last Years with the Chicago Civic Opera Company:
1923–1931   157

13 Lectures, Master Classes and Hollywood:
    1931–1937   176

14 Retirement Years: 1937–1967   190

Postscript   202

Appendix 1   Debuts   204

Appendix 2   Discography by Jim McPherson and
             William R. Moran   206

Appendix 3   Stage Technique   214

Bibliography   226

Index of Names   229

List of Plates

In all cases photographs are reprinted by courtesy of the Royal College of Music, London, except where they are otherwise acknowledged.

between pages 116 and 117

1 Mary Garden as Louise in Charpentier's opera

2 Mary Garden as Diane in Gabriel Pierné's *La fille de Tabarin*

3 Mary Garden as Massenet's Manon

4 Mary Garden and André Messager

5 Mary Garden as Debussy's Mélisande

6 Mary Garden as Fiamette in Xavier Leroux's *La Reine Fiamette*

7 Mary Garden as Massenet's Chérubin

8 Mary Garden with Claude Debussy and other members of the cast of *Pélleas et Mélisande*

9 Mary Garden as Fanny Legrand in Massenet's *Sapho*

10 Mary Garden as Strauss' Salome in the Dance of the Seven Veils

11 Mary Garden as Strauss' Salome

12 Mary Garden as Massenet's Grisélidis

13 Mary Garden as Massenet's Grisélidis

14 Mary Garden as Thaïs and Hamilton Revelle as the Baptist in Samuel Goldwyn's 1918 film *Thaïs*

15 Mary Garden as Massenet's Manon

16   Mary Garden with the composer Franco Alfano at her villa in Beaulieu-sur-Mer

17   The Garden family (Monte Carlo Beach Hotel, 1930)

18   Mary Garden at her desk as Director of the Chicago Opera Company

19   Mary Garden on her lecture tour of America

20   Mary Garden in Aberdeen

Foreword
by Neville Garden

I was still a lad in short trousers when I first heard the name Mary Garden. My mother had been given an old 78 rpm record on which Garden was singing the 'Card Song' from Bizet's *Carmen* and a sentimental ballad called 'At Dawning'. Before putting the disc onto the turntable of our ancient wind-up gramophone, mother informed me that the opera star we were going to hear was a relative. 'Your grandfather's cousin – I think,' she added vaguely.

Ten minutes later I had listened to both sides of the record and wasn't terribly impressed. The voice that emerged dimly from the sound-box didn't strike me as very interesting. But it must have had something because a few days later I returned to the record and played it again – not once but many times. Today it occupies a place of honour in my record collection.

Far from being uninteresting, Garden's voice had an understated, almost smouldering, passion which bespoke a complete understanding of the music, notably in the *Carmen* excerpt. No operatic histrionics here, simply a woman who can see her death approaching and knows she can do nothing about it. At a first hearing, I had considered the performance dull. It was an important lesson to learn and to remember when many years later I was to become a music critic.

Not much of value has been written about Mary Garden which is why this volume, carefully and lovingly researched, is so important. Once, years ago, I was invited by a publisher to write a biography of the woman who was arguably Scotland's most impressive opera singer, but the request came during a period when it was impossible for me to devote time to the project. I regret I never found that time; but Michael Turnbull has done so and his efforts make absorbing reading. He writes with warmth and admiration, but he doesn't whitewash the lady. Mary Garden was, in many ways, a selfish woman who knew exactly what she wanted and was prepared to go to almost any lengths to get it. She had, in the old Scots phrase, 'a guid conceit o' herself'. When she left the operatic stage she said flatly. 'I began at the top, I stayed at the top and I left at the top'. It was a typically arrogant statement. It was also true.

The young Scots girl who took over in mid-performance the title role of Charpentier's *Louise* in Paris, went on to star in countless productions both in France and in the United States. Her farewell appearance saw her still heading the bill.

Some of the mysteries that surround Mary Garden will never be resolved. Her relationship with the great composer Claude Debussy, for example, which, I suspect, will always remain slightly ambiguous. She always denied any kind of romantic or physical attachment to him and no evidence to the contrary has ever been found. Yet, somehow, it would not surprise us to learn that they were lovers.

What this book does, is to give a clearly told and fascinating picture of a great singer whose name is better known abroad than in her native land – a woman as unafraid of expressing a personal opinion as of walking on stage to perform a great operatic role. Once, when asked what she thought of the controversial soprano Maria Callas, Garden sniffed derisively: 'Fine actress,' she said, 'but not much of a voice!' The irony that something similar was often said about her appears to have escaped Garden completely.

I have never been remotely bothered about genealogy so, to this day, I have not found out my exact relationship to Mary Garden. To many, such a lack of curiosity will seem baffling. But I have always been proud to be part of her ancestral line. This book has made me even prouder.

Neville Garden
1996

Acknowledgements

As with my previous opera biography (*Joseph Hislop; Gran Tenore*), it was Neville Garden, journalist, broadcaster and conductor, who gave me the inspiration to write this book. Its execution was only made possible by the support of the Winston Churchill Memorial Trust, the Scottish Arts Council and Shell UK Exploration and Production.

Individuals

Bill Ashbrook; the late Harold Barnes; M. Thierry Bodin; M. Henri Bondi; Mme Robert Bourréli; Mme Anne Bessand-Massenet; Mr and Mrs Graham Bower; Bill Browning; George F. Burr; M. André Cane; the late Claudia Cassidy; Margaret G. Cobb; Dr Oliver Davies; M. Marc Doin; Neville Garden; the late Patrick Gillis; Mario Goetschel; Christian Goubault; David Grayson; Steven Heubner; Helen Hodge; Mme M. Honegger; the late Professor Demar Irvine; Mrs A. H. Julian; Tom Kaufman; Robert Long; Larry Lustig; David McKail; M. Le Maire de Peille; Professor David Mayer; Bob Monahan; Kutz Myers; Professor Thomas G. Neumiller; the late Mrs Mildred Park; Edward Hagelin Pearson; John Pennino; Susan Rutherford; Richard Schwegel; Margery Mackay Shapiro; Charles Silver; Madeau Stewart; Blanche Thebom; Robert Wallenborn; Mme Nicole Wild.

Institutions

Belgium:	Archives de la ville de Bruxelles; Bibliothèque Royale Albert 1er.
Canada:	National Library of Canada; Ottawa Public Library; Metropolitan Toronto Reference Library.
England:	Oxfordshire County Archives; Royal College of Music;

	Archives, Royal Opera House, Covent Garden; Royal Archives, Windsor Castle.
France:	Opéra du Rhin; Conservatoire de Paris; Opéra de Paris; Bibliothèque de Cessole; Archives des Alpes-Maritimes; Archives de la Savoie; Casino Grand Cercle, Aix-les-Bains; Archives Municipales, Aix-les-Bains; Les Archives de France; Bibliothèque Nationale; Bibliothèque et Musée de l'Opéra.
Germany:	Theaterwissenschaftliche Sammlung, Universität zu Köln; Oper der Stadt Köln.
Monte Carlo:	Opéra de Monte-Carlo; Archives du Palais de Monaco.
Scotland:	National Library of Scotland; City of Aberdeen Library Services; St Margaret's School, Aberdeen.
Switzerland:	Archives d'État; Archives, Ville de Genève.
USA:	Boston Public Library; Chicago Historical Society; Chicago Public Library; Cincinnati Historical Society; Cleveland Public Library; Dartmouth College Library, Hanover, NH; Department of Film, Museum of Modern Art, New York; District of Columbia Public Library; El Paso Public Library; The Daily Oklahoman Library; Denver Public Library; Enoch Pratt Free Library, Baltimore; Frank H. McClung Museum, University of Tennessee; Free Library of Philadelphia; Hewes Library, Monmouth College; Indianapolis-Marion County Public Library; Kemp Public Library, Wichita Falls; Library of Congress; Los Angeles Public Library; Loyola University, Chicago; Lyric Opera of Chicago; Metropolitan Opera Association; Mississippi Department of Archives and History; Multnomah County Library; New York Library for the Performing Arts; Newberry Library, Chicago; Oakland Public Library; Public Library of Cincinnati & Hamilton County; Public Library of Des Moines; Rochester Public Library; Roosevelt University Library, Chicago; Salt Lake City Library; San Francisco History Room; Tutwiler Collection, Birmingham Public Library; UCLA Film and Television Archive; University of Oklahoma Library; USC Cinema-Television Library; Wisconsin Center for Film and Theater Research; Yale University.

1   Discovery of a Talent: 1874–1896

Mary Garden, 'Molly' to her family, was born in Aberdeen, on the north-east coast of Scotland, at half-past ten on the morning of 20 February 1874. The first of four daughters born to Robert Davidson Garden and Mary Joss, she arrived just over a month after her parents had married – a fact which might help to explain Mary's later revision of her birth-year to 1877. Mary's father was a 23-year-old cashier at the Blaikie iron works in Littlejohn Street; her mother, fully six years younger, was the daughter of the quarry-manager at Bucksburn, to the north-west of Aberdeen.

Aberdeen, the 'Granite City', was a thriving sea-port, whipped by the cold east winds, salty with the smell of newly landed fish. The Garden home was 35 Charlotte Street, long since demolished. Although the family soon moved into 41 Dee Street, young Mary's life at home was relatively modest, even cramped. Her sister Amy had been born in 1875, only a year after Mary's birth, and a third daughter, Agnes, arrived two years later.

In Mary Garden's autobiography, *Mary Garden's Story*[1] co-written in 1951 with the American music journalist, Louis Biancolli, she tells of spending part of her childhood at her grandfather's elegant estate not far from Aberdeen and graced by peacocks and horses. However, the real childhood of Mary Garden was much more down-to-earth. The country mansion she speaks of, with its 1000-acre estate, was Pitmurchie House, near Torphins, south-west of the city. It belonged not to her grandfather but to a wealthy granite merchant, James Anderson Bower, whose son George married Mary's sister Amy after he had left the army in 1918 suffering from shell-shock. Mary's distortion of the facts stemmed from an innate tendency to exaggerate which, in combination with her failure to keep accurate records, her later highly developed skill in managing the media, and the onset of senile dementia around 1945, led to the confusion or transposition of dates, events, feelings and even people.

Mary made her first appearance in public as a singer at the tender age of

1

five. Standing shyly before her grandmother's friends, she piped 'Three little redcaps growing in the corn'. Her introduction to the world of professional song, however, would not come until some years later, when she was taken to see the great French soprano, Marie Roze, at the Music Hall in Aberdeen. The striking Parisian artiste, with her formidable aria, 'Ocean, Thou mighty monster' from Weber's *Oberon*, awakened in the small, auburn-haired girl in the audience an indefinable longing, as if for an undreamed-of previous existence.

Another strong early memory – and, inevitably, a traumatic one – dates from the day a dog leapt up and bit her below her chin. Many years later, Mary could picture herself quite vividly – a small girl in a white silk dress, stained horrifically with blood, walking downstairs towards her father's dumbstruck friends. It was, in her recollection, a scene of Freudian drama and was an early revelation to Mary Garden of her ability to shock and the accompanying frisson of power.

Piecing together Mary Garden's early days is a difficult task: Mary claimed that she never kept a scrapbook, a single clipping of herself, nor a photograph: 'I'll read a clipping about myself and then toss it away. The same goes for letters. And what is deader than a letter that has been saved for some time and then re-read? Not me. I throw them away as soon as I read them and forget them'.[2] And, in an article written for *The Ladies Home Journal* in 1930, she asserted that 'I never kept a criticism. I own no scrapbooks because I have always disregarded what people have said of me'.[3]

Like many of her claims, this is a deviation from the truth. She did keep clippings and scrapbooks, as the Mary Garden archive at London's Royal College of Music testifies. She collected photographs of herself in great number but captioned them carelessly and only sporadically in her extravagant scrawl. She kept virtually no newspaper reviews, letters or programmes. What she did keep, she did not date, with the result that such scrapbooks as she had are confusing and reveal virtually nothing about the chronology of her career.

An additional difficulty in establishing the facts is that the early signs of senile dementia are detectable in her autobiography, begun around 1947 and subsequently rejected by her publisher; and even more so in the final 1951 Biancolli version. Both books are characterized by *confabulation* – the invention of stories to fill the gaps in memory. 'The trouble was', said her solicitor, Graham Collie, many years later, 'that she didn't know herself if she was telling the truth or not. There are people like that. She was a vicious liar but she just didn't know herself what was true or not.'[4] Other typical dementia symptoms were also to be detected in her public appearances in later years – confusion over days and dates, sudden emotional outbursts, embarrassing behaviour, failure in judgement, unexpected accusations and a shallow indifference to all feelings (most of them amusingly recognizable in Madeau Stewart's 1961 interview for BBC Radio).

*   *   *

As the Garden family grew, so Robert Garden's meagre earnings proved less able to meet their needs. His eyes, like those of many Scots before him, were drawn inexorably across the Atlantic to the land of opportunity – America. So it was that in 1880 he set off ahead of his family to look for work in the New World. Three years later, the family followed, sailing from Glasgow and landing in New York after a rough crossing. Mrs Garden had been ill for most of the 12-day voyage, leaving her children free to explore the *Anchoria*, a ship bigger than any they had ever seen.

Their first American home was President Street in Brooklyn. But, in spite of the excitement of life abroad, Mrs Garden could not stifle her homesickness and wept for Scotland as she performed her daily chores. The three Garden girls were sent to the local school: 'We were very shy,' recalls Mary in the first draft of her unpublished autobiography, 'and spoke with a Scottish brogue that made us difficult to be understood. The children of the school used to make a circle around us as if we were odd little animals, asking us to say something.'

The Gardens soon moved north to Chicopee in Massachusetts where a fourth sister, Helen (later to frenchify herself as 'Hélène'), was born. Chicopee offered boundless country recreation – skating, tobogganing, cycling and early morning hunts for mushrooms.

Though an average girl in many respects, Mary did not care much for dolls, except paper ones – and these had short lives, for she devised plays of such tragic violence (using both hands to make them dance), that often a single scene was enough to see them end in bits on the floor. She loved organizing her sisters and friends into dramatic tableaux but, forgetting that pictures are meant to be silent, she would suddenly improvise a monologue – sometimes fantasies about her children who had perished in a flood or about the laird of the castle who had failed to rescue her from a dungeon. Invariably it would be something with a dramatic climax that required her to faint.

Her histrionic talent Mary attributed partly to her personality: 'Such screams! I translated everything about me into terms of drama'.[5] But her grandmother, Mary believed, had also been a powerful influence: 'One of the last memories I have of her is reciting Robert Burns in a masterly way when she was eighty. Whole pages of it. She could put what the French call *du style* in delivery with as much manner and flair as any great actress.'[6]

Music, however, still played an important part in Mary's life. Mrs Murkland, who lived next door in Chicopee and was the local minister's wife, gave her singing-lessons: thus Mary was to make her American debut at the local church festival, with Claribel's 'Five o'clock in the morning'. She also took up the violin and had lessons from a retired musician in Springfield. On 11 June 1886 she gave her first performance before an audience of the general public at the Chicopee Town Hall. Fetchingly, she sang a character song, 'Little old woman', and played violin selections from *The Bohemian Girl*.[7]

In 1889 the family returned to Aberdeen for a year where Mary and her sisters were sent to St Margaret's School for Girls. There was an international flavour to the curriculum: one of the two sisters who owned the school, Miss Jean Duncan, had studied music in Germany; reflecting the traditional 'auld alliance' between Scotland and France, it was mandatory for the pupils to speak French much of the time.

It was on this same trip to Scotland, when she had just turned 15, that Mary had her first experience of youthful infatuation, albeit completely unrequited. Her piano teacher, Walter Smith, RAM, was a noted organist. To Mary, Smith was a magnificent Scot, with a shock of red hair, icily correct in his relations with his pupils but she, for one, adored him.[8] He made a great impression on Mary: 'My career was all marked out for me then,' she recalled. 'I was to become a famous pianist. For in some way the music which filled me to the finger-tips had to find expression, but nobody had realised even then that its very soul lay imprisoned in my throat.'

Back in America, the Garden family moved again, this time to Chicago, to the Hyde Park area where many Scots had already settled. Mary's father was now on the payroll of George Pope, a manufacturer of bicycles and, in later years, cars; he even featured on one of Pope's advertisements in 1889, riding high in his breeches on the Columbia Light Roadster Safety, a tiny cap perched on his head.

One evening, her father took her to the theatre to see Clara Morris, an actress noted for her emotional delivery. The play was the French potboiler, *Article 47*. Caught up in the whirlwind of Miss Morris's dramatic intensity, her eyes glued to the stage, Mary realized for the first time the power that acting might offer. A fever consumed her: 'Deathly ill from excitement,' she remembered, 'I ate no dinner.' All night long she lay awake, her imagination reeling.[9]

There followed more concerts in which Mary performed, and then came her first light operatic role. This was with a church musical club at Rosalie Hall in Hyde Park, Chicago, where, in Gilbert and Sullivan's *Trial by Jury*, she took the leading role of Angelina. Once on stage her excitement was evident for all to see: 'I had a new costume and I was proud of it. I pranced across the stage and back again, stopping to take a squint through the peep-hole now and then to size up the crowd'. The audience proved to be 700-strong and the production raised a considerable sum. It was this appearance, albeit relatively insignificant, that confirmed Mary's interest in pursuing a theatrical career.

One evening her father's employer, Colonel Pope, came to dine at the Garden home and, after dinner, Mary was persuaded to sing for him. Impressed, the Colonel suggested she take lessons with Mrs Robinson-Duff, a former student of Mathilde Marchesi in Paris. Mrs Duff had just returned to Chicago after studying in Europe and was looking for students.

'The vision of that attractive little girl, with her gown above her shoe-tops', wrote Mrs Duff later,

> and her hair in braids down her back, will remain indelible in my memory. She entered the room with the composure of a woman of the world, and yet with modesty, and a complete lack of all self-consciousness.
>
> After a few moments' conversation, I asked her if she would sing for me and if she could accompany herself, or if she would prefer I play for her.
>
> She immediately seated herself at the piano, played her own accompaniment, and in a delightful manner, sang for me Meyer-Helmund's 'Margherita' followed by 'Annie Laurie'.
>
> Her voice at that time was small but very lovely and pure in quality. It is no exaggeration to say that she sang then with the same astounding musical understanding and remarkable phrasing which has colored her entire career.[10]

Mary duly enrolled herself as a pupil. 'She began to study with me,' recalled Mrs Duff, 'and was, in fact, my first pupil.' Mrs Duff had a manner that was wonderfully French, with her noble profile and elegant clothes. Among her other early pupils were Grace Van Studdiford, Marcia Van Dresser and Fanchon Thompson, all of whom were to become well-known on the light-opera stage.

Mary worked very hard, and learned all her exercises off by heart. 'This keen attention to her work has been the keynote of her success,' commented Mrs Duff. 'After several years with me I realised that for her artistic development and the acquisition of foreign languages, Chicago was no longer the desired field. Her voice had developed tremendously and all the difficulties of execution seemed eliminated. Paris was decided upon as the most desirable place for work'.[11]

During an end-of-season concert given by Mrs Duff's pupils at the Central Music Hall on 28 October 1891, Mary insisted on singing 'Bel raggio lusinghier' from Rossini's *Semiramide* (not in fact 'Una voce poco fà', as given in her autobiography). She adored singing trills: 'I was a coloratura in my youth. I must confess a then deadly interest in the "Caro nome" and the big aria from Ambroise Thomas' *Hamlet*.' Her performance was well received: 'One of the most brilliant successes of the evening,' wrote the *Inter-Ocean* critic, 'was Miss Garden's singing a very difficult and exacting aria not often attempted by so young a vocalist and rarely better executed than by Miss Garden.'

And there were other successes. The former theatre manager, William

Davis, (husband of the American singer, Jessie Bartlett Davis), recalled that Mrs Duff's pupils would often go to his Columbia Theater to attend a performance, or to the Haymarket Theater which he also managed, where he would arrange an impromptu concert after the play or opera. The accompanist was Mrs Nellie Skelton. Between two classic numbers they would perform a bit of ragtime or old-fashioned comedy. Mary Garden, in particular, liked the old-fashioned songs. One night, following a dinner at the Union League club, there was one such concert. Mary Garden stepped forward to sing 'My old Dutch'. 'I had heard her sing many times,' said Davis,

> but never had I seen her get so much out of a song. She was always gentle, modest and sweet... There was never any suggestion of forwardness about her, despite her magnetic personality.
> 'Mary,' I said, 'you've got a great future in vaudeville. If you just put on a coster suit and sing like that, you'll win the audience right from the start!'[12]

* * *

In 1892 the Garden family spent the summer at Pine Lake, Indiana. The family album shows the Garden girls wading knee-deep in the water or drifting with friends in a sailing-boat. These were happy and optimistic days in a new country whose natural riches seemed never-endingly abundant. Always there was the sound of laughter and high spirits.

Early in 1893, Mary was auditioned by the music committee of the Carleton Club for a part in *The Doctor of Alcantara*, an operetta by the American composer Julius Eichberg. Eichberg was born and trained in Germany. He emigrated to the United States. Mary was chosen for the part of Isabella, which she played on 30 May.

Then came a crucial turn of events. 'I have a pupil', Mrs Duff announced one day to Mary, 'who is married to a very wealthy man in Chicago. They might agree to sponsor your training.' Thus it was at Mrs Duff's studio one winter afternoon in 1894 that Mrs Florence Mayer, wife of the junior member of the dry goods firm Schlesinger & Mayer, first heard and was impressed by Mary's voice.

By that time the young singer's funds were running low. Mary's father, although he believed in her future, was unable to supply the money needed to train her voice.[13] Having spent some years in Chicago, Robert Garden was now obliged by his business commitments to move his family east again, this time to Hartford, Connecticut. In Hartford, one of the Gardens' neighbours was Hayden Eames, brother of the great American soprano, Emma Eames. Knowing that Mary had ambitions to sing in opera, Hayden spent many hours talking to her about his famous sister and the sacrifices that she had had to make in order to succeed.

In yet another move, the Gardens came to Philadelphia in 1895, where they would remain until 1907. Mary's father started his own bicycle retail and repair business at 835 Arch Street, building it up into a flourishing concern and Mary attended school in the city.

She was growing up to be a fashionable young lady. In the summer, after spending ten days in the country, she returned home to find a present waiting for her from Mrs Mayer in Chicago – her first corsets: 'What a swell figure I have with them on', she wrote.[14] Mrs Mayer, who had been following Mary's progress with interest, succeeded in persuading her to continue her musical education in Chicago. Her new sponsors invited her to live with them in their spacious home at 4544 Woodlawn Avenue, where it was arranged that she should help to look after the Mayer children and take singing lessons.

To broaden her understanding of opera, Mary accompanied Mr and Mrs Mayer from time to time to the Chicago Auditorium. On one occasion they went to hear two great artists whom Mary would later come to know much better – Nellie Melba and the tenor Jean de Reszke, in Gounod's *Roméo et Juliette*. At this particular performance there was public consternation when, in the course of the evening, a man rushed onto the stage and tried to shoot de Reszke. The tenor kept his nerve until the man was overpowered although the incident caused Melba great distress.

More concert work was to come Mary's way in 1896 – she appeared in a programme of French songs at Chicago's Salon Français on 27 February in the Auditorium recital hall. According to the *Inter-Ocean*[15] she showed 'superb taste, rare feeling and much finish'. On 8 May she sang three Brahms songs at a meeting of the Twentieth Century Club.

Mrs Mayer was delighted with Mary's progress. As the time drew near for Mrs Duff to make her annual visit to Paris, she decided to offer to send her protégée abroad with Mrs Duff.[16] Mrs Mayer duly accompanied Mary to her parents, whereupon she asked their permission to allow her to continue her studies in Paris for three years. They agreed.

And so it was that, in late May of 1896, Mary and Mrs Duff sailed for Paris.

Notes

1. Mary Garden and Louis Biancolli (1951), *Mary Garden's Story*, New York: Simon and Schuster. Mary, with the help of her sister, Amy, had begun to write her autobiography in March 1947 without the active assistance or encouragement of any musical or literary authority. Of course, she had been writing biographical articles for many years and claimed on several occasions that she had begun her autobiography. The 1947 attempt appears to have been her first serious effort to finish the job. In the author's possession is a 'copy of the original typewritten manuscript of the UNFINISHED MEMOIRS of MARY

GARDEN'. This consists of twenty pages of text, marked on the cover with the handwritten note: 'Sent to me for perusal by Miss Garden, Aberdeen, May 1948. A.A.W.' The typescript begins: 'I have decided not to ask any of my literary acquaintances to write a preface to this book...'. The other (completed) version is in the Portraits Department of the Royal College of Music, London. This version begins: 'I have written this book myself...' Having completed her manuscript, Mary sent it to New York, to her old friend the critic, Carl Van Vechten, who took it to a publisher acquaintance, Bill Raney, of Rinehart's. Both felt the text was badly written and missed out the most important aspects of her career. Van Vechten wrote to her in his most diplomatic terms to tell her so (see Carl Van Vechten papers held at the Beinecke Rare Book and Manuscript Library, Yale University). Mary seems to have persisted in her search for a publisher, however, and the typescript ended up with Simon and Schuster. They too were unhappy with the text as it stood and employed Louis Biancolli to interview Mary and to write his version of her story, presumably also drawing on her original text. Hence this final published version has been described here as 'co-written'. All quotations (unless otherwise indicated) are taken from the original completed version by Garden in the Royal College of Music.

2.   Unidentified clipping, Boston (February 1927), New York Public Library (NYPL), Music Department, #2B-2210, Reel 1.
3.   'Mary Garden: The Climb' (March 1930), *The Ladies Home Journal*.
4.   Transcript of telephone call to author from Graham Collie (23 July 1994).
5.   'Mary Garden: The Climb' (March 1930), *The Ladies Home Journal*.
6.   Ibid.
7.   *Springfield Union*, 2 May 1912.
8.   *The New Idea*, May 1909.
9.   William Armstrong (August 1911), 'The Girlhood of Mary Garden', *Woman's Home Companion*.
10.   Sarah Robinson-Duff (1919), *Simple Truths Used by Great Singers*, Boston: Oliver Ditson Co., pp.105–6.
11.   Ibid., pp. 107–8.
12.   *Chicago Tribune*, 6 November 1910.
13.   *Kansas City Star*, 26 March 1920.
14.   Letter 1. Garden to Florence Mayer, Chicago Historical Society (CHS).
15.   Chicago *Inter-Ocean*, 1 March 1926.
16.   Unidentified clipping (1901), New York Public Library, Billy Rose Theatre Collection, Robinson Locke Collection of Dramatic Scrapbooks 1856–1920, Vols 224–236, Series 1.

2 Studying in Paris: 1896–1900

The Atlantic crossing was stomach-churning. 'I have worn the complexion of an unripe lemon', Mary wrote to Mrs Mayer.[1] But she joined in with life on board, even giving an impromptu concert of German songs; she also took a shine to a young fourth officer. But the turbulence of the sea paled into insignificance for Mary at the prospect of an awakening that she knew was imminent. 'I am almost in Paris,' she sighed, 'to realize my only hope and love on earth.'[2]

In the pitch dark they arrived at Cherbourg on the French coast, then boarded a train for the Gare du Nord. After a dreary journey they trundled into Paris on Friday 29 May 1896, emerging from the station into the sunrise of a bright spring morning. En route to their hotel, the cab skirted the magnificent Palais Garnier, the fabled Opéra de Paris. On an impulse, Mrs Duff turned in her seat and gestured grandly at the theatre which glittered with gold and bronze: 'Mary, you'll sing there one day.' The cab continued on, carrying them over cobbled streets, past the back of the Madeleine where vendors could be seen unpacking their high-filled flower carts, past the curious old vegetable wagons groaning with carrots, beets and onions and so into the immense Place de la Concorde where the statues of the cities of France sat in isolated splendour.

Next morning, after a good night's rest, they set out from the hotel to look for rooms, climbing stairs until it seemed their backs would break. They were also on the lookout for a suitable singing teacher. The first they called on was Giovanni Sbriglia, a Neapolitan tenor in his late sixties. His great achievement was to have turned the fine Polish baritone Jean de Reszke into the most sought-after tenor of the day.

Sbriglia's own career had not been without its triumphs. He had toured Canada and the USA and among his most famous pupils were Jean and his brother, Edouard de Reszke, the American sopranos Lillian Nordica, Sibyl Sanderson and the French bass, Pol Plançon. At that time he was still coaching Sanderson.

Sbriglia was a small man of 67 with a very excitable and nervous manner. When Mary first sang for him, he rushed up to Mrs Duff with his hands in the air, gabbling wildly in enthusiasm. Later, at her first formal lesson, Sbriglia made Mary hum scales through her nose and succeeded, she felt, in tying her voice into knots. He inspected her teeth, peered down her throat and ordered her to unbutton the front of her dress as far as the waist, so that he could examine her diaphragm more closely. Inspection completed, he announced that he would have to build her a new 'box' (chest). His violent tugging at Mary's chest and stomach only had the effect of convulsing Mary and her chaperone into fits of laughter.

Sbriglia made Mary work with dumb-bells three times a day. He made her hum and would not allow her to open her mouth to sing. He instructed her to hold her chest up and he took her voice to high F and G. But it all proved too much of a struggle for Mary: 'I never came out of that studio,' she complained, 'without having a sore feeling in my throat.'[3] She remained with Sbriglia for only ten lessons, including French language tuition.

The second maestro on Mrs Duff's list was Jacques Bouhy, a Belgian baritone, now middle-aged. Bouhy was an impressive man: his manner was reserved, very formal and controlled. His studio was a severe rectangle of mirrors and gilt chairs and the walls were hung with photographs of grateful pupils.

As he talked to Mrs Duff, Mary could hear the word '*jolie*' repeated endlessly. When he had finished, Mrs Duff explained: 'He thinks you are very pretty. He says he can have you ready for the Opéra stage in twenty-six weeks!'

'Who on earth wants to sing at the Opéra after only twenty-six weeks?' Mary whispered to Mrs Duff. 'I certainly don't.' With that they left Bouhy's studio and did not return.

During these early weeks in Paris, Mary began to meet members of the large American colony there. Among these was the now retired soprano and impresario Clara Louise Kellogg (1842–1916). She had been one of the first top-ranking American opera singers to gain recognition in Europe. Clara Kellogg invited Mary to accompany her to the Opéra to see Saint-Saëns' *Samson et Dalila*. She also took her to hear the baritone Maurice Renaud in *Don Giovanni*, *Hamlet* and *Thaïs*. Mary thought Renaud a wonderful actor and easily the best voice in Paris.

On another occasion, Mary received a note from the mother of Emma Eames. Mrs Eames had heard from her family in Hartford that Mary was in Paris and invited her to her house to discuss singing with her daughter.

For Mary the priority was to find the teacher she so badly needed. The third teacher that she and Mrs Duff consulted was the German contralto Mathilde Marchesi, who was then about 75 years old. Not only was she elderly, but she was extremely autocratic and a woman of few words. She had been the teacher of Emma Eames, Emma Calvé, Sibyl Sanderson and Melba and had just finished writing her memoirs. Emma Eames described Marchesi as an 'ideal Prussian drill master' and observed that 'she had a head for business which, with her excellent musicianship, gave her the position she occupied for so many years – that of owner, manager and teacher of the greatest school of her day'.[4] Above all, Marchesi was hard-headed about the realities of the profession. She made it clear that 'as soon as one went into public life, all other singers must be considered enemies and that one must govern oneself accordingly and think only of protecting one-self and one's interests'.[5]

The goal of Marchesi's teaching was brilliant coloratura singing. However, Mary had decided that the last thing she wanted was to sing the coloratura repertoire exclusively, with its elaborate trills and runs, and the immobile acting technique insisted upon by Marchesi. But, in spite of Mary's misgivings, Mrs Duff persuaded her to try at least a few lessons. Mary endured it for a month. Then, in July 1896, she and Mrs Duff travelled to Karlsbad, in western Bohemia, for a holiday. There they bathed in the hot sodium sulphate springs. Massage, walks and coffee were the order of the day and Mary went crazy over the shops. By the time they returned, reluctantly, to Paris both women were refreshed and relaxed. By now, even Mrs Duff was beginning to have second thoughts about Marchesi's regime. Nevertheless, she ushered Mary once again into the presence of the formidable lady. Marchesi, it seemed, had completely forgotten who Mary was. Briefly, a flicker of recognition appeared in her eyes and she agreed to take Mary back the next day. This encounter was more than enough for her prospective pupil, however; Mary wrote at once to Marchesi and cancelled the lesson. The following day she received this sour and cryptic reply – 'Don't cry until you get out of the woods. A rolling stone gathers no moss'.

In the meantime, Paris in August was there to be enjoyed. Almost every morning Mary and Mrs Duff would get up at half-past six, dress, take a light breakfast and then venture out to the Bois de Boulogne two hours later. Mrs Duff would ride her bicycle while Mary strolled around on foot. There was scarcely anyone about at that time in the morning, just a few officers on horseback.

By this time, however, Mrs Duff was getting desperate to settle on a teacher. Back in Chicago, Mary's sponsor, Mrs Mayer, was also becoming restive as to how her money was being spent. Only one name now remained on Mrs Duff's list of approved masters – the Marquis Ange-Pierre de Trabadelo, a distinguished teacher and composer of romantic songs, with an electrifying personality.

'The moment I entered his studio and sang for him,' recalled Mary, 'I turned to Mrs Duff and said: "Here is my teacher".' She began her studies with Trabadelo on the first day of September.

Trabadelo had a cautious approach to developing the voice. He recognized registers in a voice, but did not teach them as such. He believed in working a voice in its natural register, taking care not to carry it out of its natural limits until the throat was strong, at which point he extended the middle register upwards and downwards into one continuous whole. When a voice came to him which was too open throughout, he set the singer to practise covered-tone work, and vice versa, working the extremes to achieve the mean. Trabadelo's guiding principle was: 'Beware of carrying the chest tones too high'.

Trabadelo soon had Mary studying advanced work (such as 'The Jewel Song' from *Faust*), but there remained the problem of how to improve her knowledge of the French language. Through Madame Marchesi, Mrs Duff had already found a suitable French family for Mary. La Villa des Fleurs in Clichy, the home of the Chaigneau family, was in a quiet, secluded street, shady with trees and flowers. Bordeaux-born Ferdinand Chaigneau was a respected landscape painter and etcher of the Barbizon school. He had three daughters, one of whom played the piano, one the violin and the other, the cello. It was into this charming, refined and musical atmosphere that Mrs Duff introduced Mary.

'For almost a year, twice every day,' remembered Mary, 'I sat down to table with father, mother, grandmother, three daughters and one son, with no word ever spoken but French.'[6] After only six months she was able to read her first French book, *L'Abbé Constantin* by Ludovic Halévy (1834–1908), nephew of Fromental Halévy, composer of *La Juive*. He was a writer of romantic fiction who also collaborated with Meilhac in writing librettos for Offenbach, Bizet and Delibes.

* * *

In the spring of 1897, Mary had the good fortune to meet the Californian soprano Sibyl Sanderson. Sanderson invited Mary to dinner, to show her some of the gowns and costume jewellery she had used in Massenet's *Manon*. It was to be the start of a friendship that would hold great significance for Mary. 'She is simply charming, beautiful, fascinating and clever', Mary enthused in a letter to Florence Mayer.[7] Sibyl Sanderson had great, melting brown eyes, an engaging manner, a warm individuality and such vibrancy that holding her hand gave anyone who made her acquaintance the feeling that her heart's blood was dashing through its veins. A bewitching singer and an accomplished actress, Sanderson, however, was not conventionally beautiful. Photographs show her to have been of below-average height, wide-jawed, snub-nosed and slightly stout. To disguise her lack of physical endowment on stage, she had developed striking elegance and authority.

Sanderson had studied with Sbriglia and was then coached by Massenet, for whom she created his *Esclarmonde* and *Thaïs*. She was a legendary Manon. By the time that Mary met her, however, her career was in decline after undistinguished debuts at Covent Garden (1891) and at the Metropolitan in New York (1895). She was now preparing to marry the recently-divorced Cuban millionaire, Antonio Terry.

In the summer of 1897, Mary's mother crossed the Atlantic to be with her daughter. Mary's voice by this time had become round, her diction was very much improved and she had developed real vocal style.[8] By October, Mary had completed work on the role of Ophélie (in Ambroise Thomas's *Hamlet*) and was about to prepare *La traviata* and then *Rigoletto*, singing them both in French and in Italian. The Sanderson house, meanwhile, became a home from home for her; Mary would visit every Sunday and that year she was invited to dine with the family on Christmas night. On New Year's day, while Sibyl Sanderson and Antonio Terry were spending their honeymoon in Nice, Mary dined at the home of the American attorney George Getty (1855–1930) with his daughter Gertrude.

Early in 1898 came the first of a number of attempts to persuade Mary to make her professional debut. An agent, referred to by Mary simply as 'Strackosh', came to Trabadelo hoping to engage her for Berlin or Milan,[9] but Mary had been ill with grippe and instead sent for her mother, who was by then visiting relatives in Scotland.

In an effort to improve her French diction, Mary enrolled at the Yersin School. Then, towards the end of April 1898, Trabadelo unexpectedly announced he had done as much for Mary as he could. He had arranged an audition for her with three directors from The Hague and, as from that August, placed her in the capable hands of Lucien Fugère (1848–1935), the debonair bass-baritone of the Opéra-Comique, and his colleague Jules Chevalier, répétiteur at the Paris Conservatoire.

* * *

In the summer of 1898 Mary travelled with some friends to a small village just outside Biarritz, from where they set out to tour part of northern Spain. A culture shock awaited Mary and her friends; they had not counted on the strength of Spanish rural reserve. Unintentionally, they infuriated some local farmers by paddling in a river with their legs and thighs uncovered and had to run from the scandalised farmers for fear of their lives. They sought out local bullfights and managed to see six in all. With morbid fascination Mary described to Florence Mayer the injuries inflicted on the horses, their stomachs ripped open by the bulls. Even at this early age she showed an interest in power and cruelty which would later be put to practical use in her operatic roles.

Arriving back in Paris all in one piece, Mary started stage instruction almost immediately with Fugère. He had started his own career in café-concerts, singing popular songs, and acting in sketches and pantomimes for patrons who were notoriously difficult to attract and hard to please. Fugère offered Mary the chance to learn not only how to sing and to act, but how to *play* an audience. He was to help her develop an intuitive feel for audience reaction and the self-confidence to project a role over the foot-lights.

Mary completed her study of the principal role in *Lucia di Lammermoor* and went on to learn the roles of Manon and Sapho with Jules Massenet himself. Massenet, like Fugère, was determined to bring Mary to complete readiness before they approached Albert Carré, the director of the Opéra-Comique.

By now Mary had left her lodging at the Chaigneaus and was staying not far from the Arc de Triomphe with another family in a fourth-floor apart-ment on the Avenue Marceau. There she lived with other English-speaking students. One of these was Clarence Whitehill, the American bass-baritone (then a pupil of Sbriglia's); another was Neal McCay, who would later supply a memoir to the press about his time in Mary's company.

Mary's tireless and unceasing efforts, despite her slim hopes of success, impressed McCay deeply. Her capacity for work, he later recalled, was enormous. Every morning she was the first to prepare for lessons later in the day. Her studies included every possible thing that would help her to become an opera singer. Mary's efforts were all the more praiseworthy, McCay felt, for the fact that she was working with little encouragement, and even less praise, for there were few who believed that she would ever succeed.

McCay had been asked by Mary if he would go to a concert which Fugère had arranged for his students. When McCay reached the concert venue, he found a tiny hall and a short concert programme, to be given before an even smaller audience. The programme was made up of popular exhibition arias. As it unfolded, the afternoon grew more and more tedious. Then it was announced that the duet from *Manon* would be sung by a tenor and Mademoiselle Mary Garden. As the two singers walked out onto the little six-by-eight platform they were greeted with the same encouraging applause the others had received. The music began.

When they had finished there was a warmth to the applause that made the walls of the little hall ring. Now here was something different, thought McCay. 'Mary's singing,' he recalled, 'was then, as it has always since been, subservient to a deeper influence than that found in the work of the general run of singers in emotional roles.' After the concert, McCay waited for Mary and they walked home together. He told her how delighted he had been with her singing, and that in his opinion, if she ever got the chance, there would be no holding her back. Her only reply was, 'But will the chance come – and when? Sometimes the waiting seems very long.'[10]

A major setback was to delay Mary's planned debut. Fugère's idea had been to launch her shortly after her compatriot, Fanchon Thompson, but the latter's debut was such a disaster that they were forced to hold Mary back. Fanchon's French accent was appalling and she was vocally unprepared. It was reputed she had been persuaded to resort to the 'casting-couch'. 'I assure you,' wrote Mary to Florence Mayer, 'it was not Thompson's talent that got her in, but the leader of the orchestra, who is such a *dear* friend.'[11] Mary, on the other hand, protested that she would never be prepared to use such tactics. She had been under great pressure from the English impresario, Colonel James Mapleson (father-in-law of Marie Roze, the first soprano Mary had ever heard). The Colonel was anxious for her to sign with him and go to London. Mary, however, politely but firmly refused.

In the spring of 1899, Mary's mother again joined her in Paris. Then in early May, a young relative of the Mayer's, Ed Mayer, arrived. He gallantly took Mary and her mother on a round of the fashionable places – the theatre, dinners at the Café de Paris, driving in the Bois, even the races at Longchamps where she won 100 francs. This brief episode of fashionable amusement, when inflated by gossip in Paris and reported back to the Mayers in Chicago, led to an unexpectedly hostile reaction.

For nearly a year Mary had omitted to send receipts for her tuition and other expenses to the Mayers' representative in Paris, Léon Grehier. It was all a misunderstanding, Mary claimed; a pure oversight. But it fuelled new doubts about Mary's lifestyle and the possibility that she was guilty of false accounting. Mary's allowance was abruptly terminated. She had, of course, already been in Paris for more than the two years originally agreed upon by the Mayers. There was also the possibility that the Mayers scented a romance blossoming between Ed Mayer and their protegée, which might have been socially unacceptable to them and would need to be smartly nipped in the bud.

Mary herself only discovered what had happened on the first of the month when she went as usual to withdraw her allowance from Grehier at Schlesinger & Mayer's store, 56 rue des Petites Écuries. On her arrival, Grehier, who always handed over the allowance personally, snapped: 'There is no more money coming to you. Those are my orders'. He offered no explanation but brusquely handed Mary a letter from Mr and Mrs Mayer. 'Your conduct is not as we had supposed,' complained the letter. The Mayers ended by offering to send her a steamship ticket for her return to Chicago.

Mary looked at Grehier in agonized amazement. Without a word, she turned on her heel and walked away. She was quite alone in Paris. She had only fifty centimes to her name. In later, better times she would refer dramatically to 'those dark, cruel days just before the dawn'.

She had to do something. She went to see her singing-teacher, then her elocution instructor, then her drama coach. She told them what had happened, and asked if they would allow her credit for a few months until she could sort out her finances. They agreed to do so. But all too soon her landlady's patience was exhausted: Mary came back from her lessons one day and was told to pay up or pack up. She couldn't pay so the door was firmly closed behind her. All the little cheap things she had bought in the Latin Quarter to help make her room more comfortable were kept back as security. Luckily, she remembered a little boarding-house which she had visited when she first came to Paris. Fortunately, there was a tiny room available. She took it, knowing that she would have a week or two's grace before the bill was presented.

In time all her lessons stopped. Mary was stranded in Paris and faced with destitution. 'For six months I think I was mad, quite mad! My lessons were stopped, of course – I had no money to pay for them. I set my teeth and chose to fight it out to the last ditch. I've been burned in the fires of the world's furnace, but they have taught me its lessons.'[12]

In desperation, Mary wrote one last long letter to David Mayer. 'The world is so cruel for a woman all alone!' Women needed a character of iron, she continued, to stand up against it all and emerge unscathed. And she hinted at the sexual harassment facing a woman singer: 'if you could only see the disgusting men that are there, you would have to shut your eyes and put all sense of self-respect out of the window'.[13]

Some weeks later she was handed a bill by her landlady for the third and last time, and Mary knew she had no money to pay it – she had already sold all her personal jewellery. She managed to persuade the general manager of the Opéra-Comique, Émile Bertin, to write to the Mayers about her excellent prospects. In the letter, Bertin explained that Mary had been auditioned by the director of the Théâtre Royal de la Monnaie in Brussels, and had not been engaged only because the company was already at full strength. She was soon to be re-auditioned by Massenet, added Bertin and he guaranteed that during the following year Mary would appear as a star in Paris, Brussels, London or Milan. He ended by emphasizing the importance of timing her debut adroitly, quoting the many examples of American girls whose debuts had turned into disasters because of lack of preparation.[14]

In due course, a woman came to see Mary from Schlesinger & Mayer. She explained why the Mayers had stopped her allowance. They had received letters from Paris (possibly from friends, relatives or Grehier himself) which had been full of rumours that Mary had not been studying as hard as they expected; that she was following a pleasure-seeking lifestyle and that she was living with a young travelling salesman, by whom she had just had a child.

It was a fresh, autumnal September morning. Mary went as usual for an early walk in the Bois, her head aching, trying to sort out her problems. The sight of the trees and the smell of the grass had always made her feel happy and carefree. A woman passed her, dressed in deepest mourning, her long black crepe veil trailing along the ground, catching the dead autumn leaves. Accompanying the figure in black were five little white fox terriers, which Mary immediately recognized as Sibyl Sanderson's dogs. The lady was indeed Sibyl Sanderson who turned and came back towards Mary until the two met face to face.

'Why, Mary Garden,' said Sibyl, 'what is the matter with you? How dreadful you look!' They walked arm in arm to Sanderson's carriage. 'Come into my carriage, quick, and tell me all about it.' Mary climbed in. Sibyl took Mary's hand and Mary burst into tears, sobbing her heart out. When she had calmed down, she told her story.[15]

'You call that trouble! My dear girl,' said Sanderson, 'I have troubles too, but mine can never be put right.' She was referring to the tragedies that had beset her in the two years since she had first befriended Mary: she had suffered a stroke and a miscarriage; her new husband Antonio Terry had died; and she now suffered from a debilitating illness, which would ultimately prove fatal.

They sat in the carriage, each holding the other's hands, crying like children. From that moment they were even more strongly bound together in deepest friendship. Mary was taken to the Sanderson apartment at 104, Avenue des Champs Elysées. There they had lunch together, after which Sibyl sent her manservant over to Mary's pension to pay the female proprietor everything she owed, to bring back Mary's few belongings and even redeem those things she had pawned.

Sibyl insisted Mary remain as her guest. 'She interested herself in every little detail of my history,' recalled Mary, 'and in less than three hours, she changed my whole life from utter darkness to glittering sunlight.'[16] Sanderson then made it possible for Mary to build up the contacts she so badly needed. 'Her home was one of the centres of the art life of Paris,' recalled Mary, 'and in a week's time I had met more interesting and important people than in all my two years before.'[17]

None was more interesting and important than Albert Carré, manager of the Opéra-Comique. One evening he came to dine with Sibyl and Mary, and after coffee, having learned of Mary's talent and ambitions and Sibyl's opinion on the matter, he agreed to let Mary audition for him at the opera house when the opportunity arose. In the meantime, he offered Mary the chance to visit the theatre and watch a rehearsal of the production he was preparing, a new opera, *Louise*, set in Paris and written by the bohemian composer, Gustave Charpentier.

Seeing an opera in rehearsal for the first time had an indelible effect on the young Scot. 'I had never heard such music and my eyes were watching the inside workings of an opera house for the first time. "Paris! Cité de joie, cité d'amour" went to my head like wine,' Mary commented.

> There was something in the tones of that music, as it first came to me, that set me on fire. I could hardly keep from screaming, it excited me so. The moment the rehearsal was over, I ran to a music shop to buy a copy of the score.
>
> I carried it home, locked myself in my room and simply devoured it. I did not want to eat or sleep until I knew every note of it. I had it in my head in two weeks. All day long I did nothing but sing that part, until Sibyl, who was feeling unwell, said I would drive her crazy, and had me moved into a room at the very back of the house, with four or five doors between where I continued to practise even without a piano.[18]

Beyond the Opéra-Comique there were other sources of experience which Mary hastened to draw upon. She went to see Sarah Bernhardt playing a role *en travesti* in Edmond Rostand's play, *L'Aiglon*, which had its première in the middle of March at Bernhardt's own theatre. Along with many other admirers Mary crowded into the Divine Sarah's suite after the performance. 'The first thing I saw,' she wrote, 'were flowers everywhere – exotic plants, immense vases filled with roses, while on her dressing-table lay banks of orchids, her favourite flower.'

The great actress, then 56 years old, was to be a significant influence on Mary's approach to dramatic expression. Bernhardt first played on the stage several of the roles Mary Garden would later espouse – Cléopâtre, Tosca, Gismonda, and even Pelléas. She was a master of dramatic effect, even in everyday life. Sometime later, during a lunch that Mary attended at Bernhardt's house the guests were all assembled in the dining room. Suddenly Sarah, like a beautiful dragonfly, burst in, swathed in a flowing white Greek garment.

'She took her place seated on a heavily carved wooden dais – a relic she had found in some old cathedral,' Mary recalled. 'It was closed on three sides, lined in vivid red damask and from inside the roof hung a yellow electric lamp which threw its soft rays over her radiant person.' Mary was flabbergasted. 'Her golden hair stood out all around her head, falling very low in front over her strange green eyes; heavy gold jewellery hung from her neck. She might have been a Byzantine empress of ancient time. She was one of the world's unique.'

* * *

The time came for Carré to hear Mary. In French she sang 'Ah, fors è lui' from *La traviata*. As soon as she opened her mouth, Carré stopped her and asked her what language she was singing in, as he hadn't understood one word.

'He made me promise to correct my pronunciation,' recalled Mary. She followed with the Saint-Sulpice scene from *Manon*. 'I did it, badly enough I know,' she confessed later, 'but possibly there was something about my way of doing things that interested him, so after we had had a talk he offered me an engagement to sing Micaëla in *Carmen* at the Comique the following October, beginning with a salary of 250 francs a month (equivalent to $50 at the time), rising to 500 francs by August. I had got my toe in, and every drop of blood in me was ready to fight to hold on.'

This engagement gave Mary the privilege of free access to the theatre – not only to all the performances, but to the rehearsals as well. She made good use of her opportunity. From 30 January 1900, Mary was registered as a fully-fledged employee of the Opéra-Comique.

'I went to the theatre almost every day,' confessed Mary, 'and Sibyl even allowed me the freedom of her dressing room when she was performing.' At rehearsals, Mary did not care if she had to sit on a step or stand in the corridor. She would slip unnoticed into sessions for the under-studies.

One night between the acts, Albert Carré came in to see Sibyl. He looked at Mary long and intently. 'That girl has a profile. She would make a perfect Louise,' he said, and added: 'She has the style, the figure and the sympathy.'

'Yes, and she has the voice too,' Sibyl replied.[19]

The dress rehearsal of *Louise* with Marthe Rioton in the title role took place on 1 February 1900. Mary had already been present at two rehearsals over the previous two days. The first performance of *Louise* on 2 February was a great success. However, shortly afterwards Marthe Rioton became ill and she was indisposed between 11 and 16 February. Carré was aware that Mary had mastered the vocal part of Louise and knew it by heart. He alerted the official understudy, Catherine Mastio, but also engaged Mary on 19 February to begin rehearsing the role – the first of a series of 16 rehearsals she attended with various staff conductors.

The next day, delighted with the success of *Louise* at the Opéra-Comique, the composer Gustave Charpentier had inscribed the now restored Marthe Rioton's score: 'With gratitude and admiration to an ideal Louise'. But the day was soon to come when Rioton would again begin to show signs of vocal strain.

Both in her published and unpublished biographies, Mary Garden, using her love of superstition to heighten the tension, claims that her seat number in the Opéra-Comique that evening was 113. She refers to her debut as having been on Friday 13 April 1900, even melodramatically entitling a page in the published version 'Friday the Thirteenth'. In fact, she was sitting in ground-floor box 17, her debut in *Louise* was on 10 April – and it was a Tuesday. (Perhaps she was recalling the well-known debut of the American soprano Emma Eames on 13 March 1889 at the Paris Opéra or her birth on 13 August 1865 in Shanghai?)

On that fateful afternoon, Sibyl and Mary were at home. Mary was grief-stricken at the time, as one of Sibyl's dogs had just been run over and killed. Suddenly the telephone rang. Sibyl answered it and Mary heard her say: 'Yes, she is here.' Then, 'No, of course she can't.' Realizing that Sibyl was speaking about her, Mary called out: 'Who is it?' 'It's M. Carré,' Sibyl answered. 'He wants to know if you could sing Louise this evening, and I told him that of course you couldn't.'

'Instantly I was on fire,' recalled Mary. 'I ran to seize the receiver before she hung it up and called out: "Is that M. Carré?" "Yes," came the voice. "Well, this is Miss Garden and I can sing Louise."'

Carré had had a phone call from Marthe Rioton to say that she would try and complete the performance that evening, but that she might be forced to pull out because of a severe cold. The official understudy, Mlle Mastio was also ill.[20] Carré told Mary to be at the theatre by seven.

Mary had last rehearsed *Louise* a month previously with the whole cast conducted by André Messager. She had, however, been careful to keep everything fresh in her memory by continual study of the role, as her coach Lucien Fugère had previously advised.

So, that evening, Sibyl and her sisters accompanied Mary to the Opéra-Comique, Mary dressed in the first-act costume, hidden under a cloak. She and her companions were shown to ground-floor box 17, at the back of the auditorium, directly facing the stage. Mary squeezed herself into as small a bundle as possible. Her eyes and nose, swollen with weeping for the death of Sibyl's dog, might easily have frightened off Albert Carré. 'One minute I felt hot all over,' she remembered, 'then it seemed as though someone had run an icicle down my back.'

To a full house, the curtain opened on *Louise*. Marthe Rioton made valiant efforts to sing, in spite of her obvious discomfort. She struggled through the first two acts without giving up and then, finally breaking under the strain ('*très énervée, émouvée*', as the register put it), admitted defeat.

During the performance, Garden kept her eyes glued to the small stage door that opened into the orchestra pit. As the curtain fell on Act Two, Mary was aware of the white head of a little old man, peering about with near-sighted eyes. It was the stage manager, M. Vizentini, looking over his spectacles for her. As he approached her seat, Mary got up to meet him and he hurried her backstage through a side door.

There, pandemonium reigned as management and stage crew milled about. Albert Carré rushed towards her: 'Are you ready to finish the third Act for me?' 'Certainly,' answered Mary.

In both her biographies, Mary Garden claims that André Messager had not met her until that moment and that she had never sung before on any opera stage or with an orchestra. However, the register of the Opéra-Comique (which was a powerful document which could be used as the basis for disciplinary action) makes it clear that she had rehearsed in the theatre and with Messager since 5 March. The protests she describes by Messager (at the director introducing a singer he had never heard of and who was quite untried) are certainly exaggerated, if not invented. However, he may have suggested that the audience might have preferred to have their money back.

In the event, Mary was taken up to a dressing-room, her cheeks quickly rouged, her eyes outlined with black. Her costume was adjusted and she was shown to the rear of the stage, where she took up her position with a final adjustment of her costume. Then her teacher, Lucien Fugère, stepped out to face the packed theatre and announced the substitution to the audience.

'My first realization of what I was doing,' Mary confessed later, 'came with the curious whirring sound of the rising curtain, and when, over the footlights, I saw all the black coats with gleaming white shirt fronts, I felt as though I were facing a row of tombstones. But I had no time to think.'[21]

'I remember turning my back on the audience,' she continued, 'walking upstage, saying to myself: "Now, Mary Garden, here is your chance".' Then she turned calmly and walked downstage again, steeling herself, but trying to be as relaxed as she could. She positioned herself behind the chair where Léon Beyle, the tenor who was singing the part of Julien, was seated. With a glance at Messager in the pit, she began to sing 'Depuis le jour, où je me suis donnée'.

When she finished the aria, the applause was unbelievable. To Mary's ears it sounded like torrential rain on a tin roof. 'When the curtain fell at the end of the Act, the audience went into a frenzy,' she said. 'Men and women stood shouting "bravo", waving handkerchiefs and programmes and even, in their excitement, throwing them up onto the stage. Some were calling out "*Marygardenne!*" in the French fashion.'

Messager stood transfixed. He rose, and, baton in hand, turned to his orchestra and ordered: 'Debout!' As they rose silently to their feet in salute, he held his baton high in the air – the greatest compliment a chef d'orchestre and his staff could pay.[22]

'When it was all over,' said Mary, 'I went home to my little bedroom and got into bed. My eyes would not shut. I would put my fingers over them and close them oh, so tight and – pouf! – they would fly open.'[23]

The reviews of her performance were uniformly favourable, making allowances for her unplanned debut. She had a delightful voice and pleasing appearance which quickly won over the audience, said *Le Figaro*'s music critic, adding that for her the evening ended as a great success. *Le Ménestrel* (15 April 1900), a specialist music publication, elaborated a little more knowledgeably:

From the beginning of the third Act aria her voice seemed to tremble a little with emotion. Yet, quite quickly, she pulled herself together and showed the quality of her voice. An American, Miss Garden has not rid herself completely of her accent and, like the majority of her compatriots, gives above all the impression of being a very talented amateur. In the last act she showed dramatic temperament (a little exaggerated perhaps), good poses and diction, but the musical phrase was lost from being broken up all the time. It would be premature to judge her after this improvised début. The packed hall recalled her warmly along with her teacher, Fugère.

The next day, Mary went to see Albert Carré, whose faith in her had been so well rewarded, in spite of the sceptics like Messager. He embraced her, saying he had never been so proud of anyone in his life. And he gave her a cheque for 1000 francs along with a note which read: 'With my enthusiastic admiration and eternal friendship'. Then he offered her a full-time contract for two years at 500 francs a month for the first year and 800 francs for the second, with an option for five years.

Now, at last, Mary was independent. 'I left him,' she recalled, 'thrilled with joy that in the future I would be able to make my own living.'

As an artiste she was on the way to meeting the exacting criteria the French public required of their singers: 'The French have never demanded virtuoso voices from their prima donnas. What they insisted on having was a perfection of acting artistry ingrained in the music. They also were partial to good looks. They demanded chic and beauty and the credible illusion of enchantment.'[24]

* * *

While Mary's stay at Sibyl Sanderson's apartment had undoubtedly saved her career, her weeks there had not been entirely comfortable. According to Jack Winsor Hansen, Mary had been dismayed to discover that Sibyl Sanderson was an alcoholic[25], and it has been suggested that she may also have been experimenting with drugs. As Mary rested after her triumph in *Louise*, the time came for her to leave the Sanderson home. Her friend's health had deteriorated further and Sibyl had been advised by her doctor to return to Nice. This she did, but not before finding Mary a tiny pension in the Rue Chalgrin not far away, where Sibyl paid her rent six months in advance.

Mary's one small room was on the fifth floor. It had a balcony. In the room was a bed, wash-stand, writing-table, a piano and all her clothes. Here she took stock of her progress and considered the next step forward in her career.

Notes

1.   Letter 2. Garden to F. Mayer, May 1896. CHS.

2. Ibid.
3. Letter 6. Garden to F. Mayer, summer 1896. CHS.
4. Emma Eames (1927), *Some Memories and Reflections*, New York: D. Appleton & Co., p. 52.
5. Ibid., pp. 57–8.
6. William Armstrong, 'The Girlhood of Mary Garden', *Woman's Home Companion*, August 1911.
7. Letter 15. Garden to F. Mayer, Spring 1897. CHS.
8. Letter 16. Mina Adelaide to F. Mayer, Paris, July 1897. CHS.
9. Letter 20. Garden to F. Mayer, Paris, January/February 1898. CHS. The well-known agent Max Strakosch died in 1892. If this is the person Garden had in mind, she must have been mistaken.
10. Neal McCay, untitled and undated article, Public Library, Music Department, Special Scrapbooks Vols 1 and 2, **ML46.G37R4: Mary G. Reed: Mary Garden, 1907–26.
11. Letter 24. Garden to F. Mayer, Paris, December 1898. CHS.
12. *The New Idea*, May 1909.
13. Letter 27. Garden to David Mayer, Paris, December 1898. CHS.
14. Letter 26. Émile Bertin to F. Mayer, Paris, 6 July 1899. CHS.
15. *The New Idea*, May 1909.
16. Unpublished first draft of Garden's autobiography, p. 23, Royal College of Music (RCM).
17. Karleton Hackett, untitled magazine, NYPL, Music Department, *2B-2210 Reel 1.
18. Ibid.
19. *Chicago Examiner*, 6 June 1907.
20. Memoirs of Albert Carré, unidentified magazine article, Bibliothèque Nationale, Paris.
21. *Musical Leader*, 7 November 1907.
22. *Ladies Home Journal*, March 1930.
23. *Seattle Times*, 20 November 1950.
24. Grace Moore (1947), *You're Only Human Once*, London: Latimer House, p. 78.
25. Jack Winsor Hansen, 'Mary Garden: Queen of Chutzpah', Part II, *Massenet Society Newsletter*, vol. 10, no. 1, January 1991, p. 1.

3 Debuts and Debussy: 1900–1903

Mary Garden would always identify herself with Charpentier's *Louise*: 'Only in *Louise* was I myself on stage, because she was so much like me. She was a daring sort of character. She lived hard. She believed in free love. She enjoyed everything about life.'[1] Mary also felt that *Louise* personified its composer's character:

> I have always seen it as an expression of Charpentier's own life. It is the opera of Montmartre, and he was the King of Montmartre, a real bohemian to whom money and fame meant nothing. He was satisfied if he had enough to pay drinks for himself and his friends at the Rat Mort. He lived in a dirty little garret up on the *butte*, and while he was writing this realistic picture of his own life, he was slowly starving to death. The production of his opera brought him nearly half a million francs, but he spent it all on the working-girls of Montmartre.[2]

Paris at the turn of the century was, like any great capital, a hothouse of exotic sexual display. It might have been mistaken for 'a city populated almost entirely by homosexuals, bisexuals, transvestites, male and female impersonators, prostitutes who catered to all these varying desires, and a few lonely, frustrated individuals who regretted they were unable to join the party'.[3]

Mary was all too aware of the temptations and pitfalls that existed in such an environment. During her career she was often asked the question: 'How do you get ahead in the world of opera?'. To which her answer invariably was that the 'casting couch' was a route she had never chosen. On one occasion she was asked what she thought of the claim by soprano Marguerite Sylva (1875–1957) that young women auditioning for an operatic career were forced to submit to sexual abuse from managers and impresarios. Sylva had asserted that the careers of most girls in Europe were built on the sacrifice of morals and character.

'Marguerite Sylva is a good friend of mine,' commented Mary, 'but I think she is not entirely right about this. She may have had disagreeable experiences that have prejudiced her against all managers.'[4] But Mary did have some advice for aspiring opera singers: 'As to managers and all that talk, the girl who goes into opera has to keep a level head. If she's moral at heart she'll remain moral. If she doesn't want to remain moral – why, then there's no use talking about it.'[5]

* * *

On occasion Mary loved to escape from the overheated atmosphere of Paris and the world of opera to spend time alone. In April 1900, she spent Easter Day in Dieppe. Eastertime held a special place in Mary's heart; it was an opportunity to release her pent-up tension 'and emotion'.

'To me the festival of Easter has always been the holiday of joy above all others in the year,' she confided. 'It is always spent at Dieppe because I know that at this season of the year Dieppe is deserted, and that I shall be alone for the holiday of my abandon on the sands.' Easter appealed to her love of freedom: 'I spend the day on the sands eating shrimps and walking. On no other day of the year am I so free.'[6]

Back in Paris, Marthe Rioton had again recovered and was able to sing *Louise*. But on 25 April, for the first time, it was Mary's turn to sing the part from start to finish. The unfortunate Rioton's career took a gradual downward slide from this time; she would later reluctantly quit the stage and marry. At a matinée performance on 13 May 1900 she was in the cast, but not in the leading role – it was sung by her young Scottish successor. This lesson in the fragility of operatic careers and the need to keep in the public eye was not lost on Mary.

Eight more performances of *Louise* followed – always with Mary's teacher Lucien Fugère in the cast. Then in mid-June Mary began rehearsals with Albert Carré for the first-ever role she was to create, that of Marie in Lucien Lambert's *La Marseillaise*, written for the French national day, 14 July, when it was to be performed free of charge.

Albert Carré had a great influence on Mary; the stagecraft that he taught her was to colour her whole approach to acting. Carré's method valued intelligence above all; he was insistent that before any effect was attempted (be it a sung phrase or stage business) it had to be carefully thought out and motivated. Acting, in Carré's view, was based on planned movements so precisely rehearsed that they eventually took on the spontaneity of real life.

However, in spite of Carré's best efforts, *La Marseillaise* was not a success; it only ran for three performances. Mary, who played the girlfriend of the composer of the French national anthem, was at one point required to stand up suddenly and sing 'Je suis française!' Sung in her quaint Scottish-American twang, however, this merely had the effect of making the audience burst out laughing.

*   *   *

On 27 July 1900 a milestone was reached at the Opéra-Comique: it was the 50th performance of *Louise*, 20 of which had featured Mary in the leading role. Albert Carré, Charpentier and Henri Georges Heugel (1844–1916), the music publisher, invited the whole theatre staff to a celebratory lunch at the Moulin de la Galette in Montmartre. There Charpentier was garlanded with flowers and responded with an emotional speech. But later in the afternoon the composer suddenly collapsed at his table; he was already showing signs of the illness which would hound him for the rest of his life – anaemia, caused by malnutrition.

Mary was to sing *Louise* a further 22 times between the end of July and the last day of the year. One performance, in particular, was memorable. 'I shall never forget the day when I recognized the great Madame Marchesi in my audience,' Mary recalled. 'I prevailed upon a mutual friend to go to her, and learn, if possible, what her true impression was. Well, the famous teacher was genuinely *emotionée* – in fact, she was in tears; and she declared, without reserve, that here were effects more poignant than artificial opera had ever dreamed of.'[7]

Mary's next role was to be in Mascagni's *Ratcliff* which had first been performed, with little success, at La Scala in Milan six years before. This latest venture, however, begun in late September 1900, was also destined to fail; it was abandoned a month later after just two or three rehearsals, at the same time as Mary also began work on Gabriel Pierné's *La fille de Tabarin*. Mary had by now acquired sufficient clout to be able to express her dissatisfaction with *Ratcliff* by not turning up for rehearsal. The Opéra-Comique register, while noting her presence at *La fille de Tabarin*, also records her absence for *Ratcliff* on the same afternoon (the Opéra-Comique invariably rehearsed in the afternoon).

There had now appeared a new and powerful presence in Mary's life – the composer and conductor, André Messager. For a brief time Mary enjoyed a close relationship with Messager: he was in love with her, but on her part, she would claim, it went no further than an appreciation of his dispassionate guidance within a working partnership:

> We had a tempestuous friendship for over twenty years. He had the most caustic nature and diabolic temper of any man I have ever met. As my temper was not too angelic, we quarrelled and quarrelled, but our friendship was too strongly rooted to be ever really broken. He guided me with such kind attention during the first few years of my career, never failing to discuss with me the good and bad points of all my performances.

A slightly different view is put forward by Jack Winsor Hansen, citing the unpublished private memoirs of Sibyl Sanderson's stepdaughter. Messager, already married to Hope Temple, a Dublin-born composer, was neurotic and rather ugly, but Hansen asserts that 'after several private meetings fol-lowed by a few romantic dinner-dates, the moustachioed conductor success-fully persuaded Mary to become his mistress.'[8]

There can be no doubt that, at the heart of the problems Mary faced in developing her early career in France, there loomed the creative tension between Messager and Carré as to who should have the decisive influence over Mademoiselle Garden. In her unpublished autobiography, Mary characterized her relationships with the men with whom she worked most closely as being only on the level of deep friendship and admiration. In the re-vamped, emotionally charged published version of her life, however, the impression is given that Messager and Carré both became her lovers.

According to the published biography, Carré one day called Mary to his office to tell her that he was now divorced and a free man, then he asked her: 'Will you be my wife?' Mary claims she was stunned – she had never suspected that Carré loved her. The relationship between a singer and a director or conductor has to be a close one, even intimate, but this went beyond the demands of professionalism. In order to extricate herself, Mary quickly told Carré there was another man in her life – Messager. But Carré was persistent. After an exchange of letters, he again called her to his office. He took out her contract, and, according to Louis Biancolli's biography, ripped it into little pieces and hurled it into a wastepaper basket.

As it happened, some days earlier Mary had received an offer from Heugel (Massenet's publisher) to sing *Louise* at La Scala, Milan, for Giulio Gatti-Casazza, later director of the Metropolitan Opera, New York. Mary wrote to Heugel, accepted the offer and then informed Carré. He sent for her immediately, and placed a new copy of the contract in front of her. With an inward sigh of relief, she signed it and everything returned to normal.

By the end of December, Mary was working with Messager at the Théâtre des Machinistes, rehearsing the part of Diane in *La fille de Tabarin*. Mary was fascinated by the sentimental librettist Victorien Sardou (1831–1908). He was a small nervous man with black hair, worn rather long, with keen eyes in a very pale face. Sardou always dressed in black with a velvet coat, a big white muffler round his neck and a small black velvet cap on his head. He attended all the rehearsals of *La fille de Tabarin* and some days he would be so overcome by his own writing that he would take a large white silk handkerchief out of his pocket and cry copious tears into it.

Messager conducted the première of *La fille de Tabarin* on 20 February 1901. The work was set in Poitou in 1640, most of the action taking place around the Château of Beauval. As Diane, Mary carried off her period costumes with great *élan*. She was not, however, in the best of health; she sang with a cold which turned into laryngitis the following day. But her indisposition was scarcely noticed by the appreciative opening-night audience.

In the spring of 1901, it appears that Mary endeavoured to extricate herself from Alfred Bruneau's *L'Ouragan*, a work based on a text by Émile Zola. After a single rehearsal on 30 March, she was marked absent for three subsequent weeks, sang in the dress rehearsal the following week and then missed the première two days later. Further rehearsals were held in early May but again she was marked absent. Thus ended her connection with *L'Ouragan* which, in spite of her absence, turned out to be something of a triumph.

Up to the middle of May, she sang *La fille de Tabarin* 13 times, interspersed with performances of the ever-popular *Louise*. But *La fille de Tabarin*, unfortunately, did not meet with a great deal of continued interest from the public and was taken off after just one more performance.

As summer approached, Mary decided it was time to put her relationship with Messager on a more strictly professional footing; his insane possessiveness was becoming too much for her. She knew she was not in love with him. Hansen makes the cynical comment: 'Actually, she didn't need him any more. Having been his mistress for two years, she had achieved her goal to become one of the reigning divas of the Comique.'[9] In their final showdown, Messager turned up at her apartment and flung a wad of money at her. Flinging it back, Mary showed him the door.

*   *   *

To escape the torrid summer months in Paris (the Opéra-Comique closed from 15 July to 1 September), Mary accepted an offer from the director of the Casino at Aix-les-Bains, where she would sing for the next four summers. For most of August, she rehearsed in the delightful spa town. The resort of Aix-les-Bains was at that time highly popular, frequented by European royalty who enjoyed the pleasures of the mineral waters, the magnificent lake and the grandeur of the hills, not to mention the entertainment at the Casino and the well-appointed theatre. Aix had been visited three times by Queen Victoria before the turn of the century, by the Queen of Portugal, the Emperor of Brazil, the King of Sweden and by Edward VII. At the height of its popularity the resort had 3000 English residents and 2000 Americans. As well as providing a receptive audience for Mary, Aix-les-Bains gave her access to royal patronage which could only be of benefit to her career.

Mary made her début as *Thaïs* at Aix-les-Bains. She had been assiduously coached in the part by Sibyl Sanderson, who had created the role for Massenet. Sanderson had a spacious chateau at Aix and she was the most attentive member of the audience at Mary's first performance. During rehearsals she came to Mary and said: 'Thaïs must have pearls'. With a decadent sweep of her arm she placed around Mary's neck millions of francs' worth of marvellous pearls. When Mary showed herself in costume to the conductor, Léon Jehin, the fortune round her neck made him distinctly nervous. The performance was a great personal success for Mary, but no one really relaxed until Sibyl Sanderson came backstage and the pearls were again safely round her own throat.

Messager was also in Aix-les-Bains for Mary's début. One morning some days later, he accompanied her on the rack-railway to the summit of Mont Revard, a plateau some 1550 metres high above the town. Sitting talking in a house perched on the side of the mountain, Mary leafed idly through a copy of the magazine *l'Ilustration*. As she thumbed through the pages, she spotted in the supplement a little song by Claude Debussy. It was 'Extase', the first of what were to become the *Ariettes oubliées*. Later Messager played it over on the piano and Mary half-sang it with him. As the notes of the piano died away, she marvelled at the music's sensuality and its remarkable evocation of a mood.[10]

Mary made another important discovery at Aix. She struck up a friendship with the Danish-born King George of Greece (then aged 56), the brother of Queen Alexandra of England. He had the civilized habit of inviting chosen visitors to enjoy supper in his private apartments. The king had been in the audience at Mary's début in *Thaïs*. 'Everyone adored this kind, gentle person,' explained Mary, 'and the season at Aix never began until his arrival. He adored music and never missed a performance of opera. I can see him yet, with his five gentlemen-in-waiting, always arriving before the rise of the curtain.' Impressed by Mary's performance, King George asked Mary to sing *Thaïs* in Athens. Queen Marie of Romania even wanted her to repeat it in Bucharest but both engagements, regretfully, proved impossible to fulfil.

At the end of August 1901, Mary accompanied Sibyl Sanderson back to Paris on the same train as King George. Following a conversation with the king, Mary was quoted in the American press as observing: 'I never knew before that kings were so intelligent and so human'.

*   *   *

After one rehearsal with Messager on 11 September for Massenet's *Manon*, Mary made her début in the role ten days later at the Opéra-Comique. *Le Ménestrel* commented: 'She is an artist in full control of her technique, very intelligent and very idiosyncratic. Her silhouette is delicate and charming'.[11]

Four weeks later, she was to make the first of an incalculable number of public sorties into print, astounding the musical world by vigorously denying that she had ever been a pupil of Trabadelo. Challenging the contents of a short article published in *Le Figaro* on the Berlin début of another of

Trabadelo's American pupils, Geraldine Farrar, Mary declared in a letter to the paper: 'My only teacher is Lucien Fugère, the eminent artiste of the Opéra-Comique and it is to him alone that I owe the little that I know'.[12]

'Strange!', commented the editor of *Le Figaro*, 'The article in question was given to us by M. Trabadelo himself, who has already thanked us for publishing it!' It may be that Mary's protests related more to the attention paid to Farrar's success than to any slight she felt had been made to Fugère.

In mid-December 1901, Mary left Paris for Monte Carlo where she was to appear with the French tenor Edmond Clément. He sang the part of Pierre, a French marine, in the first performances there of Messager's *Madame Chrysanthème*, conducted by the composer. The libretto of *Madame Chrysanthème* was based on a Japanese story by Pierre Loti, which anticipated, in some respects, Puccini's *Madama Butterfly*, first produced in 1904. As Chrysanthème, Mary ravished her audience with the delicate charm of her voice and the grace of her acting, as *Le Journal de Monaco* (24 December 1901) noted. The settings by Visconti were astonishing. Choubrac's gorgeous costumes were rich with embroidered silks and satins.

Resting between performances, members of the cast strolled through the ornamental gardens of the principality. In one of her photo-scrapbooks Mary preserved the occasion. She stands, a shapely figure warmly swathed in furs, a young woman of remarkable sweetness but with a certain sad awareness of both her power and her fragility. Below her, standing alert on the step, as if imitating the balcony scene in *Roméo et Juliette*, a suavely moustachioed Messager offers his hawk-like profile to the camera.

Meanwhile, in Paris, delighted by her protegée's Monte Carlo success which had duly been reported by the Parisian dailies, Sibyl Sanderson cabled Mary's parents in Philadelphia: 'Mary well. Singing in Monte Carlo. Return to Paris Monday. So glad. Good news. Love, Sibyl'.[13]

The next months were to be the most momentous in Mary's life. After her return from Monte Carlo she was called in by Carré and Messager to audition for the leading role in what was already being seen as Claude Debussy's most intriguing work to date – the opera *Pelléas et Mélisande*, written to a libretto by the Belgian poet, Maurice Maeterlinck. Encouraged by Messager, Carré had accepted Debussy's revolutionary work the previous May. Since completing the opera in 1895, Debussy had played the vocal score repeatedly to friends and acquaintances to promote the work as much as possible and persuade someone to put it on the stage.

On 29 December 1901 it was announced in the Paris newspapers that the role of Mélisande had been given to Miss Mary Garden. This was a blow for the librettist, Maeterlinck, as his mistress, the soprano Georgette Leblanc, desperately wanted the role. Stung into action by rage and jealousy, Leblanc began to exert her not inconsiderable influence over Maeterlinck to have the decision reversed.

Mary, for her part, was elated at the announcement. A few days later, all the artists who had been picked for *Pelléas et Mélisande* assembled at Messager's home on the Boulevard Malesherbes to hear the work played by the composer himself. Each singer was given a proof copy of the score to follow. Oblivious of the cast around him, Debussy sat down at the piano. Sensuous chords sprang from the instrument. He intoned the vocal parts in his deep, hollow voice which forced him sometimes to transpose the notes an octave down. The music unnerved Mary but, gradually, as the third Act unfolded, it began to fascinate her. By the time Debussy reached the fourth Act, she was filled with a depth of emotion she had seldom experienced. And when it came to the death of Mélisande, it was more than she could bear. Suddenly Mary and Madame Messager (the Irish composer, Hope Temple) were racked by uncontrollable sobbing and had to leave the room until they could regain their composure.

Some days later, Mary was called to the Opéra-Comique to be heard by Debussy alone. He greeted her with an air of resignation born of a long and fruitless search to find the ideal interpreter of the role of Mélisande. 'Sing, Mademoiselle,' said Debussy and his long, thin fingers, weighed down with rings and tipped with unbelievably long nails which rattled on the keys, began to race up and down the keyboard.[14] Debussy chanted the other roles for her. 'I sang the first two Acts; he didn't say a single word,' recalled Mary later. 'Then we began the third Act, the balcony scene. When we had finished, he suddenly buried his head in his hands and sat in silence for over a minute. Then, without a word, he got up and left the room.'

Mary could not think what had happened. She waited some time for him to return, but nobody came. Then, just as she had decided to leave, a boy came upstairs with a message from Albert Carré, saying he wanted to see her immediately. She went to the director's office; there was Debussy. He came towards her, took both her hands in his and asked (in an echo of the text of *Pelléas et Mélisande*): 'Where do you come from?' She told him and he stared at her with his deep mysterious eyes: 'Scotland! You have come all the way from the cold North to create my music.'

The first rehearsal for *Pelléas et Mélisande* was on 13 January 1902. Mary would rehearse Mélisande a total of 69 times (mostly in the presence of Debussy) before the première on 30 April. For Mary, apart from a handful of performances of *Manon* and *Louise*, it would be the year of Debussy.

The early individual rehearsals lasted between 45 minutes and an hour. They were held in one of the small rehearsal rooms at the Opéra-Comique. After an initial session with Debussy himself and the conductor Louis Landry, Mary was taken step by step through the part by Landry. With Landry, Debussy returned to hear her again on 21 January. As composer, he had the final verdict on who should or should not be in the cast. It is almost certain that this was the occasion when he irrevocably chose Mary for the role of Mélisande and decided to resist the pressure from his collaborator Maeterlinck to have the part assigned to Georgette Leblanc.

The impresario Henry Russell recalled that Maeterlinck was furious when he heard that Georgette Leblanc would not have the part. The normally unemotional Belgian arrived at Debussy's attic home, burning with rage and armed with a walking-stick. Madame Debussy opened the door and asked the poet what he wanted. Maeterlinck's reply was short and unusually direct. 'Madame, you see this cane? I have bought it to thrash your husband because he refuses to allow Georgette to sing in *Pelléas et Mélisande*.'[15]

Rumours circulated that Maeterlinck had challenged Debussy to a duel. But, instead, Georgette Leblanc initiated legal action in Maeterlinck's name to prevent the Opéra-Comique from staging the work unless she headed the cast. By good fortune, the suit failed.

Henry Russell's opinion of Leblanc as a singer was not high. 'She was a beautiful woman with a Grecian figure, large expressive eyes and exquisite colouring. But never at any time was she a great actress, and I am compelled to say that her singing was pitiable. The quality of her voice was harsh, her intonation defective, and she knew nothing whatsoever about music.'[16] Oddly enough, Maeterlinck himself had little appreciation or even love of music. The film producer Samuel Goldwyn (who was to meet him some years later in the United States) commented that: 'For me, one of the most amazing revelations regarding M. Maeterlinck concerns his indifference to music.'[17]

Although Leblanc's machinations were now, for the moment at least, effectively ended, all did not go smoothly for Mary. Progress with the rehearsals of *Pelléas et Mélisande* was painfully slow. 'When I began to work on the role of Mélisande,' remembered Mary, 'it took me a long time before I had my emotion under control, so as to be able to sing certain phrases without breaking down.'

She was absent from rehearsals on 24 and 25 January because of illness. Hearing she was indisposed, Debussy, at once sentimental and timid, was filled with pity. 'My dear little Mélisande,' he wrote from his table at the Café Riche on the Boulevard des Italiens just around the corner from the Opéra-Comique, 'I have learnt that you are ill and that pains me (as I hope you can see). I wanted very much to ask you if you would work on Friday, but I didn't dare to and so we will have to meet for *Pelléas* on Saturday.' And he signed himself quite formally, 'Claude Debussy', including his wife in the close – 'With tender affection from your two little friends'.[18] This was recognition of the fact that Mary and Debussy's wife Lily had become firm friends. The three of them often dined together, sometimes at the Rue Cardinet, sometimes at Mary's apartment. When Debussy left Lily for Emma Bardac two years later, Mary was to be inevitably affected by Lily's grief and her attempted suicide.

On 28 January Mary was back at work for an hour's coaching with

Landry and Debussy. Her tenure of the part was secure, for Debussy was convinced that only Mary, with her Scots accent and profound emotional identification with the role and with the work's brooding echoes of the Celtic twilight, could bring Mélisande to life as he conceived her. Mary's physical appearance was suitable for the part too, although her hair was not: 'for six months previous to the opening night men had been scouring the whole country hunting for a girl with red gold hair that trailed upon the ground as she walked. Five feet four inches it measures exactly and it was cut from a Breton girl's head, and sold for fifteen hundred francs, to deck the head of Mélisande'.[19]

As for Maeterlinck, he attended only one rehearsal; he was present on 19 March with Debussy to hear the third Act. For one last time, Maeterlinck tried to insist that Georgette Leblanc sing the leading role. In reply, the exasperated Debussy arranged for a jury of musicians to audition Leblanc. They agreed with the composer's decision and Maeterlinck was never seen at rehearsals again.

In mid-April there was a complete scenery rehearsal in running order, with all the sets, gas lamps, stage furniture, spot-lights, projections and testing of the curtain and safety-curtain. Then, finally, the great day dawned. The press preview of *Pelléas et Mélisande* was on 28 April 1902 at 1.15 pm. Sadly, it was marred by attempted artistic sabotage through the circulation of a satirical mock programme parodying the opera. The anonymous author of this spoof was almost certainly Maeterlinck, still smarting from Debussy's rejection of Georgette Leblanc. He had both the motive and an intimate knowledge of the libretto. That very morning, Maeterlinck had published a signed letter in *Le Figaro*, savaging the opera. He obviously hoped by this double-barrelled assault to undermine both Debussy's masterpiece and Mary's career.

During the performance, there was worse to come. When Mary delivered the line: 'Je ne suis pas heureuse' in her fetching Scottish-American accent, a man stood up in the audience and shouted: 'What do you expect?'

'All the tragic and pathetic parts of the opera,' wrote Mary later, 'were received with screams of laughter and wild hilarity. We who were singing, were numb with horror.'

During the interval, the audience boiled with controversy up and down the stairs, in the vestibules and as they spilled into the square outside. 'The many musicians present,' observed *Le Figaro*, 'were divided into two schools – the avant-garde and the bearded reactionaries. There was heated criticism from the enthusiasts, the lukewarm, the fanatics, the indifferent. Some said it was a musical event of the greatest importance; others said disrespectfully that it was just a practical joke. Among one group of people I heard the phrase "The power of orchestral sonorities"; in another, "monotonous psalm-singing" '.[20]

But the paper also added that, as a note-reading exercise, the vocal line must have been fiendishly difficult, adding that 'Miss Garden makes the best of the role of Mélisande. Her voice is very attractive and if her personality appears a little cold, it is because the part demands it'.

As for Debussy, he did not attend any of the performances, only the rehearsals. Mary recalled that he passed that fateful afternoon sitting around the corner at the Café Riche, chain-smoking, waiting nervously for a verdict on the opera he had worked at for ten long years.

On Mary, Debussy's verdict was fulsome: 'I have known cases of great devotion and great artists. Among the latter there was an artist who was curiously idiosyncratic. I had hardly anything to say to her. She painted the character of Mélisande all by herself, piece by piece. I watched her with singular confidence mixed with enormous curiosity.'[21] Later, Debussy would inscribe Mary's score with the words: 'In the future, others may sing Mélisande, but you alone will remain the woman and the artist I had hardly dared hope for'.[22]

Of course, Debussy was by no means the only composer with whom Mary was on cordial terms. Other composers also remembered her with affection. Mary's letters to Gustave Charpentier reveal that the bohemian composer of *Louise* continued to keep in touch with her. He had written to ask her to appear in a series of concerts he was organizing. 'M. Carré unfortunately has not been able to give me leave to sing on Tuesday,' Mary replied. 'He said that he needs me that evening for *Pelléas et Mélisande* at the Opéra-Comique. I am sorry, but M. Carré will only let me sing for you if he doesn't need me. Therefore, I will sing at your second concert.'[23] However, although she would not collaborate again with Charpentier in the opera house, he kept a protective eye on Mary's progress. Some years later he sent her a note which Mary proudly allowed to be published: 'Graceful interpreter,' it read, 'marvellous actress, divine singer, I feel close to you. The eloquence of the sea lulls me to sleep. I work and I often think of you.'[24]

By the fifth performance of *Pelléas et Mélisande* on 8 May, the furore caused by the first performance had all but died down. The theatre was as quiet as a cathedral. The audience sat with bated breath before the curtain rose; no one dared to cough or move in their seat, or make any noise at all. Late-comers were treated unmercifully.

Over the following weeks more and more people came to see the opera, until the box office takings exceeded all expectations. Following this great personal triumph, Mary was offered a new three-year contract by Albert Carré, beginning at 2000 francs a month and rising to 5000. On the strength of this, Mary moved out of her little room on the fifth floor and into an apartment on the fashionable Rue Washington, where she was to live for the next six years.

*   *   *

Now Mary looked for fresh fields to conquer. In the Biancolli biography she suggests that it was her performance as Manon in Paris the previous year which had attracted the interest of the Covent Garden authorities and subsequently led to her engagement there in July 1902. Another crucial factor was that André Messager was manager of the Royal Opera House.

Thus it was that she travelled to London and appeared in *Manon* at Covent Garden on 3 July, with great success. *The Times* (15 July) was admiring:

> In addition to a very charming stage presence she acts with delightful freshness, infinite variety, especially in facial expression, and grace; her voice, a very pure, rather light soprano, is extremely flexible and admirably used. In every way she is thoroughly artistic, whether in her gay or pathetic moments; and it is a rare combination of all that goes to make up an artist rather than any great predominance of one attribute that made her success so complete.

The critic went on to predict an outstanding future career.

Mary's second appearance at the Royal Opera House was in *La Princesse Osra* by Herbert Bunning (sung in French). But the new work was considered by *The Times* to have a weak libretto. Herbert Bunning's talent was defined as lyrical rather than dramatic. In spite of Mary's spirited acting, concluded *The Times*, the strenuousness of the orchestra and the rigid, inflexible beat of André Messager impeded her effectiveness and that of the other singers.

Meanwhile Claude Debussy, at home in Paris, had received an invitation from Messager to visit London. 'The success of "our Garden" doesn't surprise me,' Debussy wrote in reply. 'You'd surely have to be wearing ear-plugs to resist the charm of her voice. Personally, I can't imagine a gentler or more insinuating timbre. It's tyrannical in its hold on one – impossible to forget.' He added at the foot of the letter, 'Please will you kiss Mélisande on behalf of both of us and thank her for the charming letter I received this morning.'[25]

Debussy arrived in London on 13 July 1902 and ensconced himself for the next ten days at the Hotel Cecil in the Strand where Mary was also staying.[26] Two days later, between her operatic performances, he accompanied Mary to the Lyric Theatre to see Forbes-Robertson as Shakespeare's Hamlet.[27]

At the end of July, her stint in London finished, Mary adjourned once more to Aix-les-Bains for the summer, to resume her favourite walks along the sandy shore of the Lac du Bourget. In Aix she sang *Louise* with Léon Beyle and Fugère; then *Manon* and *Grisélidis*. 'Charpentier's work is written in prose,' observed *Le Progrès d'Aix-les-Bains*, 'something which has not yet appeared at the Opéra'. Among all the cast, Mary Garden deserved the highest praise, added the critic. As for *Grisélidis* – 'she was perfect in the part'.

It was the thirtieth anniversary of Aix's Théâtre du Cercle, and among the many celebrations was a concert at which Mary sang Messager's 'Mélodie' and Rogers' 'At Parting', as well as joining eight other singers in Gounod's 'Ave Maria'.

Among the many amusements at Aix were the festivities in honour of the King of Greece. Great numbers of people crowded into the park and then into the salons for the evening gala. After dinner, the king came down to the park. It was brilliantly illuminated with fireworks, including a triumphal arch and a cascade of fire in which fishes appeared to be swimming. The orchestra played, followed by music-hall turns and a ballet. Beaming warmly, the king acknowledged the applause of the revellers.

Her stay at Aix over, Mary a little reluctantly returned to Paris. There, in late September, she began a series of performances of *Manon* and *Louise*. At the same time she and Claude Debussy were again busy with rehearsals of *Pelléas et Mélisande* – right up to the first night a month later.

In mid-January 1903, aserts Jack Winsor Hansen, Mary went to Nice for a few days. She was having great difficulties with her turbulent relationship with Messager and needed to get away. In the Casino at Nice, Mary chanced to meet Sibyl Sanderson who by this time was in and out of hospital. Sibyl had written time after time to Mary asking for money, but Mary had always refused.[28] Hansen quotes an unpublished interview between Carl Van Vechten and Mary Garden in which she described a violent quarrel with Sanderson, after which Mary concluded: 'Why should I give her any money when she would have gone out and spent it on booze, booze and more booze?'

From Barre Hill, Mary's last Pelléas (in Boston, 1931), came the information that Mary had been avoiding Sanderson, 'because of the vicious gossip about Sibyl's unorthodox sexual tastes. Mary couldn't afford to have anything to do with her.'[29]

In late January 1903 Mary launched herself into a new role, that of Violetta in Verdi's *La traviata* which opened on 12 February. 'Miss Garden was simply delightful', wrote the critic for *Le Figaro*. Although agreeing that she had given a remarkable interpretation, the review went on to complain about the poverty of Verdi's harmonies and the thinness of his orchestration.

'Violetta was one of my favourite roles,' Mary Garden later confided. 'I never sang it in America, only in Paris and Brussels. I found the pure coloratura American brand of Violetta, a healthy, robust nightingale with a high E [in fact, a high E flat] to finish the first Act aria (if she ever missed it, God help her!), had nothing whatsoever to do with *La dame aux Camélias*.'

By now Sibyl Sanderson had come back from Nice where she had been sent on the orders of her physician, Dr Escoverso, to try and cure her infectious pneumonia. Sanderson's skin was sallow and had the texture of leather. Her body was swollen and discoloured 'and cruelly distorted by the effects of the slow atrophy of her liver.'[30] She could only eat scraps of salted meat. When Mary visited, she found Sibyl lying in bed, covered in a wicker frame to keep the bedclothes from rubbing against her. In a corner of her room sat her new fiancé, Count Paul Tolstoi (a cousin of the novelist), smoking a large black cigar, apparently oblivious to her suffering. Sibyl planned to marry him in the summer.

Then, on Friday 15 May at five o'clock in the morning, Mary was wakened by the frantic ringing of her doorbell. Hearing a male voice shouting her name, she flung on her dressing-gown and stepped quickly into the hall to see what he wanted. She found a man gesticulating wildly to her French maid. He was a *New York Herald* reporter and wanted Mary's views on the death of Sibyl Sanderson who had, he said, passed away only an hour before.

Shaking with emotion, not believing it to be true, Mary dressed quickly and went with the reporter to the Sanderson apartment – No 1 bis, Avenue Bois de Boulogne. There she discovered he had been telling the truth. Mary tried her best to console Sibyl's sisters and her maid, Lena, who had been with her for over 20 years. Lena wanted Mary to go into the bedroom and take one last look at her friend. 'I did not want to go,' recalled Mary, 'as I wanted her to live in my memory as the glorious Sibyl I had always known.'

The funeral at the church of Saint-Honoré d'Eylau was magnificent. The coffin was strewn with roses. Massenet, Carré and Saint-Saëns were present, as were many other artists. Mary sat close to the coffin with Sibyl's two sisters. Chopin's funeral march was played on the organ and then Massenet's 'Elégie' for cello. 'I had often read of a heart breaking,' Mary wrote later, 'but I never realized until that day what those words really meant.'

Sibyl's body was cremated and her ashes buried in the Père Lachaise cemetery. Later they were taken back to America and interred beside her father in San Francisco, California.

Hard practical considerations now made themselves felt. On the following day, Mary returned early to the Sanderson home, according to Jack Winsor Hansen, 'demanding her pick of Sibyl's fabulous operatic costumes, stage jewellery and other accessories. She insisted that Sibyl had bequeathed her the diamond-topped walking stick of Manon.'[31]

Sibyl's death shocked Mary into a great longing to visit America again. Shortly after the funeral she wrote to a friend in New York, who passed on Mary's thoughts about her future to the *Globe Democrat* (23 May): 'Her Paris contract holds her for another year, and after that, she hopes to go to America, which is her dearest wish.'

Notes

1. *LA Herald and Express*, 21 October 1954.
2. Frederick N. Sard, *The Musical Observer*, New York, March 1921.
3. Jane S. Smith (1982), *Elsie de Wolfe*, New York: Athenaeum, p. 120.
4. *Musical America*, 2 October 1909.
5. *Denver Times*, 15 October 1911.
6. *Washington Star*, April 1908, NYPL.
7. Mary Garden, *Theatre*, March 1908.
8. Jack Winsor Hansen, 'Mary Garden: Queen of Chutzpah', Part II, *Massenet Society Newsletter*, vol 10, no 1, January 1991, p. 2.
9. Jack Winsor Hansen, 'Mary Garden: Queen of Chutzpah', Part III, *Massenet Society Newsletter*, vol 10, no. 2, July 1992, p. 4.
10. *The New York Times*, 27 January 1935.
11. *Le Ménestrel*, 29 September 1901.
12. *Le Figaro*, 23 October 1901.
13. Telegram dated Friday 20 December 1901. Scrapbook in private possession of Peter MacPhee.
14. Jean Masson, *Candide*, 25 March 1925.
15. Henry Russell (1926), *The Passing Show*, London: Thornton Butterworth Ltd, pp. 208–9.
16. Ibid., p. 207.
17. Samuel Goldwyn (1924), *Behind the Screen*, London: Grant Richards Ltd, p. 255.
18. Letter from Debussy to Garden, held in RCM archive.
19. *New York World*, 16 February 1908.
20. *Le Figaro*, 1 May 1902.
21. Claude Debussy, *The Evening Post*, 20 February 1908, NYPL.
22. Carl Van Vechten (1917), *Interpreters and Interpretations*, New York: Knopf, p. 74.
23. National Library of Scotland, Department of Manuscripts, Accession number 4575.
24. Mary Garden Scrapbook, vol. 10, p. 25B, RCM.
25. Debussy to Messager, Wednesday 9 July 1902, in *Debussy Letters*, ed. François Lesure and trans. Roger Nichols (1987), London: Faber and Faber, p. 130.
26. Robert Orledge (1982), *Debussy and the Theatre*, Cambridge University Press, p. 186.
27. Edward Lockspeiser (1965), *Debussy – His Life and Mind*, Vol II 1902–1918, Cambridge University Press, pp. 66–7, n. 4.
28. Jack Winsor Hansen, 'Mary Garden: Queen of Chutzpah', Part III, *Massenet Society Newsletter*, vol. 10, no. 2, July 1991, p. 4.
29. Ibid.
30. *New York Herald*, 17 May 1903.
31. Jack Winsor Hansen, op. cit., p. 5.

4 Wider Horizons: 1903–1907

At the beginning of June 1903, André Messager again welcomed Mary to Covent Garden. She moved into rooms at the Hotel Cecil in the Strand, where Claude Debussy was also staying. Her first appearance was to be in *Roméo et Juliette*. It was probably during this visit that Mary made her first recordings – cylinders for the Pathé Company in London, with piano accompaniment. The American critic Richard Fletcher once recalled her reaction to the relatively primitive recording technology then in use. 'No artist could be relaxed or sing with necessary concentration,' complained Mary, 'while a recording machine sprayed wax shavings at her.'[1]

The songs Mary chose to preserve for posterity in 1903 were six Scots songs: 'Comin thro the rye', 'Annie Laurie', ''Twas within a mile o' Edinboro Town', 'Jock o' Hazeldean', 'Afton Water' and 'Robin Adair'.

At the Royal Opera House, meanwhile, rehearsals were going splendidly. Then, two days before she was due to sing, Mary happened to be sitting at an open window, admiring the boats passing down the Thames. While she sat enjoying the panorama, the Belgian tenor Ernest van Dyck (1861–1923) dropped by to see her. Van Dyck was the first Werther in Massenet's opera of that name and was then appearing as Tristan at the Royal Opera House. Immediately he warned her that no singer could afford to sit by an open window in London and admire the river. But Mary laughed and paid no attention, certain that no possible harm could come to her.

As predicted, however, disaster followed. On the morning of 6 June Mary was practising for her first appearance that season, when suddenly her voice gave out completely: she could not sing a single high note. Desperate, she rested in total silence for the remainder of the day until it was time to go to the Opera House. The opera began without incident but, when it reached the point where Juliette has to sing the Waltz, Mary was overcome by panic – she wanted to run off-stage and lock herself into her dressing-room. Fortunately the French bass, Pol Plançon, could see what she was planning.

He caught hold of her and pushed her back on to the set so that she had no choice but to sing.

The whole first act was a disaster for Mary. Every note above A had to be imagined by the audience, as not a sound came out of her throat. Happily, as the opera progressed and her voice warmed up, things improved and she just managed to struggle through to the final curtain. Next day Mary was taken to a doctor, who confirmed she had a severe attack of rheumatism in the vocal cords; she was forbidden to sing or talk for four days. She sat in her room, overcome with despair, wondering if she would ever sing again. But, in time, her voice returned and she was able to sing Juliette on one more occasion and finish the season. However, she had been so shaken by this experience that, for many years, she was unable to sing the role again.

This unfortunate return to Covent Garden was in marked contrast to her success the year before. What made it worse was that the London press was apparently not prepared to take her illness into account. 'The part is one which makes considerable demands upon a singer', commented *The Times* reprovingly, 'and if it cannot be said that Miss Garden's vocal powers are as yet quite adequate to the task, she acts with such charm and sincere conviction that it would be easy to forgive far worse singing than hers'. The critic added an elegant rapier-thrust:

> The quality of the voice is not very pleasing; and her execution of florid passages, though very neat, is not always quite to be depended upon. The top note of the cadenza in the *Valse* was omitted, it would seem accidentally. Her acting in the balcony scene and throughout the bed-chamber scene was quite admirable, though in the opening she was rather the model schoolgirl with an exemplary habit of arranging her mouth by saying 'prunes and prisms' than the child of nature with noble ardours to be kindled at a touch.

At the beginning of July she sang Massenet's *Manon* twice and at once her standing with the London critics was restored. 'There can be no doubt of Miss Garden's success,' gushed *The Times*. 'She acts with complete sympathy, wisely refraining from attempting to put too much sincerity or emotional fervour into the part, and her singing of the various admired numbers is extremely good.' But only a day or two later, Mary was again to succumb to laryngitis, preventing her from appearing in a star-studded gala before the King and Queen and the President of the French Republic. Among the performers were Emma Calvé as Carmen and Nellie Melba, singing from *Rigoletto* and then standing in for Mary in a scene from *Roméo et Juliette*.

With some success, Mary contrived to return to the Royal Opera House for *Faust*. 'The Marguerite of Mlle. Garden, heard for the first time in London, was both original and convincing,' said *The Times*. 'It is true that the part demands at times almost more, vocally, than Mlle. Garden has to give, and in the love duet she was not at her best, though she sang the 'Jewel Song' in excellent style; but in the final trio she was quite excellent, and her make-up, especially in the first acts, was very becoming – more so, in fact, than in the church scene, in which her acting was quite superb.'

In view of this generally warm reception by the English critics, one might expect Mary to have been well disposed towards London and the Royal Opera House. But her humiliation through illness and the lack of sympathy on the part of the critics rankled. 'I loathe London,' she complained, 'and would not go back for five thousand dollars a night. The atmosphere of the place is always frightfully depressing. The people lack interest and understanding as far as opera goes. I don't love the English. Possibly I don't understand them. Certainly they don't understand me.'[2]

From London, Mary hurried gratefully to her beloved Aix-les-Bains, to play *Manon*. Returning to Paris after enjoying her summer break, she started rehearsals once again with Debussy at the Opéra-Comique for *Pelléas et Mélisande*, as well as singing her by now standard repertoire of *Louise*, *Manon* and *La traviata*. At the end of October, Giacomo Puccini happened to be in Paris and came to hear Mary sing Mélisande. Afterwards, he met the company and the production team and was 'sardonically amused by the backstage acrimony'.[3]

Mary was by now working with Massenet's pupil, the volatile composer Xavier Henry Napoléon Leroux (1863–1919), in preparation for his new work, *La Reine Fiamette*. The *répétition générale* (press dress-rehearsal) two days before Christmas astounded Mary. 'One would have imagined that the eighth wonder of the world had arrived,' she exclaimed. The audience was hysterical with enthusiasm and called her in front of the curtain more than twenty times until she could bow no longer. 'The first night audience downstairs was so delirious,' she recalled, 'that Mr Leroux nearly fainted for joy and he took me out with him in front of the curtain.'[4]

What was strange was that the applause came predominantly from the expensive boxes and orchestra seats. The cheaper galleries were cold and silent – and the audiences slowly began to get smaller and smaller. Mary felt ill at ease in the role. 'I did not enjoy creating that opera,' said Mary later. 'I found the music ugly and the story too steeped in Italian politics. I have always observed that politics in opera spells failure. Nothing but the simple and eternal story of love and death is a lasting operatic success.'

Nevertheless, the critics recognized *La Reine Fiamette* as a personal landmark in her career. 'It has to be said that in this role Miss Garden has climbed to a position she has never reached before,' remarked *Le Figaro* (23 December 1903). 'She gives a performance of inexhaustible variety, composed of endlessly different aspects of personality and mood. She is at once delicious and exquisite, sad and dramatic.'

Two letters from this period to the critic Raymond Bouyer give an insight into Mary's state of mind and reveal how difficult she had found it to achieve success as a foreign national: 'I read and re-read your article in "La

Nouvelle Revue" with pride and happiness', she wrote. 'How can I thank you, Monsieur. What courage you give me! I need courage, for I am a foreigner and to obtain such a review from a French critic richly repays the four years of hard work since I came to France. Thank you, sir, from the depths of my heart.' She continued, with just a hint of exaggeration: 'You will always stay in my memory, having been the one who gave me the first word of encouragement in my work'. Then, referring to the tragic death of Sibyl Sanderson and her own unhappy return to Covent Garden, Mary added: 'I began this year with great sorrows and because of that I neglected many things. Please accept all my best wishes for 1904 and for ever.'[5]

Mary continued her run of success with *La Reine Fiamette* during the first weeks of 1904. 'Miss Garden's voice has never been so greatly and so harmoniously resonant,' wrote the *Musica* reviewer (February 1904). 'She was completely Fiamette. It is above all in emotional roles that her talent as singer and actress blossoms so strongly. Radiant, delicious, amorous and languorous, passionate and powerful, she has a voice of the highest and most impeccable clarity.'

Looking back at *La Reine Fiamette* in her autobiographies, Mary dismissed the piece as an aberration. But, in her retrospective judgement she undervalued very considerably the success of the work and its importance as a milestone in her own career. She claimed that the work was taken off after 20 nights, but in reality the register of the Opéra-Comique shows that it was given on more than 30 occasions.

*   *   *

On 18 July 1904, Mary Garden and Claude Debussy decided to cross the Channel to see Sarah Bernhardt and Mrs Patrick Campbell in a special matinée performance of Maeterlinck's *Pelléas et Mélisande* performed in the original French text at the Vaudeville Theatre. They took the night train, arriving in London early on the morning of the performance and then had a good lunch at the house of one of Mary's friends. The play, however, was a disappointment to both of them. Mary thought Bernhardt miscast and was horrified to see that when Mélisande let down her tresses from her tower bedroom, the hair was jet black! Leaving the theatre immediately after the performance, Mary and Debussy quickly returned to Paris.

Nevertheless, Sarah Bernhardt had been a considerable influence on Mary's development as an actress and to some extent Mary's future career would parallel Bernhardt's. Like Bernhardt, Mary had a great flair for publicity. Oscar Wilde's play, *Salomé*, had been written in French for Bernhardt and was produced in Paris while Wilde was still in prison (suggesting perhaps that Wilde saw himself as Jochanaan); while Richard Strauss' *Salome* would later become one of Mary's great roles. Bernhardt played several other parts that Mary would later take, and like Mary, she was especially effective in *travesti* roles.

The master actor Benoît Constant Coquelin (1841–1909) also influenced Mary, as she admitted in the year of his death, remembering what 'that master player upon human hearts' had taught her:

> One night, tired and overwrought he was playing the lead in *Les Misérables*, when, to his own surprise, he burst into a flood of tears. Himself so deeply moved, he lost sight of the supreme moment, and his audience sat as if carved in stone. Another night, warned by his previous error, he held himself aloof from the throbbing woe of the character he acted, and his audience shed the tears. So Art triumphed over Nature. Doesn't she always?[6]

Coquelin's approach to stage technique also had similarities with that of Bernhardt. Both stressed voice as the actor's principal weapon. Both were equally skilful at using silence. Both co-ordinated sets and costumes to lavish total effect. But despite these parallels there were also significant differences. From the playwright Victorien Sardou and the tragedian François Talma (1763–1826), Bernhardt had learnt to employ a specific order in miming a climax – glance, followed by gesture; finally, speech. Coquelin, on the other hand, was noted for facial expression, centring on his eyes. Bernhardt's effects were a blend of traditions – the classical and the melodramatic. She used the *contrapposto* (S-curve) beloved of mannerist painters, posing with her shoulders in one direction and her hips in the other. Coquelin, however, avoided exaggerated visual effects; he relied on internalizing his characters.[7]

Mary Garden's mastery of flamboyant external gesture and her deeply internalized characterization can be seen in part as the result of watching both Bernhardt and Coquelin at work and discussing their methods with them off-stage.[8] This can be seen as one of the principal benefits to Mary of spending the early part of her career in Paris, a cosmopolitan melting-pot of traditions and influences from all over Europe and the East.

In 1904 Mary again entered the recording studio, this time in Paris for the Gramophone & Typewriter Company Ltd, with Claude Debussy accompanying her at the piano. First to be recorded were the *Ariettes oubliées*, texts from poems by Paul Verlaine set to music by Debussy – 'Il pleure dans mon coeur'; 'L'Ombre des arbres'; 'Green'. Then came 'Mes longs cheveux' from *Pelléas et Mélisande*.

Listening to these recordings in 1954, with the benefit of hindsight, Richard Fletcher commented:

> It is said that Debussy greatly admired a 'dry' singing tone. Perhaps in deference to Debussy's taste, perhaps because she herself considered such tone appropriate for the songs, or perhaps merely by nature of the recording apparatus of the day, Garden managed to achieve an extreme *sécheresse* [dryness; coldness; leanness] in certain portions of these recordings.
>
> At any rate, the delivery here tends more towards dryness than in any of her

later recordings. It is possible that this characteristic of her early discs derived from tenseness which disappeared as her voice mellowed, and as her approach to singing and to the recording process relaxed.

In all of these recordings the voice is clear and perfectly pitched, though Debussy's piano sags throughout.[9]

Desmond Shawe-Taylor, in 1984, is less sanguine: 'a woefully inadequate and primitive G & T of 1904, in which her singing of the unaccompanied quasi-folksong at the start of Act 3 is interspersed with some wavering piano phrases played by Debussy himself.'[10] These are sentiments echoed by the tenor Hugues Cuénod: 'Alas, the small solo from *Pélleas* certainly does not give an idea of Garden at her best. I still have in my ears the enchanted sounds she fluted out even as late as 1927 and the strange charm floating over Mélisande. These virtues are not present in the recorded excerpt, and are to be found still less in "Il pleure dans mon coeur", sung to a tinkly piano (one hopes it is not Debussy himself).'[11]

As for 'L'Ombre des arbres' and 'Green', these drew the disapproval of Richard Fletcher. 'In the songs, Debussy tends to race some of the tempi, especially in "Green", causing the singer to sound hurried and breathless. Garden in later years used this number as a standard recital item, taking it much more slowly to convey an impression of woodsy languor.'[12] If this is so, it appears to contrast with Garden's normal practice in later years, which saw her profess to measure performances of Debussy's works according to their fidelity to the composer's customary playing style.

Thirty years after Fletcher's judgement, Desmond Shawe-Taylor again contradicted him, adopting criteria of a quite different kind and approving, this time, of the result. 'We note the decisive clarity of the tone and the remarkable freedom (by tame modern standards) of tempo and phrasing.'[13] But while critics may disagree on the success of an interpretation as preserved by an admittedly primitive process, there can be no argument as to the historical value of these recordings.

*   *   *

As was her custom, Mary spent August and September of 1904 at Aix-les-Bains, this time singing Thaïs. After one performance, the artists were called four times in front of the curtain – evidently unique in the history of the theatre. In a single performance of *Thaïs* in late October, Mary's grace and charm were remarked upon by the critics.[14]

Back in Paris her schedule in November and December that year was, apart from a single rehearsal of Mozart's *Les Nôces de Figaro*, marked by preparation for only one new work – Saint-Saëns' *Hélène*, the première of which had taken place in Monte Carlo the previous February, with Melba in the title role.

The dress rehearsal of *Hélène* was given at the Opéra-Comique on 16 January 1905 before the assembled press. 'I praise Miss Garden unreservedly,' said *Le Figaro* (18 January 1905). 'In the role of *Hélène*, she gave evidence of exquisite sensibility, of harmony and proportion in her movements, of admirable vocal security and the finest intelligence in musical expression.'

Another new role followed a month later in Monte Carlo, where she sang the leading *travesti* part of the 17-year-old Spanish boy, Chérubin, in the première of Massenet's opera of the same name. The soprano Emma Calvé had been at the rehearsals and the most influential critics in Europe were present including Gabriel Fauré who was covering the work for *Le Figaro*. Sitting with Prince Albert in the royal box were Massenet and his wife.

It was a triumph. Commenting on Mary's performance, Fauré wrote: 'It would be impossible to conjure up more bravery, gaiety and spirit', adding that her success was swift and complete.[15] 'Miss Mary Garden, who lends her delicious voice to the role of Chérubin,' wrote Fernand Platy in *Le Journal de Monaco* (21 February 1905), 'performed the role with charming mischievousness and astonishing verve. And how jaunty she is dressed as a man – she carries it off with suggestive ease. She seems to be at one and the same time an adorable child and possessed by a demon. Her acting is pure art. The audience could hardly stop applauding her throughout the whole opera.'

The sopranos Lina Cavalieri as L'Ensoleillad and Marguerite Carré as Nina were also greatly admired. Equally so, Maurice Renaud as the Philosopher.

Mary's success in the role of Chérubin was repeated at the Opéra-Comique in May 1905 – again singing with her rival Marguerite Carré and, this time, Lucien Fugère. Massenet was present for most of the rehearsals. Mary sang the role that May and June, until the end of the season. The effect of her performance on the Paris audience was as seductive as ever. A front-page cartoon in *Le Figaro* shows two young women discussing the opera: 'Garden – she was adorable! My father says that it was like Virginie De Jazet in *La Belle Époque*'. The caption concluded coyly: 'Daddy was very worked up about Garden – so excited even that he gave Mummy a very fine present!'

Mary ventured once more into recording. Her Edison Cylinders date from this period in Paris. With an orchestra she recorded 'Le chanson du duc' (*Chérubin*); 'L'amour est une vertu rare' (*Thaïs*) and 'Chant Vénitien' by Bemberg – this last with piano accompaniment.

Midsummer 1905 was spent as usual in Aix. 'Miss Garden is still the Thaïs full of charm and grace whom one never wearies of applauding,' wrote *L'Avenir d'Aix-les-Bains* (10 July 1905). 'Her voice is clear and pure as crystal', commented the critics on a subsequent performance. They also admired the beautifully sinuous line of her figure. Changing roles, she became a delicious Manon, a part she interpreted, said the critics, with 'the characteristically bizarre and piquant originality employed by one of the most interesting of artists – and consequently, one of the most patronised of our age.'[16] Her success appeared complete.

Late in October, Mary went to Rome for the first time, soaking in the atmosphere of *Tosca* at the Chapel of the Attavanti in Sant' Andrea della Valle and noting 'something quite indescribable and mysterious in my inner self, being conquered at once by Rome's imperious magnificence'. She visited the country home of a friend, Count Giuseppe Primoli, in the bathing resort of Fiumicino, where in 1885 Debussy had written a large part of his 'Diane au Bois' while still a Prix de Rome scholar. Primoli was the son of Charlotte Buonaparte and had been brought up at the Tuilleries in the circle of the Empress Eugénie. He was a patron of the arts well known for his hospitality. He would later introduce d'Annunzio to Paris and pave the way for the triumph of Eleonora Duse.

But after ten days in Rome, Mary received a telegram asking her to sing at a soirée for King George of Greece to be held by King Edward VII at Windsor Castle. Very reluctantly, she left Rome. Passing through Paris, she stopped only to buy a beautiful new dress for the occasion. Then she went to London the day before the soirée and settled into her room at the Savoy Hotel.

Strolling through the Strand, she heard the newsboys announce that the King had sprained his ankle while hunting. Mary hoped the soirée would be cancelled 'for I must tell you,' she wrote later, 'it was always torture for me to have to sing at any private function'. However, there was to be no such relief: the soirée at Windsor Castle went ahead the following day (17 November) despite the King's injury.

Mary arrived at Windsor Castle with Melba and was ushered into a long, cold room. At the far end was a small fire which they both hugged desperately – for hours, it seemed. They were then taken upstairs to a small circular room off the drawing-room where the concert was to be given. The large doors into the dining-room next door were open and, through them, they could see the crowned heads standing drinking someone's health. Shortly afterwards, all the guests came flooding into the drawing-room for the concert. Edward VII seated himself between Queen Alexandra and King George of Greece in the middle of the front row, resting his sprained ankle on a red velvet cushion. Among other members of the audience were the Archbishop of Canterbury and Viscount Churchill.

'Melba sang like a bird from *Rigoletto* and *La bohème*,' recalled Mary. Mistakenly, she writes in her autobiography that the other singer on the programme was the baritone, Sammarco. In fact, it was the tenor Giovanni Zenatello (1876–1949). With Landon Ronald at the piano, the Australian diva partnered Zenatello in one of Puccini's love duets, while Mary sang

'Vissi d'arte' (*Tosca*) and 'Depuis le jour' from *Louise*. Sir Walter Parratt conducted, assisted by the composer Francesco Paolo Tosti.

After the entertainment was over, the two kings and the Queen chatted to the artists and thanked them. As the royal party left the room, King George of Greece, with whom Mary had become acquainted at Aix-les-Bains, presented her with a magnificent pearl necklace; its value was later reputed to be $1.5 million. The artists were invited to join some of the ladies and gentlemen-in-waiting at supper. About 20 people sat down to the meal, Lord Farquhar taking his place between the two sopranos.

During a pause, while everyone was eating their asparagus, Melba complained in a loud voice: 'What a poor concert this would have been if I hadn't been singing!' Lord Farquhar tried to smooth over the embarrassment as best he could by paying Mary a compliment but in fact Mary rather enjoyed the situation; Melba's rudeness amused her. She liked Melba for her outspoken and forceful Australian manners.

After supper, the artists were offered accommodation for the night in the Castle or a swift return to London in a special train. Melba and Mary took the train. 'Before we reached London,' Mary recalled, 'we had become fast friends and this friendship lasted until she died.' Their mutual liking was such that Melba apparently tried to persuade Mary to join her opera company in Australia to sing *Louise*, but Mary had no desire to work so far away from Europe. Some years later Melba visited Mary in Monte Carlo. 'A more charming companion would have been hard to find,' commented Mary. 'She entered into all our fun and, like me, adored to play roulette. I have often heard that she was not kind to her fellow-artists, but I never saw that side of her character. She had nothing to fear from me, as my voice was not *coloratura* and I did not threaten her career in any way.'

*   *   *

In 1906, from 3 January until its première on 27 March, Mary rehearsed Camille Erlanger's new opera, *Aphrodite*, with a libretto based on the highly popular novel by Pierre Louÿs (1870–1925). The part would require her to play a lesbian, a prospect at which Mary was unperturbed in spite of Carré's misgivings, and for the rest of the season her energies were devoted exclusively to this work. Erlanger's opera 'winds its pernicious way through a tale of prostitution, murder, theft, sexual inversion, drunkenness, sacrilege and crucifixion and concludes, quite simply, in a cemetery.'[17]

By now, Mary was having to work extremely hard to maintain her position as leading soprano of the Opéra-Comique. But there was one challenge she could scarcely fight on its own terms. It came from Albert Carré's wife, Marguerite, whom he had married in the autumn of 1902.

In her old age the soprano Maggie Teyte would enjoy repeating the anecdote about the two leading sopranos meeting one evening underneath the opera house stage along the narrow passage that gave access from one side of the wings to the other. 'Let me pass,' said one soprano to the other. 'Don't you know who I am?' said the other, 'I am Madame X, the wife of the director.' Whereupon the first soprano replied: 'Oh, don't be silly, I was Madame X long before you'. According to Teyte, the sopranos concerned were Mary Garden and Marguerite Carré.[18] Carré himself always vehemently denied that he had ever been motivated in his relationship to Mary by anything other than strictly professional criteria.

Jack Winsor Hansen goes further. He suggests that Marguerite Carré was determined to topple Mary from her pre-eminent position at the Opéra-Comique. This she attempted to do on three fronts: first, she put it about that Mary was suffering from tuberculosis and would infect other singers if they came too close; second, she circulated the rumour that Mary was a lesbian, again with the object of frightening off other artists, by intimating that Sibyl Sanderson had introduced Mary to a bi-sexual lifestyle. Third, she instigated a stream of hate-mail which arrived regularly at Mary's door.[19]

While rehearsing for *Aphrodite*, Mary had to put this rivalry out of her mind. Carré was trying hard to convey an aura of sensuality and abandon in the opera. He tried to angle lights in such a way that they shone through Mary's evanescent costume and revealed her nakedness under it. Much to his frustration, the lamps available to him were not nearly powerful enough.[20] But, as he hoped, at the première Mary's Chrysis was a sensation. Popular enthusiasm was unbounded, as a cartoon in *Le Figaro* (28 March 1906) demonstrates. In it, an old bald man in the audience is speaking to a young lady who is holding a pair of binoculars and scrutinizing the singers on stage. 'How do you like the costumes?' asks the old man. 'There are too many of them,' she replies. 'Blast!' he exclaims, 'I was led to believe there wouldn't be any!' And in a photograph on another page in the same issue, Mary is shown wearing a very low-cut dress. Underneath runs a quotation from *Chérubin*: 'Je suis li ... bre!'

Le Figaro wrote that Mary 'played the role of Chrysis as a great lyric tragedienne. She could not be more beautiful, more seductive, more touching. No greater enthusiasm could be aroused – the evening was a triumph for her'.

During one performance of *Aphrodite*, a calling card was brought to Mary's dressing-room at the Opéra-Comique from a gentleman waiting below. Mary glanced at the card, which read: 'Oscar Hammerstein'. The name meant absolutely nothing to her, so she sent back word to tell Mr Hammerstein to telephone her in the morning. Hammerstein was, in fact, anxious to secure Mary's services at his Manhattan Opera House in New York for the coming season. When eventually she did give him an appointment, he climbed the five flights of stairs to her apartment; he had to sit on the top step to recover from the effort. While he was recovering, Mary's maid came out and said her mistress was very sorry but she was too tired to see anybody; she had been rehearsing all day and was resting. This was too much for the impresario, who mopped his brow and started off downstairs. The maid vainly endeavoured to get him to make an appointment for some later date. 'I'm too tired to make another engagement,' Hammerstein called back, 'I walked up five flights of steps and I'm resting now – as I go down.'[21]

* * *

Marguerite Carré's efforts to oust Mary Garden from the Opéra-Comique became more determined, and would culminate in Mary looking further afield for work. According to Jack Winsor Hansen, the scandalous stories circulated by Mme Carré, who had apparently hired private detectives to expose Mary's lack of morals, included that she had sold her body to a man in Chicago (presumably, David Mayer) in return for financing her studies in Paris and had done the same for Sibyl Sanderson in Paris in order to gain entry to the Opéra-Comique.[22] In order to avoid the adverse publicity threatened by his wife's allegations, Carré took the part of Mélisande away from Mary, giving it and that of Chrysis in *Aphrodite* to the 19-year-old Maggie Teyte as soon as Mary left for America, and he severely limited Mary's contractual appearances – in 1907 Mary would sing only some 25 times at the Opéra-Comique.

This seemed an appropriate moment for Mary to spend some time abroad. At the beginning of 1907 she appeared in Maeterlinck's native land, in Brussels, at Le Théâtre Royal de la Monnaie, in *Pelléas et Mélisande*. Unlike the Gothic settings used at the Opéra-Comique (of which Maeterlinck did not approve), the opera at La Monnaie was set in early Renaissance Italy.

Debussy presided over the final rehearsals with the orchestra and the singers and Mary went on to make 14 appearances there as Mélisande. Exceptionally, according to *L'Éventail* (6 January 1907), the composer was seen to be smiling and in good humour. As for Mary, she was 'an actress in a class of her own – original, a singer with a strangely attractive voice and crisp diction. She is the ideal incarnation of the character dreamed of by the poet. She is Mélisande, from her toes to the crown of her head, supple, fine, disturbing, deliciously and innocently wayward and seductive because she is unaware of her waywardness'. The critic Georges Eekhoud added his compliments: 'What a fascinating voice, fluid and full of hidden strength. What diction, what movement and what poses! The Théâtre Royal audience was never so hypnotised. Its enthusiasm turned to delirium, with countless recalls.'[23]

This was to be the last time Mary and Debussy worked together in the theatre. 'Debussy,' she wrote many years later, 'was not easy to know. He was intensely timid and unsociable. I never observed in his nature any real exuberant expression for anyone or anything. It was quite impossible for him to reveal his inner self to anyone. He was mystery itself.'[24]

In March 1907 the music publisher Gustave Schirmer arrived in Paris to see Mary. He had been sent over to sign Mary by Oscar Hammerstein, who was planning an artistic counter-offensive at the Manhattan Opera House against the onslaught of the Metropolitan's German and Italian repertoire, by providing a rich diet of the finest French operas; Mary had a key part to play in his plans. She was aware that she had angered and humiliated Hammerstein and was keen to make amends. She read over the contract that Schirmer had brought and agreed to sign it but, she stipulated, only in Hammerstein's presence.

As the summer of 1907 approached, Mary was at the peak of her powers. To one enquirer she revealed: 'I have to sing tonight and I always rest quietly beforehand'. The reporter observed that 'She smiled with a soft languor that really masked a perfect arsenal of energy'.[25] She was the toast of the Paris opera public. Her maid revealed that Mary was being pursued by princes and barons. 'There was a host of them, all offering titles and estate and jewels and their hearts'.[26] Mary often reacted in unexpected ways to this adulation. According to one American correspondent, she ejected the elderly Marquis de Castellane – who had managed to invade her boudoir with a bunch of orchids – by kicking him down the stairs into the street.[27] But one admirer of her art whom she did not dismiss was the composer Richard Strauss.

Strauss had come to see a performance of *Pelléas et Mélisande*. He arrived during the first scene and sat alongside the novelist and musicologist, Romain Rolland, with Maurice Ravel and Jean Marnold, a music critic. During the performance, Strauss chatted freely to Rolland, emphasizing points, yet listening to what was happening on stage 'with the greatest attention and, looking through a lorgnette or my opera glasses,' said Rolland, 'he didn't take his eyes off the actors or the orchestra for an instant.'[28]

In his diary, Rolland described the dinner which followed next day at the house 'of a certain X who is, I don't know how, a friend of Strauss. I find there Strauss, [the composer Gabriel] Pierné and his wife; one of Briand's [Aristide Briand (1862–1932), French socialist politician] secretaries and his wife; the Z's; Lord Speyer, to whom the score of *Salome* is dedicated, and Lady Speyer; Mary Garden (yesterday's Mélisande) and a rather pretty American woman, who has been playing (very badly) the part of the page in *Salome* – Strauss speaks to me again about *Pelléas*, from one end of the table to the other'.[29] Describing the two singers, Rolland adds that their dresses were 'cut so low as to show their navels'.

Strauss had written *Salome* in 1905 after an 1893 text of Oscar Wilde. Its first production was at Dresden on 9 December 1905 with Marie Wittich and Carl Burrian, conducted by Ernst von Schuch. New York had recently seen it for the first time on 22 January 1907 at the Metropolitan with Olive Fremstad and Burrian, conducted by Alfred Hertz. London would not see the work until Sir Thomas Beecham conducted Aino Ackté in 1910. Mary, interested in the title role, faced determined opposition in Paris; a theatrical clique, led by Marguerite Carré, had formed to prevent her securing it. Mary was 'struggling for her very existence as an artist on the European operatic stage'.[30]

In the midst of all this strife, Oscar Hammerstein, seizing his opportunity, finally arrived. He had bought the American rights to *Louise* as well as to *Pelléas et Mélisande*; indeed, he had engaged the four other singers who had created the work with Mary and had had an exact copy of the Opéra-Comique scenery made.

Mary decided to take Hammerstein for a drive in her automobile. As they passed through Versailles and neared Boinville, a front wheel suddenly came off. The car lurched against the curb and both of them were thrown violently against the side of the vehicle.[31] Hammerstein was severely shaken and bruised. He spent the next day in bed and could not walk in comfort for several days. Mary was sore also, but not seriously hurt.

In the Biancolli version of Mary's autobiography, the location is transposed. Hammerstein decides to go not west to Versailles but east to Fontainebleau. His reason for that destination is that Mary should sign her contract in the palace where Napoleon I had abdicated in 1814. When the car overturns, he and Mary fall out, laughing, into a meadow of poppies and, ravished by the beauty of the flowers, they decide to sign the contract in the middle of the field. The scene is obviously contrived and artificial. In reality, the contract was signed the day before the automobile accident.

Mary's last appearances at the Opéra-Comique, for the time being, were first *Louise* and then *Aphrodite* (Biancolli reverses the order to make her end conveniently with the opera in which she made her début). Meantime, anticipating her arrival in the United States, the musical press there was already subtly talking her down: 'Her voice is a brilliant soprano – brilliant in a little theatre like the Opéra-Comique; very clear, and with a vibrancy, an elasticity, a sort of undulation that at first is thrilling'. They revealed the magnitude of the artistic prejudice she would have to fight against: 'Then you discover that this undulation is its pervasive quality and that it lacks much variety of tonal color. She has finesse in detail and she gets her high notes through her nose. But the vibrancy of the tones is electric when you first hear them. I fear the Manhattan will swallow her. Operatic acting doesn't count for much with American audiences.'[32]

Mary passed the summer at Thun in Switzerland. She took advantage of the proximity of Germany to go directly to the home of Richard Strauss.

There, to his piano accompaniment, she sang part of the score of *Salome*. 'No person but you will sing it in Paris,' Strauss declared vigorously when she had finished.[33]

In the autumn she was again at La Monnaie, this time for *Faust*. 'She created a delightful personality,' wrote *L'Éventail* (6 October 1907). 'The childish and charming joys of the girl who awakens to love; the enchantment of a woman who discovers her growing playfulness. Then the sadness at being abandoned. Frequent curtain calls showed how much the audience appreciated the originality of her acting, her powers of expression and the charm of her singing'.

La traviata followed at La Monnaie. So did the appreciation of the public and the critics: 'The piercing timbre of her voice, warm in quality, had the appeal of freshness and youth. She moved from touching passion to tragic agony'.[34]

* * *

On 18 October 1907 Mary, accompanied by 16 trunks of the finest costumes ever made in the city, finally prepared to leave Paris for the United States. A host of friends were at the station to give her a rousing send-off.[35] She had now completed the first phase of her career. She had assimilated the incisive traditions of French opera and of the French theatre. She had developed her own startling interpretative powers, both as singer and actress. From her début as a resident performer at the Opéra-Comique to her final year there, her reputation rested mainly (quantitatively, at least) on three works: *Louise* (108 performances); *Pelléas et Mélisande* (59 performances) and, surprisingly, perhaps, *La traviata* (37 performances).

The Garden repertoire had been judiciously chosen. One of the most astute comments on the direction she had decided to take came from the impresario Henry Russell. One-time general manager of the Boston Opera Company, Russell had coached Mary when she had only just begun her brilliant career at the Opéra-Comique. He points out that crucially Garden avoided the mistake of dedicating her studies and her voice to the *bel canto* operas of Mozart, Rossini, Bellini or Donizetti. Had she done so, she would probably have achieved only a mediocre reputation.[36] Instead, being well aware of her own strengths and limitations, she directed her energy more towards the histrionic and interpretative side of her art. She treated her voice rather as a medium of expression than an instrument on which to play.

The nature of that instrument was an important consideration. Merle Armitage, assistant to Garden's American manager Charles Wagner, concluded that the Garden voice was impossible to catalogue or describe.[37] It was not a voice in the true operatic sense, he suggested; it was an instrument of interpretation and projection. It was a metallic instrument, whose most striking characteristic was its intensity. It was the vehicle for the projection of an intense conviction – the ideal equipment for the complex new opera of which she was the pioneer exponent. It was also a chameleon-like instrument, capable of taking on the character of its environment.

The critic and music historian Richard D. Fletcher drew attention to the multiplicity of the Garden voice: 'She proclaimed she had had not one, but twenty voices,' remembered Fletcher. 'For each new creation, Garden managed to undergo complete psychological transformation, bending her voice, like the actor's other instrument, her body, to the requirements of the new creation.'[38]

As she sailed back across the Atlantic for the first time since she had left Chicago in 1896, Mary prepared herself for a full assault on the American opera-going public, confident that her vocal and dramatic techniques were secure and, more important, that she knew how to make the most of them by singing the roles in which they would appear to the best advantage.

Notes

1. Richard D. Fletcher, 'The Mary Garden of Record', *Saturday Review*, 27 February 1954, p. 47.
2. *The American Magazine*, August 1914.
3. Stanley Jackson (1974), *Monsieur Butterfly*, New York: Stein and Day, p. 113.
4. Mary Garden, 'The opera singer and the public', *American*, August 1914.
5. Located in Département de la Musique, Bibliothèque Nationale, Paris.
6. *The New Idea*, May 1909.
7. Marguerite Coe (1984), 'Sarah and Coq: Contrast in acting styles', in *Bernhardt and the Theatre of Her Time*, ed. Eric Salmon, Westport: Greenwood Press.
8. For details of Garden's dramatic and vocal technique in a variety of roles, see Appendix 3.
9. Richard D. Fletcher, op. cit., p. 54.
10. Desmond Shawe-Taylor, 'A gallery of great singers: 15 – Mary Garden (1874–1967)', *Opera*, October 1984, p. 1079.
11. Hugues Cuénod, 'Remembrances of an enchantress', *High Fidelity Magazine*, July 1964, p. 37.
12. Richard D. Fletcher, op. cit., p. 49.
13. Desmond Shawe-Taylor, op. cit., p. 1082.
14. *Le Progrès d'Aix-les-Bains*, no. 619, 8–22 October 1904.
15. *Le Figaro*, 15 February 1905.
16. *L'Avenir d'Aix-les-Bains*, 20 July 1905.
17. Carl Van Vechten (1917), *Interpreters and Interpretations*, New York: Knopf, p. 72.
18. Garry O'Connor (1979), *The Pursuit of Perfection*, London: Victor Gollancz, p. 85.
19. Jack Winsor Hansen, 'Mary Garden: Queen of Chutzpah', Part V, *Massenet Society Newsletter*, vol 11, no. 3, July 1992, p. 22.
20. Garry O'Connor, op. cit., p. 70.

21. *Musical America*, 30 March 1907.
22. Jack Winsor Hansen, op. cit., p. 25.
23. *L'Éventail*, 13 January 1907.
24. Mary Garden, Manuscript notes made for a lecture/recital, 29 January 1935, at the Plaza Hotel, New York, pp. 4–5. New York: The Pierpoint Library.
25. *Musical America*, 18 May 1907.
26. *Chicago Examiner*, 6 June 1907.
27. Ibid.
28. Alan Jefferson (1973), *The Life of Richard Strauss*, Newton Abbot: David and Charles, p. 112.
29. Fragments from Romain Rolland's diary, in *Richard Strauss and Romain Rolland: Correspondence and Essays*, ed. Rollo Myers, Editions Albin Michel, 1951 (Calder and Boyers, 1968), pp. 156–7.
30. Untitled clipping, 23 December 1907, NYPL, Billy Rose Theatre Collection, Robinson Locke Collection of Scrapbooks 1856–1920, vols. 224–234.
31. *New York Globe*, 28 May 1907.
32. *Musical Leader*, 11 July 1907.
33. *Chicago Examiner*, 13 June 1907.
34. *L'Éventail*, 6 October 1907.
35. *New York Herald*, 19 October 1907.
36. Henry Russell (1926), *The Passing Show*, London: Thornton Butterworld Ltd, pp. 168, 275.
37. Merle Armitage (1965), *Accent on Life*, Ames: The Iowa State University Press, p. 61.
38. Richard D. Fletcher, op. cit.

5 The Creation of a Legend: 1907–1908

New York society, jaded from a heavy diet of Italian and German opera, awaited the arrival of the cream of French operas and French singers with bated breath. People knew that Hammerstein's recent French acquisitions for the Manhattan could only intensify rivalry with the Metropolitan. Competition just had to be good for the consumer.

A French fifth column was already preparing the ground. Speaking in Boston, Emma Calvé applauded the rivalry between Hammerstein and the Met:

> I think it will be very helpful to the interests of music in America, by bringing the newer French music to the foreground. Mr Conried evidently thinks that there are only two operas of the French school: *Carmen* and *Faust*. Mr Hammerstein is going to show some of the newer school of operas, notably *Pelléas et Mélisande* and *Louise*.[1]

On the night of Saturday, 26 October 1907, Mary sailed in past the Statue of Liberty. On board was the pianist Ignacy Paderewski but Mary overshadowed her celebrated fellow-passenger. She skipped down the gangplank, 'bubbling with vitality and radiating temperament', as the *New York Telegraph* put it. She drove straight to the Loreley, an apartment house she had taken for her family at East Fifty-Sixth Street. Svelte, cologned, distinguished in his goatee beard, her father Robert Garden was by now a prominent figure in the New York automobile trade. He was the first to notice that Mary's years in France had changed her irrevocably.

'It was Paris did it for her,' he later explained, regretfully. 'When Mary went over there she was a jolly, laughing girl who never used her head unless she had to. Now it's her head that never stops working. Paris has made my daughter cold and calculating.'[2]

One immediate and very visible change was the inauguration of Mary's uniquely symbiotic relationship with the American newspaper industry. No sooner had she settled into her apartment but a pack of newshounds fell upon her. Attempting to answer an avalanche of diverse questions, she told the newspapers that her favourite artist was the Croatian soprano, Milka Ternina (1863–1941), because of the magnificence of her gesture, the pride and stateliness of her stage movement and her majestic presence. In the next breath Mary was asserting her own total independence as a woman. 'How few women live by their own light! They lean this way or that, but never stand upright. I have always followed my own light. I have made many mistakes, but I always suffered my way out'. Next, tongue in cheek and savouring the effect on her audience, she announced to an astonished *New York Telegraph* reporter exactly the opposite of what he and his colleagues were expecting to hear. 'I want to sing Wagner. I shall probably start with *Lohengrin* and hope to sing *Tristan und Isolde*.'

'But one cannot sing Isolde', slyly riposted a *New York Times* reporter, 'until one has had a great many love affairs'. Mary laughed. 'I fancy I can manage that'.

Mary's sister Agnes rather indiscreetly drew media attention to Mary's lifelong fascination with fortune-telling. 'Every day a new one. Long-haired ones, short-haired ones; crystal-ball gazers, trance-mediums; palmists, tea-leaf artists'. Mary promptly took her cue and began to tease the newspapers unmercifully. 'Oh, that astrologer was great. He told me I would commit suicide this year and for a – what do you think? a Man. But I don't believe in fortune-telling. It's perfectly silly, of course'.

In mid-November, the papers had an opportunity to report a more dramatic incident: visiting her sister Amy in Philadelphia, Mary stepped into an elevator. As she descended, the car suddenly slackened speed. Then Mary noticed that the man in charge had lost control and seemed to be fainting. Quick as a flash, she seized the lever, guided the car to street-level, opened the door and then alerted hotel staff to get medical help.

Thus Mary's daily life was beginning to become the stuff of American legend – even before she had sung so much as a single note on stage.

*   *   *

Mary's contract with Hammerstein was for five years. Her salary was said to be $1800 a night, with a stipulation that she sing twice a week. It was also rumoured that she had promised André Messager to promote French music by acting as a talent scout for him among young American singers.

A month after her return to the United States came her first appearance in front of an American audience. In the theatre were many friends (such as the famously lesbian actress and interior decorator, Elsie De Wolfe) and well-wishers. Also present were those who might well have had reasons to resent her success. It was not an auspicious beginning – Mary was suffering from the effects of a cold. Nevertheless, Cleofonte Campanini conducted her in

Thaïs with a cast which included Maurice Renaud and the tenor Charles Dalmorès, soon to be the father of her nephew, Mario, by Mary's sister Hélène.

As Thaïs, Mary wore a dress of pale pink crêpe de chine. It hugged her body as if she had been vacuum-sealed and made her look completely naked. When she threw off her cloak, there were audible gasps from the audience. As for her performance, it was received with disparaging critical discernment but some flashes of admiration. The much-feared New York critics put her under the microscope and she emerged with considerable honour, in spite of being handicapped by her cold and beset by nerves at having to live up to all that was expected of her.

The press reaction after the première highlighted the pronounced difference between critical analysis in France and America. Where the Continental critics drew back and focused rather on an opera as a total composition and less on the detail of the performers, those in metropolitan America submitted a leading singer to examination in close-up.

'Only Chaliapin's Mephisto surpasses Thaïs of Alexandria in economy of wearing apparel,' smirked *The New York Globe*.[3] 'In gesture she was exuberant rather than sure. Her poses were always picturesque, not always dramatically significant. And as Thaïs turned saintly her impersonation became progressively less convincing. The Mary Garden that won her audience was not so much an actress of certain and resourceful technique as a woman of extraordinary temperament and superabundant vitality, with a beautiful lithe body, who held you by sheer force of personal fascination.'

Then the critics proceeded to probe further into her performance. *The Globe* (December 1907) dissected Mary's vocal technique:

> Certainly her singing was a hindrance rather than an aid. The voice itself was a pleasant surprise. It was not the close, pinched, metallic voice that Paris so often tolerates, if it does not actually favor. Rather, it was free, rich, and of individual timbre, but it seemed to have been badly trained and sounded somewhat worn. A continual slight tremolo marred its tone. The high notes were forced and shrill. When the singer would use half-voice the tone became pale and lifeless. There was no true 'legato'. The phrasing was often a blur. Even the diction, which in singers of French training is traditionally excellent, sounded indistinct and otherwise faulty. In the final scene the redeemed Thaïs shrieked like a lost soul. And yet, through a medium of imperfect singing, the natural beauty of the voice did shine forth.

Perceptively, the magazine *Human Life* (26 November 1907) saw that in her personality there were two opposing halves. 'On-stage there is no great singer so *risqué* and so daring. But off-stage there is none more chaste than Mary Garden'. This was an antithesis which Mary herself never tired of emphasizing.

There were endless interviews at her apartment over the next few days. The press had a chance to drink in her personality. The interior decoration of her drawing-room had by now received the strong stamp of her character. It was predominantly floral with a touch of fashionable decadence. All about the room there were tall vases of waxen white lilies and bowls of soft pink roses. The air was heavy with perfume and the pungent smell of a wood fire. Through this botanical splendour, the eager reporters stared with fascination at the signed photographs of Camille Erlanger, Claude Debussy and Gustave Charpentier which decorated her piano.

Smiling indulgently at their expectant expressions and their quivering hands poised to cram her every remark into stenographers' notebooks, Mary began by explaining that her artistic aims and methods were not to be confused with those of other singers: 'My art is one quite separate from that of other operatic singers, and the success I have won is not the success of vocal cords. It is by an art quite different and I want to be judged not alone by my singing or my acting or my stage appearance, but by these combined into one art.'[4]

But her sizzling media relations soon took their toll. Succumbing to a bout of influenza, Mary was dispatched by Hammerstein for a few days' rest in Atlantic City. When she next played Thaïs at the end of November, the critics remarked that she sang much better and was more at her ease, the better to loose her undoubted charm upon her audience. But in the theatre that night there was an unexpected backstage drama. Towards the end of the second Act, a four-inch steam pipe suddenly burst behind the scenes; within an instant, the house was filled with the hiss of escaping steam. Half the chorus stampeded and the audience was poised to make a rush for the exits. Mary, on the contrary, steeled herself and continued to sing as if nothing had happened. The panic was averted.

* * *

The new year of 1908 saw Mary's first American performances of *Louise*. Astonished audiences were introduced to what became known as the 'Louise Kiss' – a '25-second dreamy half-Nelson', as *The Kansas City Post* put it, with 'no hint of slurring or shirking full duty'. The American première of *Pelléas et Mélisande* followed towards the end of February at the Manhattan. Mary was at pains to explain that the opera was set in medieval Scandinavia – everything was intended to be dark and sombre. 'Mrs Patrick Campbell, when she acted the play, placed it in the Renaissance period, when everything was bright and gay. I find that all wrong'.[5]

The critics were dazzled. Reginald de Koven, for example, found it an impersonation so mystic, so subtle, so full of half-explanation and hidden suggestion of mood and feeling, as to stamp it as intellectual and emotional to a rare degree. Her voice, he added, was admirably suited to what she had to sing and the expressive quality, finish and artistic repose and sincerity were practically beyond praise.[6]

Mary's success had by now earned her the public admiration of her former Chicago sponsor, Mrs David Mayer. 'Mary has risen in the world since I became interested in her,' commented Mrs Mayer proudly to the *Chicago Tribune* (1 May 1907). 'She deserves it'.

Hammerstein, anxious to press home his advantage over the Metropolitan, began the first of a series of regular appearances at the Academy of Music, Philadelphia, including *Louise* with Mary and a largely Parisian cast. He sent Philadelphians into a frenzy by announcing that he planned to construct an opera house for the city. However, signs of internal division in the Hammerstein camp were already drawing public attention. America was being given the distinct impression that Mary had declared war on Luisa Tetrazzini. On one occasion the previous year, Tetrazzini, a supreme exponent of the coloratura style Mary publicly professed to abhor, had thoughtfully sent a basket of roses to Mary's dressing-room. But this touch of personal kindness had not prevented Mary from publicly proclaiming her opinions about Tetrazzini in an article in *Everybody's Magazine*.

Entitled 'The Debasement of Music in America', Mary's article was a frontal attack on the state of opera in America and on the immobile postures of coloratura singing as personified by Tetrazzini, who was then taking the Manhattan Opera House by storm. She argued that America was still satisfied with *tone* as opposed to interpretation. This was shown, Mary claimed, by the great popularity of Melba and Sembrich – perhaps the last, and certainly the greatest exponents of the coloratura school which charmed the world until the first quarter of this century.

Now, announced Mary, a great modern school had been founded, the music of which dealt with deep human truths and carried them to the hearts of its audiences. This modern music was aimed not just at the senses, but also at the mind. Mary continued her assault in the daily press by proclaiming that in France a fine large woman walking more or less stiffly through a long opera and occasionally emitting a few glorious tones was no longer considered a great artist. Singer and music had to strive to interpret the impulses and motives of the human mind, heart and soul. Modern opera, she added, represented not persons but passions.

In response, while agreeing with her that America was still satisfied with *tone*, as opposed to interpretation, *Musical America* confirmed the enormous scale of Mary's endeavour. 'It is hardly too much to say that the engagement of Mary Garden marks the beginning of a new operatic era in America.'[7]

Hostilities between the two divas became evident as they set out over the Atlantic on the *Kaiser Wilhelm II* at the end of March. The coolness between them apparently continued throughout the voyage, although Mary, when pressed, vehemently denied its existence and laughed it off. 'There is nothing in it at all. It is true we did not speak during the voyage from New York, for the reason that we both remained in our beds speechless with sea-sickness.'[8]

Mary spent the second half of April singing at La Monnaie, Brussels. Two potentially exciting engagements in Europe did not, unhappily, come to fruition. First, Mary had been preparing for a Paris revival of Chabrier's *Gwendoline*. Second, in London, an operatic combat between Mary, Melba and Tetrazzini had been announced for Covent Garden during a gala performance of *Les Huguenots* on 26 May. But Mary took part in neither. Instead, she marked her return to Paris by switching her allegiance to the larger house, Le Palais Garnier, the Opéra de Paris. Between May and October, she sang at the Opéra fifteen times.

Even though she had left the Opéra-Comique partly to escape from the machinations of Marguerite Carré and the quarrelling over her by Marguerite's husband and Messager, a very warm reception marked her entry to the larger stage, and fulfilled Sarah Duff's almost-forgotten prediction of 1896. Mary began with *Thaïs*, which had been Sibyl Sanderson's debut there also. 'A début very eagerly awaited,' wrote Robert Brussel in *Le Figaro*, 'especially as her successes in America have kept her far from us. It was interesting to see how her art would fare on such a huge stage as that of the Opéra, an art so personal, so generous in melodramatic feeling, composed of myriad nuances and informed by an intimate understanding of the characters she portrays. I hasten to confirm that the outcome for Miss Garden was dazzling. She completely won over the Opéra audience.'

Mary astounded Paris with a Thaïs of flesh and blood, given to enthusiasm, living an intense and agitated life, with a heart and a soul full of sensuality. She expressed Thaïs' fervour, said *Le Figaro* (2 May 1908), 'with infinite artistry, with power and with authority. Her enormous success as a singer was multiplied by her equal triumph as an actress'.

On the evening of 4 May she had been due to sing Thaïs, but it was announced that she had suddenly been taken ill at her Rue Washington apartment: 'It was gas,' she told an interviewer, 'part of which I used for reading in bed and the other part I inhaled. It was a narrow escape. Next week I am moving into a new apartment in the Avenue Malakoff. There will be no gas there.'[9] The fashionable new home she referred to was furnished entirely in the Empire style and its decoration included original sketches by Watteau, Boucher, Tiepolo, Fragonard and Reynolds.

When she came to portray Marguerite in *Faust*, Mary was not quite as successful as in her other roles. One American observer regretted 'the vocal defects of a rather hard voice in a role almost beyond her powers which she supplements with intelligence and a sense of dramatic fitness'.[10] Another critic dryly castigated her French accent:

Miss Mary Garden is evidently an artist whose very individual nature moves the public deeply. Her interpretation yesterday evening glowed with life; it was animated, original, full of intelligence and interest. I will only make one criticism – by mistake, she sang the wrong opera. She sang in what appeared to be an English opera, in which she sang the English with a strong French accent![11]

Squeezed between Mary's work in Paris came a single performance of *Pelléas et Mélisande* at the Königliche Hofoper, Cologne. Reviewing the occasion, the critic Paul Hiller felt that Maeterlinck had dressed up an ordinary tale with a web of mysticism and mystery. Debussy's music was, in his view, wearily monotone, like the intoning of psalms; Debussy seemed to be reacting against Wagner and Richard Strauss. But Hiller enjoyed Mary's performance. 'Miss Garden was even more riveting as an actress than as a singer. But the latter skill could not be shown to advantage because of the dreadful monotony of the score. In everyone who heard her, she produced a desire to experience her highly individual artistry again.'[12] Hiller added that the performance had been poorly attended because a lecture given on the work two days before had frightened the public away.

While Mary was in Cologne, the Opéra-Comique in Paris had stolen a march on the Opéra. Mary found herself prevented from singing Mélisande at the Opéra because Maggie Teyte (1888–1976) was already playing the role with great success at the Opéra-Comique.

So instead, in July, Mary broke new ground in her career by singing Juliette for the first time in Paris to the Roméo of the Russian tenor, Ivan Altchevsky (1876–1917). The audience was magnificent and applauded Mary repeatedly. The critics were of a like mind. Even the normally pernickety L. Vuillemin seemed to be won over: 'Miss Garden holds the secret of how to sing the most charming tones. I do not exaggerate in confirming that she is an artist gifted with unimaginable originality and fantasy in her movements, her facial expressions, her vocal inflexions'. He added, tongue-in-cheek: 'Miss Garden returns for several months every year to the country of her birth in order to perfect the delicious pronunciation with which Nature endowed her'.[13]

*　　*　　*

Having completed her engagements in Paris for the time being, Mary set off for her usual summer haunt of Aix-les-Bains, her mind full of plans for *Salome*. The previous March the composer Richard Strauss had been in Paris to discuss the production of his work with the Opera managers, Messager and Broussan. *Salome* had already been produced in German at the Théâtre du Châtelet the previous season, where it had been sung by Emmy Destinn and Olive Fremstad. It had appeared that there were problems which would prevent Mary from playing the role in Paris; Mary, however, fully expected to play the part. She had already arranged with Madame Mariquita, the choreographer of the Opéra-Comique to teach her the *Salome* dance; she also spent part of that summer at Versailles in preparatory study of the score. Now, on her departure for Aix, she revealed that her costume for *Salome* had been ordered and would be ready when she returned to Paris in September.

Aix-les-Bains was idyllic. 'One rises and retires early,' noted Mary languidly, 'and is lulled to sleep at night and awakened in the morn by the tinkling of cowbells'. There were her old friends to visit. The ever-present journalists reported that: 'There again was His Highness of Greece and not far behind him Mary Garden just returning from rehearsal. She is seen almost daily in the Bois Vidal'.

Leaving Aix-les-Bains, Mary travelled to Switzerland where, partly to tone up her breathing, she set off to climb Mont Blanc. Dressed in men's clothes and accompanied by two guides, she made the ascent in two days, stopping one night at Grands-Mulets, and pushing on at two the following morning. She stayed only ten minutes at the top, because it was 50 degrees below zero. 'For two days after,' she explained, 'I felt absolutely exhausted, and my eyes hurt from the glare of the snow. But now I feel splendid, and my lungs seem twice as strong and in fine shape for *Salome*.'[14]

From Switzerland she caught the train to Munich and then took a car up to Richard Strauss' new villa at Garmisch. At this meeting with Strauss all the difficulties surrounding her casting as Salome evaporated. He first gave her his permission to sing the role, handing her a letter to that effect and then, from the piano, coached her in the part. But Strauss cautioned her: he did not think it possible for Mary to sing *and* perform the dance.

'My favorite operatic composer is Strauss,' Mary was to comment later. 'There's a man for you; a real man. He lives in the mountains with his family and he is very happy.'[15]

Strauss' librettist, Hofmannsthal, had also suggested Mary for the part of Octavian in his new work, *Der Rosenkavalier*. He had written to Strauss suggesting 'a graceful girl dressed up as a man, à la Farrar or Mary Garden'.[16] According to Mary, Strauss did indeed offer her that role also. There are three versions of why she never sang it on stage. In the first, to be found in the Biancolli biography, Mary herself supplies her reason for not playing Octavian: 'Making love to women all night long would have bored me to death'.[17] This is amusing but unconvincing, since Mary had already played a number of *travesti* roles. In the second version, supplied by Vincent Sheean, Mary tells Strauss that she would never have time to learn Octavian. It would take a year to learn German and another year to learn Viennese dialect, so she had to decline the honour.[18] However, in view of the fact that Mary had been learning German for some years (albeit not too successfully) this also seems a weak explanation. A third explanation is given by costume designer Ernest de Weerth: 'Her contract was signed, she studied the role;

but the rehearsals were suddenly stopped by the outbreak of World War I and the production in Paris was cancelled for ever'.[19] This has the ring of truth.

*   *   *

Mary returned to Paris. She settled back into her spartan daily routine, as regular as clockwork. Her day would begin at nine with breakfast in bed – an egg, a bit of bread and a cup of chocolate. After finishing her toilette, she dealt with her correspondence and then practised, perhaps until lunch at one o'clock. This meal, like the dinner at eight in the evening, was invariably simple but filling. In the middle of the afternoon she went for a walk. Later, at five o'clock tea, she would chat with friends.

However, on days when she was performing, she altered this routine. After breakfast she might write a few letters. But then she returned to bed and stayed there reading, until the time came for her to go to the opera house. Immediately after the performance she would go straight home for a light supper.

On 25 September 1908, shortly before leaving France once more for America, Mary appeared at the Opéra in *Hamlet*. Her Ophélie opposite Maurice Renaud's Hamlet was a triumph. Equally successful were her rehearsals for *Salome*, as Carl Van Vechten recalls:

One afternoon in the autumn of 1908, when I was Paris correspondent of the *New York Herald*, I received the following telegram from Miss Garden: 'Come this evening at 5.30 to Mlle Chasles, 112 Boulevard Malesherbes to see me as Salomé.' Mlle Chasles's *salle de danse* I discovered to be a large square room; the floor had a rake like that of the Opéra stage in Paris. There were footlights and seats in front of them for spectators. This final rehearsal – before the rehearsals in New York which preceded her first appearance in the part anywhere at the Manhattan Opera House – was witnessed by André Messager who intended to mount *Salome* at the Paris Opéra the following season, Mlle Chasles, an accompanist, a maid, a hair-dresser and myself. ... The seven veils were of soft, clinging tulle. Swathed in these veils, she began the dance at the back of the small stage. Only her eyes were visible. ... On this occasion, I remember she proved to us that the exertion had not fatigued her, by singing the final scene of the music drama, while André Messager played the accompaniment on the piano.[20]

As Mary's star climbed upwards, there came news that stunned America. It was rumoured that she would shortly leave the operatic stage and become the wife of Prince Mavrocordato, a Russian living in Paris who had a fortune estimated at five million dollars. It was said that the Prince and Mary were frequently seen driving together on the Champs Élysées and in the Bois de Boulogne. The Prince, it was whispered, made frequent morning calls on Mary. He occupied a box every night when she sang and left the theatre when she was not on stage. The gossip columnists revealed that the Prince had for years occupied bachelor apartments in the Chaillot quarter of Paris. The fact that he was now having a large house built for him near the Trocadéro made more plausible the report that he was contemplating matrimony.

Such reports did no more than amuse Mary. 'I hope some day to marry a prince', confirmed Mary to them archly, 'but whether it will be the particular prince you refer to, I decline to say'. And on another occasion she commented:

> To be a Princess? A fig for titles! It would take more than a title to make me give up my beautiful independence and liberty. It's one thing to have a proposal of marriage from a prince, but to marry a prince – Ah, that is another thing. You see, a woman who has a successful career, more or less talent and a big salary, isn't so mad to marry as she might be.

Later that October, Mary Garden made her second triumphal return to New York, this time with a change of supporting cast. On board ship she had become acquainted with the Scottish ironmaster millionaire, Andrew Carnegie. He had sent her his card and they had chatted together, exchanging Scottish stories. Carnegie promised to attend her opening night: 'She is an admirable woman', he commented.

By the time Mary returned, the Manhattan had increased its subscription list six-fold. The Metropolitan, stung by Hammerstein's success, began to fight back by bringing over Giulio Gatti-Casazza from La Scala, Milan, to replace Conried as director and engaging Arturo Toscanini as conductor.

The first American production of *Le jongleur de Notre Dame* followed at the end of November, giving proof of the way that Mary could not only transform her character on stage, but her sex and her age. 'So excellent was her makeup,' wrote Reginald de Koven, 'that I think the audience hardly recognised her at first. As always, the detail and finish of her art in gesture, facial expression and by-play was remarkable'.[21]

Katherine M. Roof, commenting on a performance of *Pelléas and Mélisande* around this period, made the perceptive remark that:

> her voice is the least of her equipment – the curious Parisian habit of singing a little flat, the trick of slipping *below* the tone, especially at the end of a phrase is definitely suggested by Debussy's intervals and it is deliberately employed by Mary Garden whose own natural personality is one of tremendous vitality and energetic expressiveness.[22]

Making an appearance in her old home town of Philadelphia, Mary tried hard not to let her audience down. She sang Thaïs against her doctor's advice, stricken with a cold. She persevered, so hoarse, she could not speak except in whispers. She overcame her handicaps by sheer determination and willpower.

But Philadelphia was hard to please – even in its new Opera House, which was now open for business. Her voice was cold, white, said the press. It had a lack of volume, of richness and of resonance and was not well suited to Massenet's music. Her juggling feats were primitive. In sum, they were disappointed.

Notes

1. *New York Herald*, 19 October 1907.
2. *Actresses of Today*, February 1909, NYPL, Billy Rose Theatre Collection, Robinson Locke Collection of Scrapbooks 1856–1920, vols. 224–234.
3. Chaliapin sang the title role of Boito's *Mefistofele* semi-nude.
4. *New York Herald*, 1 December 1907.
5. *New York Times*, 15 February 1908.
6. *The World*, 20 February 1908.
7. *Musical America*, 25 January 1908.
8. *Musical America*, 11 April 1908.
9. *Musical America*, 16 May 1908.
10. *Musical Courier*, 1 July 1908.
11. *Comœdia*, 14 June 1908.
12. *Neue Musikalisches Rundserau*, 15 June 1908.
13. *Comœdia*, 7 July 1908.
14. *Musical America*, 5 September 1908.
15. *Musical America*, 20 November 1909.
16. Letter of 11 February 1908, quoted in Alan Jefferson (1973), *The Life of Richard Strauss*, London: David and Charles, p. 124.
17. Mary Garden and Louis Biancolli (1951), *Mary Garden's Story*, New York: Simon and Schuster, p. 204.
18. *Opera News*, 4 February 1967.
19. *Opera News*, 5 April 1954.
20. Carl Van Vechten (1917), *Interpreters and Interpretations*, New York: Knopf, p. 81.
21. *The World*, 28 November 1908.
22. Katherine M. Roof, 'Borderland Art', *The Craftsman*, vol 15, November 1908.

6 *Salome* and Scandal: 1908–1910

A frisson of anticipation swept through New York in the autumn of 1908: Mary's most titanic role – Richard Strauss' *Salome* – was fast nearing its debut. The opera had first been seen in America the previous year, sung (in German) by Olive Fremstad at the Metropolitan, where the Dance of the Seven Veils had been performed by Bianca Froelich.

Mary made it known that in her appearance at the Manhattan she would be executing the Dance herself. But she was quick to counter rumours that her interpretation would in any way scandalize public opinion. She would neither dance in bare feet nor would her costume be of a character to invite intervention by the police. She planned to discard the veils one by one, but there would definitely be no immodesty and no shocking finale. While she hoped they would not protest, she strongly suspected that the religious authorities would be judging her by the Salome dances which were then already infesting the theatres but which the churchmen, hypocritically, did nothing to oppose.

As for her characterization, Mary believed Salome to be a paradox. She was complex. She was Vice and yet she was archetypal Woman. In Mary's view, Salome was a child of nature, thin and very young and red-headed.

The new year of 1909 came and, with it, more flashes of rivalry between leading sopranos. During a benefit concert given on 17 January at the Manhattan Opera House for sufferers in the Italian earthquake, Mary shared the billing with the tenor Giovanni Zenatello and Luisa Tetrazzini. 'Miss Garden's voice has a certain metallic quality', reported *The Toledo Blade*. It was thought that she lacked charm; her stage presence was considered most unpleasant. Mary was stung by the marked difference in the applause given to her and to Tetrazzini – and she showed it.

Three days later, there was more discord. Mary had discovered that Hammerstein planned to give *Thaïs* with the beautiful Lina Cavalieri in the title role. Mary savaged Hammerstein. She was determined to maintain a monopoly on her French repertoire and sent him the following acid reprimand:

> When you told me that you were to engage Mme Cavalieri to sing *Thaïs*, I said to you that the day this announcement was advertised in the newspapers, I would leave the Manhattan Opera House. This morning the published announcement appeared and accordingly I hereby send you my resignation.

She added, ironically given her own nationality: 'I will not allow an Italian to sing my French roles.'

The following day, Mary refused to attend a *Salome* rehearsal scheduled with the orchestra of 115 players. Fortunately for her, Hammerstein knew on which side his bread was buttered. Cavalieri diplomatically announced she was too ill to sing, thus saving the day and Hammerstein's face. He renewed Mary's contract, giving her exclusive rights to her existing roles and an option to appear at any time till her contract expired.

Mary made her début as Salome on 28 January 1909, singing in French. Her performance knocked New York cold. After the Roman soldiers crushed Salome to death under their shields, the audience sat in stunned silence for fully thirty seconds as the curtain fell. A conception of incarnate bestiality so powerful, howled *The New York Herald*, had been realized by Miss Garden that it was a dreadful thing to contemplate.

After the curtain-calls, Mary gathered her cloak over her bare shoulders and groped her way through the semi-darkness at the back of the stage to the dressing-room with GARDEN painted in black letters on its forbidding metal door. There, she explained to the press exactly how she had conceived the dance. It was not the conventional *Salome dance* – the Oriental dance – which she used, but a Greek dance, which was perfectly authentic in the crowded little court of Herod Antipas. She had first examined the visualizations of many great painters, then had decided to depart from all of them. She had decided to follow Oscar Wilde, who had Narraboth describe Salome as pale and pallid: 'She resembles the reflection of a white rose in a silver mirror'.

Public reaction began to make itself felt in her next port of call – Philadelphia. Two days before her appearance there as Salome, there were official protests from many of the local churches – Methodist Episcopal, Lutheran, Protestant Episcopal, Congregational. But the Sunshiners (nudists), misunderstanding the nature of Mary's costume, endorsed *Salome*: 'We look upon it as the greatest force for true morality that has ever come to Philadelphia. 'Clothes,' they announced, 'are only shams.'

Perhaps realizing that, as hostilities increased over *Salome*, she would need as many artistic allies as possible, from whatever quarter, Mary now began to adopt a somewhat less confrontational attitude towards her fellow sopranos. She had recently been reported as saying that before she would modify her interpretation of Salome, she would let Luisa Tetrazzini sing the part. Mary denied she had ever said such a thing and sent a note to Tetrazzini to that effect, accompanying her message with a basket of flowers. Tetrazzini at once responded with an equally courteous note.

* * *

During this period a potentially much more serious confrontation spilled into the daily press. Allegedly it had all begun when, one night in an adjoining box at the Manhattan, Mary publicly snubbed her former Chicago patrons, Mr and Mrs David Mayer. Angered, Mrs Mayer threatened to go to law for recovery of the money she had advanced Mary to study in Paris. 'She became inhumanly ungrateful,' said Mrs Mayer, adding that she had never received so much as a note of gratitude from Mary for her patronage.

A ten-year-old can of worms now opened and was seized upon by the press, with a host of allegations about Mary's life as a student in Paris. She was said by *The Chicago Tribune* to have been the mother of an illegitimate child and to have climbed to her unique position in the world of opera 'on the skeleton of a vividly and tempestuously sinful past'.

In 1899, members of the Mayer family had heard first-hand stories about their protegée's apparently profligate life-style in Paris which had led to their termination of Mary's allowance and her subsequent penury. Amplifying the tale, Amy Leslie, an American theatre critic based in Paris, now wrote a series of articles which sought to explain the Mayers' actions. Ms Leslie also claimed to have received the full story from Sibyl Sanderson herself:

> A dull man with a blonde friend took the pain to tattle irritating tales about the goings-on of Mary. The Mayers travelled to Paris and found Mary with a drummer [slang for a travelling salesman] from Waterloo with a twirly moustache and a Gascon accent and a baby a few weeks old, and she had a sad story and not much voice, and Mrs Mayer wept; also Sibyl Sanderson wept and the American colony wept, because Melba did not approve of the way the little American had treated her benefactors.[1]
>
> The Mayers now limited the wife of the little salesman to a small competence, covering her expenses as a student. Then Mary thought the proper thing would be suicide. Mary ricocheted her shoulder with a tiny pistol.[2] Sibyl Sanderson rushed to Mary, discharged the young salesman and found a home for the sad-eyed progeny. With Sibyl, Miss Garden learned many things, one of which was to wear just as little covering as possible!

The Chicago Record added the information that the two young lovers had subsequently divorced!

Amy Leslie, while admitting she herself did not meet Mary or the drummer or see the baby, asserts that, when she was a journalist in Paris, the story about Mary, the drummer and the baby was common knowledge in the American community there. Leslie added that Sibyl Sanderson had been her chief informant. Sanderson, of course, had died six years before and could therefore not corroborate Amy Leslie's story. Melba certainly was alive in 1909 and Americans in Paris would also have been able to corroborate or refute Leslie's story. However, neither the 'drummer' himself, Nellie Melba nor any of the very large group of Americans in Paris at the time seem to have left any record of such a tale, so casting considerable doubt on its authenticity.

Other sources suggest that it was Sibyl Sanderson who had slipped into a life-style of which Mrs Mayer would certainly not have approved. There was a rumoured affair with Massenet which was public knowledge in Paris and another with the American critic James Huneker, who was said to have been sleeping with Sanderson. Mary is alleged to have walked into her apartment and found the two Americans in bed together.[3]

Jack Winsor Hansen writes that Sanderson's stepdaughter Natividad recalled that 'Sibyl told me that Mary recently had a baby, and Sibyl had taken the child and placed it with a Catholic orphanage'.[4] Sanderson, adds Hansen, evidently asked her stepdaughter not to discuss the incident with her and she never did. However, this desire for secrecy appears to conflict with Amy Leslie's assertion that she had been told the whole story by Sanderson and that it was public knowledge among the American colony in Paris.

Thus the sorry tale unravelled simultaneously in New York and Chicago. The Mayers filed a lawsuit against Mary for $20,000, which was the original amount plus compound interest at six per cent for all the years intervening – the interest itself amounted to almost the original sum. She was advised that if the sum was not paid by twelve o'clock the following day then matters would be pushed to the extreme.

As it happened, Mary had $10,000 in her account and, by good chance, the president of Mary's bank being a box-holder at the Manhattan, the bank lent her a further $10,000. 'First thing next morning,' Mary revealed, 'my lawyer took $20,000 in crisp, new banknotes and paid the last cent. I was flat broke but I was the happiest girl in New York.'[5]

And as for the Mayers: 'I met Mrs Mayer in the lobby of the Manhattan Opera House,' said Mary. 'She came up to me, smiling, with her hand held out, but I could not see her. I looked straight through her at the wall, and then I knew I had done it.'

There still remained the accusations that Mary had slept her way to the top and had borne a child. Mary, lying back on her pillows (ill with the grippe and the effects of a heroic effort to sing *Salome* for the Campanini benefit on 26 March), declared in phrases worthy of any of her greatest roles:

As God is my witness, I deny that I have ever been the mother of a child. I do not say that I have lived the life of a saint, for I have loved life. I have had my loves; I have known great joy; I have been in the depths of as great sorrow, but in all my life I have never had a child – never, never! Do you think for one instant that if I were the mother of a child – I say that little one would be here – right here at my side. I am no coward. I could face anything that was mine – a child, a sin, a sorrow, a joy.[6]

Unexpectedly, Mrs Mayer made a dramatic *volte face* and confirmed Mary's innocence: 'Why, it is true, every word of it – what Mary says. She has been the victim of malicious gossipers. I know that she had her romances. No woman so graced by nature could have escaped them.'[7] And the *New York Star* publicly exonerated Mary: 'The *Star* states unhesitatingly that the recent vile and groundless attack on Miss Garden is due to an organised band of blackmailers, who having been foiled in their attempts to wrest money from Miss Garden, have resorted to the methods of the gutter.'[8]

The truth of the matter is that there is no evidence that Mary had a child. Judging by her correspondence of the period with the Mayers, she seems to have been eager for them to come to Paris to see for themselves how she was progressing. In the letters there is an underlying awareness on Mary's part that the Mayers' reliance on reports from Ed Mayer, the over-zealous Léon Grehier or friends such as Mina Adelaide would never be satisfactory and might well lead to serious misunderstandings.[9]

However, Mary did learn at least one hard lesson from this traumatic episode – the power of malicious gossip when it was turned against her and how it could be magnified by an eager American press. Her awareness of its power may well have made her realize that she would have to learn how to manipulate public relations in her favour; this was the point at which she began consciously to bend information to suit her own agenda. She was becoming one of the earliest and most successful modern 'spin-doctors'.

By way of light relief came a different type of publicity for Mary. In what was to be the first of a stream of phantom liaisons appearing in the gossip columns, the rumours about Mary's impending engagement to Prince Mavrocordato re-surfaced. By now he had been courting her for over three years but she vehemently denied reports that she had married him. 'I marry? Why, what would I do that for? What would I do with a husband, travelling about as I do? Why should I marry anyone when I am perfectly happy as I am? It is true that the Prince has been after me. He has besought me repeatedly to become his wife, but I have refused him'.[10] The only private corroboration of the numerous newspaper stories about her relationship with the Prince occurred in a postcard that Mary sent to Carl van Vechten on 4 October 1908, which confirmed that she had been dining with Prince Mavrocordato and her sister at Versailles.

She then injected a measure of hard-headed reality into the argument. 'I do not think the husband of a prima donna has a fair show at all. He loses his individuality, his personality. Who would marry a man and reduce him to the status of "Miss Garden's husband"? I am wedded to singing and I do not think that any woman who is a mother should continue to be a prima donna.'[11]

In spite of these protestations the rumours persisted that she would shortly become Prince Mavrocordato's bride and was to sail for Russia on 13 April to marry him. Unable to turn down an opportunity to tease the American press, Mary now launched into a series of disparaging observations about the amorous qualities of the American work-obsessed male who was, she maintained, literally perpetual motion – knowing not art nor literature nor romance. 'He has no time,' she concluded. 'Now,' she added mischievously, letting her voice drop to golden, caressing notes, 'the Latin gentlemen make love per-r-r-fectly [sic].'[12]

* * *

In the late spring of 1909 Mary planned to spend a few days in Paris then to take a motor trip through the chateau district; then on to Nice at the end of May; then to Florence. In Italy that summer she would study with Lombardi. Later she would go to Marienbad or perhaps Carlsbad and then Switzerland until 5 September when she would return to Paris. She could not leave New York, however, without a few last tweaks at the press: coquettishly she revealed that Jules Massenet was writing an opera for her about the Egyptian queen, Cleopatra. And she made a final vitriolic swing at David and Florence Mayer: 'Those Chicago Mayers! They are simply too horrid for anything'.[13]

On 28 April Mary left for France. Her return to Paris was an anti-climax, however. On 21 May she was said to be ill and couldn't sing Ophélie. Then she failed to appear at the Opéra on 25 May in a Gala Beethoven programme where she had been due to sing a group of the 'Chansons écossaises'. Advertised as singing in *Roméo et Juliette* on 4 June, she again failed to materialize. It was reported she was indisposed for the rest of the season. *Le Figaro* wrote with some scepticism that two days previously she had rehearsed brilliantly but was stricken by a sudden return of the illness which three times already (and always at the last moment) had prevented her from singing.

By chance, Paris was at that time packed with Mary's rivals: Lina Cavalieri was playing Thaïs; Lucienne Bréval was appearing in *Monna Vanna*; Marguerite Carré was at the Opéra-Comique and Georgette Leblanc was in a play by Maeterlinck. Even Geraldine Farrar was there on holiday.

A confusing account of Mary's activities appeared in *The Boston Telegraph* of 5 June. It claimed that Mary was in Constantinople at the time she was failing to appear at the Opéra. The report added that the new grand vizier was Mary's warmest admirer and that her health had suffered because she had attended too many receptions and was only averaging five hours' sleep a day. Although this report was probably a red herring, what is curious is that, following the siege of Constantinople and the overthrow of the Sultan, the new Turkish cabinet's minister for agriculture, mines and forests was, coincidentally, 'Mavrocordato effendi'. This was clearly not the Russian prince Mary was rumoured to be marrying. However, the following year Mary would declare herself amorously linked to a 'wealthy Turk, a friend of the former sultan, a pasha 38 years old whom she had met in London'.[14]

Whatever the unfathomable reality behind this web of intrigue, there does seem to have been a significant and time-consuming liaison of some kind with a man from Eastern Europe, which may have affected Mary's health to the extent that it forced her to cancel her engagements in Paris.

Ever-solicitous, *The Boston Telegraph* announced that she was seriously ill and that her recovery would mean many months of care. It was believed that she was suffering from an oriental fever. Other explanations were more mundane. It was said that as a result of using hair-dye, she was nearly blinded and her whole nervous system shattered; her eyes were bandaged and she had been placed under doctors' orders in a darkened room. The accident had occurred, it was said, because Mary had taken a dislike to her sandy hair. She had stained it repeatedly with a preparation guaranteed to give her hair that was golden, with red highlights. Having applied the dye several times, she discovered only too late that her optic nerves had been affected. She had continued to use the hair-dye until her whole system was badly damaged and she was forced to cancel her engagements.

Mary was highly indignant at this latter version of events – the reported stories of her blindness were false and she would like to see them repudiated. When interviewed by a newspaper correspondent, she was neither ill in bed nor was there any sign of hair-dye. The reason she did not appear, she herself explained, was that she was suffering from rheumatism in her shoulders, which made acting too painful. Except for this she was perfectly well. She was preparing to go that week to Aix-les-Bains for the cure, and would return for her engagements in September.

Perhaps one reason for this trip to Aix-les-Bains was that Luisa Tetrazzini was coming for the first time to sing at the Trocadéro. Also in Paris was Oscar Hammerstein busy completing his special Opéra-Comique troupe. There would be 'no Tetrazzinis,' he declared, 'no Mary Gardens, no Renauds, no Dufrannes in the company'.[15]

At Aix-les-Bains, at the Villa des Fleurs, on the long, green gaming-tables where the 'little horses' ran, Mary indulged her passion for gambling. She played for high stakes and without much success. Where others played silver, she played gold – and lost. But the enforced vacation restored her natural exuberance; it was said that nervous energy surrounded her like an aureole, that she fairly radiated with dynamic personality.

*   *   *

Returned from Aix-les-Bains, she nevertheless led a quiet life in Paris. Horse-riding in the Bois was her favourite relaxation. For the Opéra, she was studying the title role in Henri Février's *Monna Vanna* (after a libretto by Maurice Maeterlinck) in which she was due to make her début on 11 October. Her coach was her old teacher, Trabadelo.

Between the beginning of September and the end of October 1909 Mary appeared at the Opéra in *Thaïs* (her performances achieving record receipts – the last performance netting $4500 from a packed house), *Faust, Hamlet, Roméo et Juliette* in addition to *Monna Vanna*. Her Monna Vanna left Paris in two minds. General agreement was that her interpretation was supremely interesting from the standpoint of idealism and that it was exceedingly well liked by her audience. But there were misgivings insofar as Mary had taken the liberty of changing the opera, doing away with the long final tableau and making the opera end in the same way as the play.

The critic L. Veuillemin condemned the improvisatory nature of Mary's performance.

> I know of no artist as disturbing as Miss Mary Garden. Having charmed the spectator, she proceeds to shock him; having stirred his heart, she makes him laugh. She plays as she happens to feel and is only concerned with giving utterance to one of her singular intonations. She turns, she jumps, she pirouettes and ties her arms into knots that give the lie to all the laws of anatomy. All this is not the result of study or deliberation but the proof of intuition which is sadly at fault – or of chance.[16]

Meanwhile the rumours of marriage persisted. Late that September she was quoted in a number of papers as saying that she would soon be married. Other reports insisted she was tired of the vanity and pomp of the world, and was studying the Roman Catholic religion with the intention of taking the veil as soon as her opera career closed – indeed, in her Avenue Malakoff apartment she already had incense burning, with a prie-dieu placed below a crucifix. *The Cleveland Plain Dealer* (6 October 1909), true to its title, hit the nail on the head by commenting: 'There is no better self-advertiser in the world than Mary. She is a great artist and she fixes public attention chiefly by the force of her art. The personal gossip directs attention to her; she holds it by her interpretation of some of the most difficult roles in the world of music.'

In an unexpected shift of opinion, Mary suddenly revealed a distaste for America. She dismissed the United States as an immense railway station, not a country. Referring to her next scheduled visit there, she complained: 'Everything in America is money. I am bound by contracts this time. Then I shall never leave Paris.'[17]

Arriving in New York, Mary declared this would be her last season in America. Her disembarkation was marred by an investigation into her resident status, perhaps caused by her rather undiplomatic remarks before she left Paris. 'Miss Mary Garden is not a non-resident of class A or of class B', wrote the critic for *The New York Herald*, owned by the intrepid James Gordon Bennett, a journalist of Scots descent who would later be one of Mary's expatriate neighbours at Beaulieu-sur-Mer on the Côte d'Azur. 'She is not a foreigner at all,' continued the paper. 'At least that is the opinion of the Customs experts of the Treasury Department, reached today'.

Mary, still a parsimonious Scot in many ways, was finally forced to pay duty on the wardrobe she brought over from Paris in a dozen or more trunks. She was not amused. Later, it was reported that she would sue. She bullied the Customs unmercifully but it took all of eight weeks for the New York Customs to decide that Mary really was a resident of Paris. This saved her the sum of £2000 in duty on costumes and jewellery.

Meanwhile, Mary had settled into an apartment on West Fifty-Sixth Street and started to indulge her passion – titillating the press. Her appearance was dramatic enough: her hair was now red; there were diamond horseshoes on her slippers, emeralds on her fingers and a large pearl hung from each ear. She would expound at length, contradicting herself frequently, on her favourite topic – herself. She confessed she was madly in love with a man in Paris and it was only a contract with Mr Hammerstein that brought her to America. Then she changed her mind, saying: 'Married life is not for me'. As easily as she had once declared herself a suffragette, she now repudiated the movement: 'I am not a suffragist or a suffragette. Why should I want to vote? I have no time to vote'. She said she believed in dissociating the theatre and the home – she was one woman in the theatre; quite another outside. She had plans for the future: she would buy an estate in Scotland and there, a nice, respectable old lady, would settle down for good. She planned to keep every kind of animal there except the human animal, and would be perfectly happy and would live to a ripe old age, far from the madding crowds. And to an enquiring reporter who asked her how many people she had cared for in her life, she revealed: 'I could count them on one hand'.

As to the immediate future, she was wild to visit Russia, and had had a magnificent offer to go there, which she might accept. She had always dreamed of making an appearance at St Petersburg and she always got what she wanted. She wanted to go there, sing and succeed. But she never did.

Instead, she went to Philadelphia, where she sang in *Sapho* and *Le jongleur de Notre-Dame* and then returned to the Manhattan to sing in *Thaïs* and *Salome*. In December 1909, her Marguerite in *Faust* at the Manhattan produced an uneven assessment. The sheer power of her conception and her stage art were applauded. The limitations of her voice were evident, but she acted so well that her vocal shortcomings were forgiven. At times, she was obliged to force her voice and it had become strident. It seemed to be her production that was at fault, not the voice itself.

Meanwhile, Oscar Hammerstein continued to wage his war of attrition against the Met. During the Opéra-Comique troupe's autumn season in Chicago, Hammerstein had spoken to the music critic, Karleton Hackett, who had long been advocating the formation of a Chicago opera company. Hammerstein told Hackett he would be willing to form a company and build an opera house, provided Chicago could finance it. When, however, Hackett insisted on a board of seven directors, Hammerstein refused, saying that he always managed his businesses alone and withdrew his offer. Immediately on hearing the news of this meeting, New York financier Otto Kahn, then chairman of the board of the Metropolitan, stated that he would provide both an opera company and an opera house.[18]

On 9 December 1909 the organization of a Chicago Grand Opera Company was announced, some six months after negotiations had first started. Karleton Hackett and publisher John C. Shaffer of the *Chicago Evening Post* persuaded 50 businessmen to contribute $5000 each to a subscription fund. Harold F. McCormick of the International Harvester Company was appointed president of the new Chicago Opera Association and Otto Kahn subscribed $50,000 to become vice-president. Metropolitan backers generously supported the new venture in the hope of preventing Hammerstein from forming his own Chicago company.[19]

While these skirmishes moved backwards and forwards on the managerial front, Mary continued to bemuse audiences in New York. Her *Sapho* at the Manhattan, according to *The New York Times*, was felt to be a distorted portrayal – 'a gross exaggeration of all the mannerisms of gesture and posture and bodily writhing that she has made familiar in other parts. She lapsed frequently into the speaking voice. Her singing has never been so bad. The strident quality that used to reside in the upper tones was heard last evening in them all'.

Then, in another performance of *Faust*, Mary confounded all the critics. While Mary had admitted Marguerite was not a role that interested her greatly, no sign of this could be seen across the footlights. The *Musical Courier* wrote that she had given a very sympathetic performance, singing always with intelligence of phrasing and enunciation and with perfect control. There was none of the brittleness or shrillness of tone which sometimes marred her performance, nor did she force her voice. She triumphed through the naturalness and beauty of her acting. But there was one notable dissenter. The composer Charles Cadman, condemned her vocal style: 'in many episodes she talked rather than sang'.[20]

Amidst her performances in Pittsburgh, an old rivalry briefly flared up. Rumours emerged from the city that Luisa Tetrazzini and Mary had quarrelled because Tetrazzini had received less applause than Garden. Mary was said to have called Tetrazzini's coloratura style 'antiquated'. Mary denied the story. Tetrazzini made no comment.

Before she left Cincinnati, Mary had given the journalists good copy and a timely pronouncement on her marital ambitions. Divorce should be made as easy as possible, Mary believed. If a man and a woman were mismatched, it was proper that they should separate; it was wrong for them to live together without love. But, she proclaimed, she did now believe again in marriage. She claimed she had seen Prince Mavrocordato in Paris not long ago and told him that she really thought they would have to get married, as the American press had it all arranged.

This constant publicity-seeking exasperated the *Musical Leader* (6 January 1910), which gave her this advice: 'Mary Garden, the artist, the actress and grand opera singer, should throw off Mary Garden, the inter-viewee and notoriety-seeker.'

Another appearance as Marguerite at the Manhattan led once again to the verdict that she was a better actress than singer. She was not entitled to serious consideration as a singer, said the critics; her voice was thin and acid in quality, and she had little regard for the technique of vocalization. Her success was due to the fact that she understood the apparatus of the theatre and if she could sing such parts as Thaïs or Salome, it was because she composed them with a splendid knowledge of effect, and interpreted them with great cleverness.

In spite of such belittling comment, the need to promote opera in America appeared to be uppermost in Mary's mind. While playing the Belasco Theatre in Washington, Mary and the other members of the Manhattan company visited President Taft at the White House. She discussed with the President the advisability of an opera house for the national capital and he was interested enough to go and see her in *Thaïs* and *Le jongleur de Notre Dame*.

Mary's next important American première was Massenet's *Grisélidis* at the Manhattan. Reviews were generally favourable: 'She makes of Grisélidis,' wrote the critic for *The Musical Leader* (27 January), 'a passion-less, ethereal creature. Much of the music lies where her voice has that golden, luscious glow.'

Meanwhile Hammerstein, drained by losses in Philadelphia, had begun to cut rehearsal time. Anxious to support him in his struggle against the Met, Mary suggested to the press that the two companies should divide the reper-toire between them; the Met should confine itself to Italian and German operas, while the Manhattan should specialize in French opera. And she added that the Manhattan would have to release its Italian singers and recall Campanini – who had resigned in protest at the end of the previous season. Paradoxically, however, Mary claimed that she still hankered after the German repertoire, and was still studying German. She was not at this time (as she would later be in the case of Victor Herbert's *Natoma*) a supporter of opera in English.

*   *   *

April 1910 proved to be a watershed in Mary's career, in her domestic affairs and in American operatic history. Mary was planning to sail for France early in April and was going to sing in *Salome* at the Paris Opéra a month later; she had also been asked to sing the role in a Strauss cycle in Brussels.

After a gala concert in Philadelphia where Mary performed with John McCormack, Oscar Hammerstein announced that he was ready to sell the Philadelphia Opera House to the Metropolitan. Morale was at rock-bottom in the Hammerstein camp; it was the end of Hammerstein's final season. Things were not going well, and Mary, his trump card in attracting new audiences, had been overworked. She was, on one occasion, forced to sing five nights in succession between the New York, Boston and Philadelphia houses.

A dispute erupted between Mary and Hammerstein over Mary's contract; he was threatening her with a court case because of alleged over-payment. Mary hurried to outwit him: she would have to make sure that her costumes and household goods were packed and placed quickly aboard the steamer in case Hammerstein impounded them – Mary would need these costumes to sing at the Paris Opéra as soon as she arrived in France. The packing was done with only her sister and the cook to help her; fortunately, the costumes reached the steamer.

As she sailed on the *Adriatic*, reputedly with $100,000 in her purse, Mary accused Hammerstein: 'He has treated me like a servant. I, his leading lady – I might have been one of his chorus girls.' Hammerstein rebutted: 'Her contract called for a payment in francs, not dollars. A fool of a man paid her, by mistake, in dollars. It is an overpayment of $4000. Besides that she owes the box office $500 for tickets. Miss Garden's contract has two years to run. She will come back.'[21]

From Crookhaven a week later, Mary sent a telegram to Hammerstein, claiming he owed her $2500. When she arrived in Paris, she announced haughtily that she had no intention of ever singing again at the Manhattan or in Philadelphia until Hammerstein backed down and apologized.

Notes

1. *Chicago News*, 25 March 1909.
2. The story bears a strange resemblance to a section in Biancolli's, *Mary Garden's Story*, p. 45, in which a young doctor shoots himself for love of Mary and is sent to Biarritz to recover.
3. Arnold T. Schwabb (1963), *James Gibbons Huneker – Critic of the Seven Arts*, California: Stanford University Press, p. 256.
4. Jack Winsor Hansen, 'Mary Garden: Queen of Chutzpah, Part 1', *Massenet Society Newsletter*, vol. 9, no. 2, July 1990, pp. 13–14.

5. Karleton Hackett, untitled magazine, January 1911, NYPL.
6. Untitled clipping, 27 March 1909, NYPL, Billy Rose Theatre Collection, Robinson Locke Collection of Scrapbooks 1856–1920, vols. 224–234, Series 1.
7. *Philadelphia Times*, 29 March 1909.
8. *New York Star*, 3 April 1909.
9. Letter 16, Garden to F. Mayer, Paris, July 1897, CHS.
10. Untitled Philadelphia newspaper clippings, 3 April 1909, NYPL, Billy Rose Theatre Collection, Robinson Locke Collection of Scrapbooks 1856–1920, vols. 224–234, Series 1.
11. *Musical America*, 10 April 1909.
12. Philadelphia newspaper clippings, 18 April 1909, NYPL, Billy Rose Theatre Collection, Robinson Locke Collection of Scrapbooks 1856–1920, vols. 224–234, Series 1.
13. *Los Angeles Examiner*, 28 April 1909.
14. Untitled newspaper, 19 October 1910, Mary Garden scrapbook, vol. 1, RCM.
15. *New York Herald*, Paris, 14 June 1909.
16. *New York Telegraph*, 24 October 1909.
17. *New York Evening Times*, 3 November 1909.
18. J. Bulliet, *How Grand Opera Came to Chicago*, privately published c.1930, pp. 5–6. Located in the Music Information Center, Chicago Public Library.
19. Robert L. Brubaker (1979), '130 years of opera in Chicago', *Chicago History*, VIII, No. 3, Chicago Historical Society, p. 157.
20. *Pittsburgh Despatch*, 24 December 1909.
21. *Boston Herald*, 9 April 1910.

7 *Salome* in Paris and On Tour in America: 1910–1911

Back in Paris, Mary settled into her spacious apartment at 148 Avenue Malakoff. The Garden finances were in a healthy state; in 1910 she claimed to be earning $200,000, some of it made in speculation on the Paris Bourse.

Towards the end of April that year, she sang from the second act of *Roméo et Juliette* at a reception in the Elysée Palace, to an audience which included Colonel Theodore Roosevelt, former United States Republican president, Rough-Rider and explorer; in later years, Mary would say that Roosevelt had thrilled her more than any celebrity she ever met. Then, from May to October, she launched herself into an extraordinary run of 20 appearances at the Opéra as Salome, with an average of four days' rest between performances.

Paris was no stranger to the *Salome* of Richard Strauss. It had been first heard at the Petit Théâtre on 30 April 1907, with Mme Jacques Isnardon playing Salome; she, like Mary, had performed the Dance of the Seven Veils herself. To prepare for her own dance at the Opéra, Mary had gone to the ballet mistress Mme Stichel and together they devised steps which would fit into the production by Paul Stuart and the conducting of André Messager.

Public reaction in Paris to Mary's performance showed none of the protests or moral censure she had experienced in America. The critic Henry Gauthier-Villars picked on what he felt to be Messager's dynamic exaggeration and a Dance of the Seven Veils which seemed to have been deliberately restrained to conserve the soprano's vocal powers. But he was captivated by Mary's interpretation:

> Her studied poses, her gestures copied from famous paintings, her dress shimmering with precious stones, like a light veil over her thighs; her nervous energy, her untamed sensuality, are not normally to be found in the opera house. She had the very literary notion of playing Salome right from the first scene as a dancer who knows that the eyes of all the men, inflamed with desire, will not leave her body. She acted the whole opera with bare arms, heaving loins and voluptuous legs.[1]

Gauthier-Villars went on to identify Mary's interpretation as that of Oscar Wilde and of the Symbolist painter, Gustave Moreau, adding that Mary's unqualified success was the highest pinnacle of art ever offered by the National Academy to the French public. Louis Handler, however, was totally bemused by the gymnastic complexity of Mary's performance: 'Miss Garden has not taken three steps but she has made 133 gestures with her right hand, 76 with her left arm and 314 with the rest of her body!'[2]

Paris now had three Salomes: Mary at the Opéra; Lucienne Bréval at the Gaiêté Théâtre in Mariotte's one-act work; and, at the Casino de Paris, Sahary-Dejeli, as beautiful and sensual as her sisters in a striking and voluptuous *mimodrame*.

Meanwhile, as Mary danced from success to success in Paris, riding a wave of public acclaim, there were ominous rumblings across the Atlantic. In an act of final resignation, and bowing to financial reality, Oscar Hammerstein sold the Philadelphia Opera House to the Metropolitan. In Paris, Mary gave her reaction. Sitting beside her new griffon dog, Salome, which she had recently bought in Brussels, she mused: 'Wasn't it odd about Hammerstein? I really never believed he would have given up. The horrid man says it was I and Renaud who broke him. Ridiculous. I was not mercenary when I went to Hammerstein. I may be now, but I was not then.'

She added nostalgically: 'Hammerstein is a nice, kind old man. We were always quarrelling. But I like him. He was badly advised by his son, and several snakes he had in his employ. My opinion is that he should never have given up.'[3] Later, she added: 'Oscar Hammerstein! What a man! What a wonderful man! If he had only come into my life earlier – say when he was 50 or 60 instead of 75 – ah, then it would have been lovely! Ah, if –'[4]

What Mary perhaps did not reveal was that she had learnt a great deal about the techniques of public relations from Hammerstein. He had a saying: 'Praise me if you can; roast me if you must; at any rate mention me'.[5]

So, looking towards her own future, on 23 June Mary cabled from Paris to general manager Andreas Dippel, agreeing to join his newly formed Chicago Grand Opera Company at the Auditorium Theatre for an initial ten-week season that autumn. Dippel accordingly announced that he had closed the contract with Mary on the same terms she had made with Oscar Hammerstein – $1400 a performance. This acquisition of Mary Garden put the finishing touch to Dippel's plans; he already had Renaud, Dalmorès and Dufranne under contract. Along with Mary, they would also appear at the Metropolitan in New York during the winter while the Chicago company was based in nearby Philadelphia; featuring as special stars they would give performances of French opera.

In Paris, the receipts of Mary's 13 Opéra performances in June were 247,000 francs – an average of approximately $3800 a performance. Yet even this paled beside what the Metropolitan Opera had recently taken in

Paris. In both cases the audiences were largely American. Critical opinion of Mary's work, however, continued to be mixed: at the beginning of September Marc Bertoni complained that, in the vast Opéra, her voice did not carry over the fantastic orchestration of Strauss. She seemed to be trying to compensate by forcing her chest notes and exaggerating her acting.[6] But others thought her talent was like no other. The critic for *Musica* (September 1910) was struck by the disconcerting originality of her acting and of her singing – a certain exoticism out of which, by means of intelligence and intuition, she had been able to create art. One could dislike her artistry, but no one could fail to find it interesting. Mary was, along with Lillian Nordica, Sibyl Sanderson and Emma Eames, the best of the singers America had shown to Europe.

Yet others protested the barbarity of her style. Writing about her Thaïs, *Comœdia* (10 October 1909) was astonished and alarmed: 'What gestures, what poses! Their exaggerated, even shocking use is not compensated for by the crudity of vocal effects to which the singer is given. In her, everything is taken to extremes, for the sole purpose of astonishing and achieving an eccentric musical and dramatic impact.'

In October came *Monna Vanna* in which Mary's contrasts of extremes unnerved L. Vuillemin: 'I don't know any artist so disturbing as Miss Mary Garden. One has to, in turn, love her and hate her; praise her and criticise her. She sings, then she speaks. She shouts, then she is silent. She stays still, then she runs about. Everything about her is violent contrast. She is scarcely on the stage when she turns, leaps, pirouettes, twists her arms against all the laws of anatomy.'[7] And he ended with a spiteful dig at her successes across the Atlantic: 'Those who liked Mélisande will not like Monna Vanna. And that, I think, is the only moral profit of the two visits Miss Garden has made to America.'

Having made a triumphant final appearance as Marguerite in *Faust*, Mary sailed for America on the *Kaiser Wilhelm II*, promising to return the following April to create a role in Giordano's *Siberia*.[8] She had ended her season at the Opéra with a new box-office record.

By this time Mary had taken steps to upgrade her own personal staff by engaging a new agent, Arnold Daly. It was not long before his skills were called upon. She was ordered to pay 1000 francs to the impresario Markus for breaking a contract between them in 1907 for appearances in Germany, Austria and Romania. She had refused to start the tour, she claimed, because he had not made the proper advance arrangements.

But, leaving such matters to Daly, she arrived back in New York in her inimitable style, stepping breezily down the gangplank sporting a fashionable monocle. She was accompanied by her sister Agnes and had spent the voyage with the tenors Charles Dalmorès and John McCormack and the composer Gustav Mahler.

To the waiting journalists Mary announced provocatively: 'Marriage agrees with me'. Wearing a band of plain gold on the appropriate finger, she declared that she was wearing a wedding ring but she could not talk about the man yet. She asserted that she had married a poor man. On the other hand, there were wild rumours of an immensely wealthy Magyar nobleman. It had been a beastly voyage, she complained. She had eaten nothing but eggs and drunk nothing but ginger ale. She needed some rest.

Over the following days it emerged that flying was Mary's new passion. She was discovered at New York's Belmont aviation field, where she chatted in French, German and Russian in one breath as she accepted the homage of Baron Schlippenbach, Fernand de Lesseps and Herr von Krafft – who was said to be watching the flights of the sky-ships in the interests of the Kaiser. 'I am mad, quite mad, about aviation,' said Mary. 'Last year at Rheims when I saw forty flying machines take air at one time like a flock of marvellous great birds, it took me a week to come down to terra firma myself.'[9]

In New York Mary signed a contract with R. E. Johnston for a concert tour the following spring, beginning in March; she then left for Chicago. Arriving in the Windy City, she walked straight into an operatic skirmish. Five sopranos were clashing over who would be the first to sing Thaïs and three arguing about who would play Carmen.

Mary moved into her beloved Blackstone Hotel and began feeding the newshounds her tales – about the Turkish pasha who was languishing in the fastnesses of his native mountains, about his romantic person, his slavish devotion. It was the Turk's ring circling one of Mary's white fingers. He was due to come to America in December and had asked her to marry him. But no man ever could come between her and her art. As for her, she wouldn't want a man to be faithful to her. Love came and went. It was repugnant to think of having anyone bound to one by hateful ties. 'I am a man, not a woman,' she declared to the startled journalists. 'I have fought for everything I possess. It has all come out of this throat of mine and it pleases me to live as I choose. I believe in a single standard for men and women.'[10]

The New York Times, however, insisted that Mary was to be the 'Bride of a Bey'. Her intended was now said to be James Bey, a high-born Englishman in the service of the Egyptian government. Mary continued to fascinate and infuriate – she always had an eye for public relations. As Edward Moore points out: 'There were two camps in all opera seasons, those for whom Miss Garden can do no wrong, and those who are never satisfied with anything she does. She never scorned the artful aid of newspaper publicity. She always managed to say the right thing at the right time to get it printed.'[11]

By now Mary's red hair had been replaced by brown but she still continued to have an immense theatrical impact. In *Pelléas et Mélisande*, in Chicago in early November 1910, her 'dominating and delightful personality reached out beyond the footlights to the heights of the gallery, with power far more effective than merely vocal pyrotechnics could have attained. Her conquest was complete and the great audience gave all the honor that many recalls could compel'.[12]

But there was also theatricality of a different kind. She walked out of the Lyric Theater because she had been asked several times by the usher to remove her hat of champagne velvet decorated with plumes. Questioned about the offending hat, she said: 'It is fairish in size; but then I was sitting at the back of the box'.[13]

There were also defeats. She gave up her new role of Minnie in Puccini's *La fanciulla del West* ostensibly because she did not know Italian well enough. She had resisted the entreaties of Andreas Dippel and Tito Ricordi: 'The opera is rotten!' she announced. 'I mean it. I've said it before and you must not modify my word. I think as I may and I say what I think. You know I was to have created Minnie in Chicago, but when I read the score I absolutely refused to take the part.'[14]

Her first Chicago performance of *Salome* was on 25 November 1910. It stunned the audience. She was seen to be 'the acme of devilry, an unusual type of sensualist whose power extended beyond the footlights. Her dancing of The Seven Veils was a vision of grace but the ferocity of her passion that finally consumed itself was strange and terrible'.[15] Then, at the end of November, the third performance of *Salome* had to be called off as a result of a violent protest by Chief of Police Leroy T. Steward: 'It was disgusting. The whole show lacked high class. Miss Garden wallowed around like a cat in a bed of catnip. I think that the way Miss Garden rolls on the floor with the decapitated and supposedly bloody head is revolting.'[16]

Mary's response was a full-blooded attack: 'I never in all my life read anything so disgusting as what your Chief of Police said about me and my Dance. If there's going to be any more trouble over this I will simply refuse to give *Salome* here again,' she added. 'Some horrid person sent me a package of catnip. Wasn't that disgusting?'[17]

Others joined the chorus of complaint started by the Chief of Police: 'I am a normal man, but I would not trust myself to see a performance of *Salome*,' said Arthur Burrage Farwel, President of the Chicago Law and Order League.[18]

The banning of *Salome* infuriated Mary:

> I don't like to be crushed out in this way in a matter of such importance to my art. I'm convinced it is a minority that opposes the opera, and a very tiny one. I'd rather that they close *Salome* down altogether than ask me to change my interpretation. I won't change my art for anyone in the world. We were to have presented it once a week until the end of the season. Anyway, we are going to produce it in Milwaukee, and I feel in my bones that Milwaukee will know real art when it sees it in *Salome*.

But Mary suspected that there were powerful figures behind the ban: 'It is a

plot, a deep, sinister plot. There is someone they are afraid of, these directors. This someone doesn't like me or is jealous of my triumph. Someone
who is a power has said "No more *Salome*".[19] The implication was that it
was Mrs Harold McCormick – she was said to have objected to the opera at
the beginning of the season.

'Mary Garden's refusal to tone down performance closes house' was the
announcement of *The Toledo Blade* (30 November 1910). When arrangements were made to put on another production, the artists revolted and
said they would not appear in any play. But, while the view of the police
authorities of *Salome* was that 'Lust is its keynote and its consummation',
Chicago, judging by ticket sales, was thirsting for another glimpse. By 1
December Baltimore, however, had banned *Salome*, but in Milwaukee
tickets for the 9 December performance were booming. *Salome* had now
become a national issue. The critic Carl Van Vechten recalls that at this
point Mary sent a series of characteristic telegrams. One of them read: 'My
art is going through the torture of slow death. "Oh Paris, splendeur de mes
désirs!"'[20]

In spite of having become Chicago's 'Our Mary', she had decided that she
would never sing in Chicago again: 'Chicago is a little too unsophisticated. It
has a little too much mock modesty. It stands for all kinds of vice, all kinds
of *risqué*, cheap theatrical productions, but it was too nice to accept
Salome.'[21] As for the prospect of ever singing in London again – 'My dear,
what should I do in London? They wouldn't let me in. I'd have to camp on
the outskirts – me and my immoral shows.'[22]

Trouble loomed in Milwaukee where a committee of men aged 75 and
over had been appointed to vet the performance and Archbishop Messmer
had advised his flock to stay away. His admonitions were countered by one
Jeremiah Quin who argued that 'However revolting the cuddling of Salome
over the dripping head of St John may be to Catholics, it cannot be more
shocking to faith, than the scenes of Oberammergau, where our Lord himself is depicted nailed to a cross, in view of priest and people'.[23]

Those who went to *Salome* for titillation were disappointed: 'Why, it
wasn't *risqué* at all', wrote *The Milwaukee Morning Telegraph*. Where was
all that spice Chicago roared about? Nevertheless, *The Toledo Times* (13
December 1910) noted that 'Salomania' had hit America: 'prudes and puri-
tans, preachers and policemen all over this broad land send up a sympathetic
cry of horror at the abomination'.

Local critical judgement in Milwaukee was not favourable. Morality
must come before art:

> Mary Garden is not a voluptuous figure. She looks like a splendidly built young
> man. Her portrayal of the barbaric girl's bald passion thrilled and fascinated. The
> Dance was an amazing thing. The immorality lies in its suggestiveness – the
> underlying motive. Miss Garden's pantomime was dramatic, primitively virile.

There is still the inartistic episode of a young girl caressing in an ugly rhapsody the dissevered head of the man whom she has pretended to love, and whose death she commanded! Can the musical apotheosis of such a scene be anything but inartistic – insincere as well as horrifying? Truly, *Salome* is 'grand opera gone quite mad!'[24]

*   *   *

Returning to Chicago, in mid-December Mary appeared as Marguerite in *Faust*:

A rather frequent tendency to 'scoop' the tone bore witness to her limitations in the matter of vocal technique. In other words, her attack is habitually uncertain. She does not impale the tone with that mechanical certainty which belongs to a Melba or a Sembrich but approaches it tentatively from below, reaching up to it slyly and with stealth. On the other hand, Miss Garden balances this intervalic circumspection with a delightful certainty in the matter of tonal quality.[25]

An interview with William Armstrong during this period illuminates Mary's state of mind and explains her method of preparing for a role. In some things, it seemed, she was mentally more like a man. Impulse she had in abundance; without it, she could not be an artist:

Wagner I shall take up later. That is why I study German every day. I shall commence with Elsa. At forty-one or two, when my art is matured to its fullest, I shall take up Isolde… When I read a new role, it unfolds itself like the coil of a cinematograph. Its every picture I see in my mind, I memorize the whole thing together – music, words and action. That first conception I never change.

Unable to resist slipping in a word on the subject of men:

A man who would interest me must interest me through his intellectuality. It is only for that that I would marry. Men have never interested me greatly; few of them keep my illusions. There is an artist in the north of Europe who comes now and again to Paris to see me in some role at the Opéra. Each time he writes me his impressions, each time he sends me flowers. He has made no attempt to meet me; I have no desire to meet him.

Mary went on to explain her attitude to her audience:

Nervousness is a pose. From the stage, the audience before me is no more than the stones in the street; it does not exist. I mean this in the sense that my whole mind is on my work. Sometimes I am exhausted at the close of the opera but always my sleep is wonderful. That gives me great force.[26]

In an article in *Century* (February 1911) Mary elaborated on how she built up a character: 'I can speak only of myself, and I cannot exactly describe my condition. I know that for the time being I am the character to the last note, till the curtain drops: then I am myself again.

'The inspiration, the feeling of a part,' she continued, 'comes to me first through the music. There are three elements in operatic interpretation – beauty and expressiveness of musical tone; the communication to the audience of the exact significance and color of the words; the expression of action.'

She gave her reasons for avoiding the coloratura repertoire and the Italian language: 'The expression through tone is of course a part of the coloring that gives meaning to the words, yet often the utterance of every word in itself is important. For that reason I do not care to sing in Italian, a language I understand incompletely. Yet if it were not that the public demands the very high notes, the perfect coloratura in the old Italian roles, it would interest me to undertake them.'

Discussing *Le jongleur de Notre-Dame*, she observed that she was the only woman singer who had Massenet's permission to sing the part. Speaking about *Thaïs*, she explained that she did not research the story by Anatole France, because the woman presented in the libretto of Massenet's opera is not precisely the Thaïs of Anatole France. Instead, she read books describing the life and atmosphere of the period in which Thaïs lived. Then she commented on *Carmen*, saying that she was studying the novel by Prosper Merimée upon which the libretto was based. She believed Merimée's Carmen was not the character usually seen represented in the opera house. Carmen was not the mere vulgar coquette sometimes portrayed.

Finally, in respect to *Pelléas et Mélisande*, she revealed that she had not long before been working with Debussy. His compositions were very difficult to learn; his musical intention was so individual that, in learning, as she recently had, some of his new songs, she attempted no more than the actual committing of the notes before seeing him. Yet, once mastered, his music remained fixed in her memory.

It was around this time that Mary announced a new project: she would write a book during her vacation, covering the previous ten years: 'Shall I go into my love affairs? Good gracious, no! Do you think I am going to write volumes?' The first chapter of her book was to be devoted to American women: 'I shall show how the American woman is lazy. I despise a woman who lacks ambition. That is the trouble with all women. They don't know how to train a man. They don't know how to appeal to him.'[27]

Early in 1911 Mary agreed to auction boxes at the Auditorium for a charity performance in aid of the Firemen's Relief Fund. The auction took place in the Chicago Stock Exchange. She stood high up above the crowd, taking bids, when suddenly there was a commotion and a gun fell at her feet. Mary turned to see a policeman dragging off a man with long grey hair and shabby clothes. Later Mary sent a friend to speak to him in prison. In reply to the question as to why he wanted to shoot a famous soprano, the man answered: 'She talks too much'. Needless to say, the auction raised $1000.

From this period an intimate glimpse has been preserved of Mary's attitude to her colleagues on stage. She had been in Philadelphia preparing for the première of Victor Herbert's new American opera, *Natoma*. Charles Bancroft, who sang in the chorus, recalls that:

> Mary Garden was at her prime. She was in her early thirties – vivacious and sparkling and unusually friendly. She took us under her wing and did everything to cure us of stage-fright. She made some very clever rapid pencil sketches of one or two of us. Those of the cast who performed with her said she was an inspiration to work with. She made the members of the chorus feel she was their friend. The second Act grew in intensity when I, as one of the soldiers, dashed across the stage to rescue Mary Garden, the Indian maid, from the mob. Unfortunately, I over-played my part and if it had not been for Miss Garden catching me, I would have gone off the apron of the stage into the orchestra-pit![28]

Unhappily, *Natoma* was not a great success. The story of *Natoma* was melodramatic in tone and scrappy in treatment and only slightly related to American life.[29] 'Natoma is as much a puppet as all the rest,' wrote George Rogers in *The Philadelphia Inquirer* (26 February 1911), 'and not even Miss Garden's unequalled genius for characterisation could transform this cigar-store figure into a breathing, suffering, loving human being. Miss Garden sang the music of the title role with much fervor of emotion. In the Dagger Dance she managed to invest her gliding, sinuous movements with the aspect of a sinister intensity.'

Her characterization was considered to be finely observed: 'The Indian always sings either a little flat or a little sharp', commented the *New York Times* (8 March 1911). 'Miss Garden reproduces this striking trait of Indian song. Her dance technique was something which would have filled Isadora Duncan with envy.'

Heightened realism had its penalties. In Baltimore Mary was slightly wounded during the Dagger Dance. The dagger slipped as she made a lunge with it, cut her arm near the elbow and sliced the skin from the tip of her finger. But, despite the mishaps and the shortcomings of the work, *Natoma* was a good vehicle for her talents: 'There is in Miss Garden,' pointed out *Musical America* (27 March 1911), 'exactly the strain of French theatricalism which knows its moment and its effect and equips her to appeal to the spectacular sense in the observer.'

At this time, Mary completed a number of recording sessions for the Columbia Phonograph Company in New York. 'Quel est donc ce trouble charmant?' and 'Pour jamais ta destinée' from *La traviata* drew comment from Richard D. Fletcher that:

> the most rewarding and astonishing of the Columbia operatic excerpts are the two Act I soprano airs from *La traviata*. Here Garden displays a coloratura which may stand proudly alongside Galli-Curci's. Though the tone does not carry the italianate throb of the latter singer, the display work is delivered with an ease Galli-Curci never surpassed and much of the passage work is dashed off with greater smoothness.[30]

Desmond Shawe-Taylor echoes this assessment:

> Among the most valuable is her double-sided 'Ah fors è lui' [sung in French] from *La traviata*. Surprisingly perhaps, Violetta was one of her favourite and most successful roles, and the record certainly shows that she was a more technically accomplished singer than is often supposed. In spite of the French translation and of traditions of phrasing that are strange to us, she shows a solid technique and good tone: a shade thin perhaps around the transitional notes, the higher E and F, but enviably secure in the upper regions [her effective range was from C to C], and she contrives to 'suggest' a D flat at the beginning of one of the roulades of 'Sempre libera'.[31]

Hugues Cuénod adds: 'The *La traviata* item (in French) is really wonderful. Excellent style, fantastic attacks, fresh voice throughout, amazing virtuosity, the staccato high Cs wonderfully accurate, especially when one considers the very quick tempo.'[32]

Her 'Liberté' from *Le jongleur de Notre-Dame* and 'Il est doux, il est bon' from *Hérodiade* also drew commendation from Desmond Shawe-Taylor: 'we note her naturalness and simplicity of manner, allied with purity of tone; the "Liberté" excerpt from *Le jongleur de Notre-Dame* also supports her claim to have made no change in the music – except, of course, that she sings it an octave higher than Massenet's tenor line.'[33]

Hugues Cuénod, however, had reservations: 'The selection from *Hérodiade*, that dull piece, is sung with her bell-like purity of voice, but with sudden inexplicable chest tones, very well executed but musically unnecessary.'[34]

*   *   *

In March 1911 it was announced that Mary would for the very first time make a four- to six-week concert tour of the cities of the Atlantic seaboard and some of the middle states. She had at first refused to undertake the tour as she was postponing her return to Europe in order to write her autobiography as she had promised. A solution was found: a special private Pullman car was provided, with three porters, a chef (who had formerly cooked for her in Paris), two maids, a secretary and an amanuensis to take dictation. Her book was to be in the hands of the publishers by 1 July. A week later she also hired a secret service agent to guard her jewellery.

The tour began at Carnegie Hall in early April with the baritone Mario Sammarco and the violinist Arturo Tibaldi; the pianist was composer Howard Brockway. Appearing later in Atlanta, Mary dazzled the audience in a gown of pearls and sequins over white satin; many diamonds and several large emeralds glittered about her.

In Toledo her concert was very nearly cancelled because of low ticket sales and a religious revival meeting. But Mary saved the concert through positive thinking:

I saw the tent of the famous evangelist Billy Sunday who was saying all those awful things about me. So I went to his tent one day and there he was – just a little boy not even as tall as me. He didn't know quite what to do, so he offered me a drink of water. I said, 'No thank you. But I'll tell you what I would like – I'd like a nice big chocolate soda, wouldn't you?' So off we went, Mary Garden and Billy Sunday, and had a chocolate soda together. That was the only man I ever stood up to.[35]

The critic of *The Rochester Union & Advertiser* (26 April 1911) noted Mary's good points and her faults:

She has been spoken of as the Sarah Bernhardt of opera, the same strange combination of hard metallic tones and moments of soft, luscious quality. In listening to Miss Garden, the thought is repeatedly brought to mind that here is a voice whose possibilities of sheer beauty of tone have never been realised. Faulty technique and incorrect vocal production have laid many pitfalls and the result is that already there are frequent indications of wear, of a voice that lacks freshness. In concert singing Miss Garden is out of her sphere. She requires the glamour of stage accessories, the inspiration of the dramatic side of the picture to show her at her best. Her great forte is acting. Her marvellous versatility and the very great power of her art as an actress are displayed to greatest advantage in the exacting demands of the modern French school of opera.

Arriving in Indianapolis, Mary was suffering from the effects of a bump with the engine which had jolted her car, 'Iolanthe', and smashed her china, spilling her wines. On her right hand, she wore a yellow solitaire diamond as large as a walnut. Flanked by her manager and treasurer, Max Hirsch, and her new personal representative, William F. Chauncey, Mary launched into one of her grand public statements: 'Women vote? I should say I don't believe in it. Only those uninteresting and old women, who have ceased to have anything else to do in life, are agitating for suffrage. Woman is made to be loved, not to vote.'[36]

'We'll take her to the vaudeville show this afternoon,' said Chauncey, who had been the soprano Lillian Nordica's secretary until her recent marriage. 'She is so enthusiastic about it, and I hear they're to have clog-dancing. She'll go wild about it', he added, as he picked up her furs and coat from where she had flung them and hung them up where they belonged. Chauncey, in the *Indianapolis Star* (3 May 1911), explained her relative lack of success in Rochester: 'She was like a bird in a cage, struggling against the concert stage restrictions that held her and her art. Miss Garden needs the pomp and circumstance of opera to be at her best. She needs a grand opera orchestra, the scenery and atmosphere, the freedom of the whole stage – and the opera itself.'

In the town of Peoria, Mary refused to sing from *Salome* – 'it loses its whole effect when taken out of the music drama and accompanied on the piano'. The organizers cancelled the concert. She promptly transferred to the Masonic Hall. On her arrival in Peoria she found the whole town placarded with enormous signs reading 'Mary Garden WILL sing tomorrow night.'

There were even streamers which reached across streets with her name in black or red letters. Even though she didn't sing *Salome*, she walked away with all of the takings!

At the end of her concert in Denver, Frances Wayne of *The Denver Times* (12 May 1911) extolled her power on the concert platform:

> The woman who stood before us last night, shimmering in white and silver, diamonds and pearls, has what others lack – the power of dragging her audience into the innermost chambers of the heart and soul of the characters she portrays. Miss Garden's voice is topographical. In it one encounters chasms and peaks; peaceful valleys are there, and still, comforting waters for the refreshment of weary hearts; volcanoes burst and glacier pits yawn. It is Nature – that voice of Mary Garden's – Nature, naked, unafraid, magnificent, comprehending. Miss Garden is first and foremost an interpreter of character and passion.

In the Park of the Red Rocks near Denver, Mary made the trip to Creation Rock. There, in the natural auditorium at Mount Harrison, she sang the Bach-Gounod 'Ave Maria'. 'Never in any opera house in the world,' she commented, 'have I found more perfect acoustical properties.'

*　*　*

As the tour drew to a close, Mary was anxious to get back to Paris. 'You see I broke a contract with Messager to sing at the Opéra in order to go upon my first American concert tour,' she explained. 'Now Messager has been cabling me almost daily since the end of the Philadelphia Opera season. He seems to be angry. What he will do when I get to Paris, I don't know.' She made known her plans to return to the United States by the beginning of October, to sing in the Maine Festival at Bangor. In the spring she hoped she would be able to make an even longer tour.

She sailed for Europe on 13 June 1911. After a champagne supper for breakfast, Mary, resplendent in yellow stockings, a feather boa and a big blue hat, nearly missed the *Kaiser Wilhelm II*. Her manager, Max Hirsch, trailed behind while a reporter interviewed her on the run: 'I'm taking over 45 pairs of American shoes with me,' she confessed.

Arriving in Paris, Mary arranged for a lesson with her old teacher, Trabadelo. She then surveyed herself in the mirror and decided she was too fat. Normally she weighed 139 pounds. She found she weighed 30 pounds more. Over the next six weeks she set about losing the extra weight. Every morning she rowed and then took an ice-cold bath. After a ride in the Bois she rowed again, then showered. Before going to bed she rowed for a third time and showered.

She proceeded to reveal more secrets of her regimen to the *Louisville Herald* (29 October 1911):

> I have never been out to an after-theatre supper in my life. My first thought after a

performance is to get home. When I get to my rooms I eat a small piece of chicken or 12 crawfish tails, drink two glasses of water with lemon and go to bed. I never drink anything stronger than water. An invariable rule of mine is never to eat between meals.

Then there were details about her figure:

In 1900, when I made my debut as Louise, I wore a narrow little black skirt that fitted me well. Whenever I sing Louise, I wear the same skirt. It has not been altered a particle. That means that in fourteen years my hips have not varied an iota in size. But in that time my chest has expanded twelve inches. That change has all been due to my vocal lessons.[37]

There were a number of setbacks for Mary at this time. In preparation for performing *Carmen* in Philadelphia the following November, she travelled to Marseilles to try to persuade Marguerite Sylva to sell the famous silk shawl she had worn the previous year as Carmen. It was valued at $2000 but Sylva refused to sell it.

There were also stories of ill-feeling between Mary and the Russian soprano, Maria Kuznetsova. Wonder was expressed at Mary not singing *Salome*. Illness, said the rumours, had been mentioned as a pretext to the management but Miss Garden was far from ill. She had simply delivered an ultimatum to the management and *Salome* as a result had had to be taken off the boards for an indefinite period. The root of the problem, however, appeared to be jealousy between Mary and Mme Kuznetsova. While Mary was making her concert tour in America, her favourite roles at the Paris Opéra had all been given to the Russian. Mary enlisted the sympathy and help of the tenor, Lucien Muratore, without whom it was impossible to give the opera. She succeeded in convincing Muratore to declare that his vocal chords had been so affected by the current heatwave that he would be unable to sing in *Salome*. The managers of the Opéra, Messager and Broussan, were accordingly obliged to announce an indefinite postponement.

But even before she would appear in *Salome*, there again arose objections from various quarters as to the way Mary proposed to handle the head of John the Baptist and to her crawling on the stage. 'I read what those foolish old duchesses in Paris said about my methods being better fitted to the Moulin Rouge than to the Opéra because of the way I handled the head of John the Baptist,' Mary retorted. 'What do I care. I'll be singing at the Opéra after most of them are gone, and I'll handle that old head just as I please.'[38]

Meanwhile, in America, criticisms were being aired about her public relations techniques: 'Mary is the best press agent in the world,' wrote *The Cleveland Plain Dealer* (8 August 1911). 'She has old Barnum beaten and as a self-advertiser could teach Theodore Roosevelt a thing or two. In Europe she thinks up "stunts". Mary wants first pages of the press – and she manages to do things or say things that land her in that position.' Comment as usual was passed on her romantic affiliations: 'Private dispatches from Paris indicate that she is the wife of William Chauncey. According to a report she has legally taken his name.' Mary, of course, denied the story of her marriage. Resting in Aix-les-Bains, she was scathing about those 'damned stupid reports'.

In Munich that summer, before she motored away to Switzerland, and despite having been previously a staunch opponent of opera in English, Mary declared that after appearing in *Natoma* she had become a convert to opera in English. She asked for her name to be added to the list of members of the National Society for the Promotion of Opera in English.

She returned to Paris after her summer break and, after two performances of *Faust* and one of *Thaïs* (all conducted by the composer Henri Rabaud), Mary threatened that for *Salome* she would wear so little, Americans would be astonished. Messager conducted all five of her September appearances as *Salome*, in which Mary enjoyed herself so much that she threatened to stay away from America. But in spite of this Parisian success, trouble was again brewing. A row between Lina Cavalieri (later to become Lucien Muratore's wife), and Mary was now said to be raging like a prairie fire fanned by a western whirlwind. Cavalieri, generally considered to be the most beautiful woman on the stage, although not the greatest of singers had held an anti-Garden reception at her home on the Rue Messina on the night Mary was singing *Thaïs* at the Opéra.

The wily southern prima donna, entertaining her guests, showed them her pictures. In the most prominent place in the room was hung a painting of a giraffe. Fierce electric lights beat upon its long neck and some mischievous anti-Gardenite uttered the phrase 'The American Thaïs'. The uproarious fun which followed this could not be halted for a long time. Then Cavalieri herself, clothed in white and wearing her $30,000 rope of pearls and with emeralds as big as hazelnuts in her ears, stood next to her cream-and-gold piano and sang snatches from *Thaïs*.

Mary's counter-attack consisted, it was rumoured, in telling her friends that Lina Cavalieri ate a raw onion before retiring, so as to give her skin its creamy white colour.

At the end of September 1911, in preparation for her return to America, Mary wrote from Paris to Andreas Dippel, manager of the Chicago-Philadelphia Opera Company, asking for an assurance that she would not be arrested before she agreed to appear as Carmen! She claimed she had always been afraid of playing *Carmen* in Philadelphia as the police there did not like her.

*   *   *

Mary arrived back in America during the first week of October, remarking that she was going to make the tailors of America, and the tenors of everywhere, jealous by wearing pants. She had not met Oscar Hammerstein in Europe, but, she claimed, although he had treated her like a dog she still had a tender feeling for him and regarded him as the greatest impresario that ever lived.

Mary's new hotel rooms in New York had been made into a suite that was henceforth named the 'Mary Garden' apartments. They were draped and papered, rugged and upholstered in her favourite colours – soft, pale shades of pink and green.

From New York she set off on her concert tour, beginning in the Bangor Auditorium at the Maine Music Festival. She sang the 'Jewel Song' from *Faust* and the *Bangor Daily News* (16 October 1911) captured the carefully calculated phases of her interpretation:

> Her demure pensiveness as she sat by the spinning wheel; her start of surprise as she caught sight of the casket, almost hidden beneath its covering of roses; the girlish delight, blending into eager rapture, as she held up the jewels in glittering cascades, fastening them upon her bodice and twining them in her hair. Then she snatched the casket and ran past the cheering chorus like a streak of light. Finally, she swept on in a long, red opera cloak, throwing kisses to right and left as she vanished in the direction of her waiting carriage.

There were the occasional lapses, as in Hartford, Connecticut, where she forgot the words of Bemberg's *Chant Vénitien* and had to ask her accompanist André Benoist for them in the most charming French. 'Her manner,' wrote the *Hartford Courant* (17 October 1911), 'is not that of the perfect repose that belongs to the concert – or recital – singer, there being always, apparently, the desire for motion, for action, on the singer's part.'

As soon as she reached Boston, the press commented on one curious fact – there had been no rumours that year of betrothal to a foreign suitor, but rather an ominous silence on the question of marriage. She was more forthcoming on a variety of other topics, however. To *The Boston Telegraph* (20 October 1911) Mary ventured her opinion that composers were often not good conductors of their own work: 'In Paris, Messager conducted *Salome*. I have never heard anyone conduct the opera as he does. Strauss conducted *Salome* for me and I assure you the opera was scarcely recognisable. The same thing happened with Charpentier and *Louise*. It was a dreadfully tiresome, lagging performance.' Then, taking a new tack, Mary announced that were she not a singer she would be a detective. She was following with the utmost interest a recent murder case in Boston. All such reports were carefully preserved by her family for her bedside reading. Innocently, she revealed that she longed to meet a murderer, a real cold-blooded criminal – not just a passionate man who murdered his wife or sweetheart in a fit of rage.

Particularly memorable for Bostonians was her concert late in October.

'She has seldom, if ever,' commented *The Boston Herald* (23 October 1911),

> displayed here in opera as full a voice as she displayed last night, when she sang for the first time in concert in this city. Only a great artist could deliver the opening line of 'C'est l'extase' as she breathed it forth. These *Ariettes oubliées* were composed as far back as 1888, and in them the true Debussy was revealed. As sung by her, the melodic contour did not seem strange and inexplicable, nor the harmonies too subtle and elusive. In these songs, the voice of Miss Garden, except in the upper part, was of wondrous beauty. In them she was poetic, not too evidently dramatic.

Shortly afterwards, Mary travelled to Philadelphia to begin rehearsals for *Carmen* and *Cendrillon*. 'I do like the women's roles better,' she revealed to the *New York Telegraph*. 'I am really three-quarters feminine and only one-quarter masculine. I shall not do any stunts with Carmen, but stick to the classic interpretation.'

Her Philadelphia *Carmen*, in which she insisted on using real Spanish playing cards, was outstandingly successful in financial terms. It was the 29th anniversary of Cleofonte Campanini's first conducting engagement in America; the attendance figures were the highest ever, exceeding by 200 those for *Salome* two years before.

Mary had conceived Carmen as an impulsive, wayward, passionate woman; not vulgar, like the drab suggested by Maria Gay; not quite so pretty as Sylva's gypsy or turned into a cocotte like Calvé's Carmen. *The Musical Courier* (3 November 1911) focused on the care with which she had studied the psychology of the role. She had never been content to delineate merely the externals of a character, but studied their psychological and sometimes even their pathological aspects for the purpose of fathoming completely the nature of the person she represented and understanding the true springs of her actions, as a woman and as a dramatic character. This thoroughness stamped Mary as a painstaking artist, and the fact that the newspapers tried to manufacture sensationalism from her desire to be theatrically truthful in her acting in no way lessened her artistic standing. Often in interviews she had pointed out that acting in opera was too much neglected, and she had even been quoted as saying that she was striving to establish a standard which would regard the acting of an opera role as of more importance than the singing.

Mary had also worked on the external appearance of the part. She had coral hoops in her ears, a coral necklace reaching to her waist, and a coral-coloured carnation, stuck straight and rampant in the stiff twisted knot of hair on top of her black wig. In the first five minutes of the first act her use of her hands alone broke all the conventions of the romantic Carmens. Carmens normally stood with their arms akimbo. Mary's hands, with all five fingers spread, lingered across the pit of her stomach.

In one of her usual discussions with the press about her private life and personal opinions, Mary was adamant on the subject of marriage: 'I think no woman ought to marry unless the man is more important to her than her art. I have never seen a man like that. Artists are wedded to the public anyway, and the public is an exacting and inconsiderate husband, but jealous to the point of murder if neglected.' She added airily, as if an afterthought: 'I'm going to have my apartments papered in Nile-green. Wallpaper serves as a fair substitute for a husband, to my mind.'[39]

The performance of *Cendrillon* on 6 November in Chicago featured not only Mary but Maggie Teyte, who had already become something of a rival by taking over the roles of Mélisande and Aphrodite at the Opéra-Comique. Then, replaced in *Carmen* by Gerville-Réache on 23 November (because her face was swollen by an ulcerated tooth), Mary passed her time by firing darts at the New York critics. Pointing the finger at Henry Krehbiel, the dean of musical journalists, she complained that the New York critics were the most senseless writers in the world. 'How sharper than a serpent's tooth it is to have an ungrateful Garden,' retorted Charles Meltzer. 'At the very thought of me,' said Sylvester Rawling in verse, 'Miss Garden still will freeze / for once I blamed her shoes, false in *Louise*'.[40]

William F. Chauncey, now her secretary, to whom she had so often been linked romantically, became the particular butt of her mischief. In *Vanity Fair* (11 November 1911) she confessed with peals of laughter that she had managed to engage herself to four different men that summer, under the very eyes of poor little Chauncey, who acted as unconscious gooseberry while she captured a Spanish grandee, a German princeling, a French tenor and an Italian duke. But the irritation was visible in her voice when she was speaking in Cleveland. She was tired and looked it. Her secretary said that Mary had been so besieged, she hated the sight of a newspaper. 'I am not married, and I am not going to marry Mr Chauncey or anybody else,' she declared.[41]

Notes

1. *Comœdia*, 7 May 1910.
2. Ibid.
3. *Chicago Examiner*, 19 June 1910.
4. *Seattle Times*, 16 December 1934. Hammerstein was actually 61 when Mary came to Manhattan and 64 at the time of this quote.
5. Edward Moore (1930), *Forty Years of Opera in Chicago*, New York: Horace Liveright, p. 54.
6. *New York Telegraph*, 25 September 1910.
7. *Comœdia*, October 1909.
8. Unidentified clipping, Mary Garden Scrapbook, vol. 1, RCM.
9. *New York Telegraph*, 28 October 1910.
10. *Chicago Record Herald*, 30 October 1910.
11. Edward Moore, op. cit., pp. 64–5.

12.   *Chicago News*, 7 November 1910.
13.   *Chicago Herald*, 13 November 1910.
14.   *Boston American*, 11 March 1911.
15.   *Musical America*, 3 December 1910.
16.   *Chicago News*, 29 November 1910.
17.   Ibid.
18.   Edward Moore, op. cit., p. 75.
19.   *The New York Times*, 30 November 1910.
20.   Carl Van Vechten (1917), *Interpreters and Interpretations*, New York: Knopf, pp. 82–3.
21.   *Philadelphia Times*, 9 December 1910.
22.   *Chicago News*, 29 November 1910.
23.   Letter to Editor, *Evening Wisconsin*, 10 December 1910.
24.   *Evening Wisconsin*, 10 December 1910.
25.   Glenn Dillard Gunn, *Chicago Daily Tribune*, 14 December 1910.
26.   *Ainslee Musicland*, January 1911.
27.   *Los Angeles Examiner*, 3 February 1911.
28.   Letter from Charles Bancroft to Miss Hartman. Mary Garden: clipping files, Music files, The Free Library of Philadelphia. It should be noted that, in fact, she turned 37 five days before the première of *Natoma*.
29.   Edward Moore, op. cit., p. 98.
30.   R. D. Fletcher, 'The Mary Garden of Record', *Saturday Review*, 27 February 1954.
31.   Desmond Shawe-Taylor, 'A Gallery of Great Singers, 15 – Mary Garden (1874–1967)', *Opera*, October 1984, p. 1082.
32.   Hugues Cuénod, 'Remembrances of an Enchantress', *High Fidelity Magazine*, July 1964, p. 37.
33.   Desmond Shawe-Taylor, op. cit., p. 1083.
34.   Hugues Cuénod, op. cit., p. 37.
35.   *Seattle Times*, 20 November 1950.
36.   *Indianapolis Star*, 3 May 1911. See also J. Ardoin (1983), 'Namara: A Remembrance', *Opera Quarterly*, vol. 1/4, pp. 77–8, where Chauncey is described as Garden's 'charming former lover'.
37.   *Louisville Herald*, 29 October 1911.
38.   *Music Review*, August 1911.
39.   *New York Telegraph*, 27 October 1911.
40.   *New York Telegraph*, 23 November 1911.
41.   *Cleveland Leader*, 20 November 1911.

8 Praise and Criticism: 1912

The year 1912 began with an embarrassing moment for Mary. During a performance of *Carmen* in Chicago, her costume began to fall apart on stage. She had to use both hands to keep her skirt up. It was said that her frantic efforts to keep on that skirt while she was dying were worthy of the highest callisthenic art. Afterwards, Mary blamed it on the carelessness of her maid. There were others, however, who thought she had done it deliberately so as to hit the headlines in the press.

Costumes were not the only problem – sometimes it was the stage-lighting. Mary explained to the *Chicago Tribune* (14 January 1912):

> Not often have I warred with the electrical forces of the Auditorium. Once was when poor old *Salome* was produced last winter – the blues and greens, which at first were arranged to carry out the weird, uncanny effects of this great opera, simply served to hide me, not render me mysterious.
>
> On that account I protested. The German opera houses and theaters are so far, far ahead of American and French playhouses in lighting systems. It is almost magical how the *Herr Direktor* behind the scenes can press a few buttons and scenery will rise and descend and lighting effects of day or night will be instantly produced.
>
> Here at the Auditorium there is no end of fuss before every scene is ready. Such banging and slamming and confusion! It is disturbing to the artiste who is on the alert to give forth golden melody and to whom every bit of friction means another step toward nervous collapse. Give me amber lights! My soul, my art, my voice demand them.

During a production of *Natoma* in January, Mary appeared as Natoma at an upper window. Her room was supposed to be lit by two candles but the effect was achieved with two baby spotlights. Mary insisted that the lights were not strong enough and she would not be satisfied until two full-power lights were aimed at her from the bridgework at each side of the stage. The rays from each machine were 15,000 candle-power in strength.

Mary continued to find invaluable photo-opportunities, such as the day when she donated $1600 to the Chicago Home for Boys. She kissed several. Confessed one of their number, 'Tough' Darnum: 'It lasts a long time,' he gasped, 'and, believe me, it transports you into a regular paradise and makes the world seem sort of different. She doesn't make much noise about it and seems to cover your entire mouth with her lips. She looks squarely into your eyes and, believe me, she is some kisser.' Another boy, Billy Denby, added: 'Miss Mary Garden is the champion kisser of the world.'[1]

Then, having announced that she would henceforth wear old-time Grecian costumes for both street and house wear (because she had found them so comfortable), she appeared at a Chicago reception in a wonderful silver gauze garment of diaphanous texture. Under the flimsy tunic Mary wore a white satin robe, which reached to her feet in the front and trailed over the floor a yard or so at the back. It was observed that she did not wear corsets with the costume. She declared, however, that she had never felt more comfortable.

At the end of January, Mary appeared in St Paul, but was not well received: she was thought not to be in good voice and to lack control, and there was a harsh character to her higher notes, but her talent as an emotional actress saved the day. The disappointment of the occasion was exacerbated when, after the performance, Mary lost her handbag containing her jewels and a large amount of money.

In St Louis, her Thaïs revealed a certain hardness of voice in the upper register which developed early in the evening. But later, the softness and beauty of her intonation restored her reputation in the eyes of the audience. Her Carmen in St Louis was little appreciated: 'Mary Garden has no clear notion of the gypsy of Prosper Merimée, nor quite the deftly-attuned ear and voice for the Bizet score. Garden's Carmen was a bit of Salome, a trace of Thaïs, an infusion of the style and carriage of the grande dame, a glimpse of a calculating wanton. Whenever it suited her, she was robustly off key.'[2]

In Cincinnati, her appearance in *Natoma* was thought to have been an error of judgement:

> Mary Garden, in the title role, was effectually disguised in an ugly and elaborate Indian costume and makeup. The music permitted her to declare her emotions in a species of manlike contralto, from which her voice rose, through an evident break in the scale, towards piercing heights. The role is unworthy of this fine artist. Natoma's psychology is of the most elemental and manifests itself in crouching, staring and brooding.[3]

At the end of February she gave the first of six performances at the Metropolitan Opera House, New York, under Campanini. Here, her Carmen was a success. According to one critic, the audience was delighted to find all the well-loved traditions of the Carmen role preserved, and yet supplemented with a large number of dramatic touches. The shrewishness of Carmen, overlooked by many previous interpreters, stood out. But Charles

Henry Meltzer felt she was too old for the role: 'Miss Garden lacks the youth which one associates with the character. Her movements are a thought too set and studied for the capricious cigarette-maker. Her passion, though quite real, is sometimes deliberate.'[4]

The final assessment of her performance was a positive one. People who went for sensation were startled first when Mary appeared on the bridge clad in a blue dress dotted with white, and a priceless shawl. She again startled the audience when she began her wooing of Don José with a slap in the face, and when she all but scalped her girl adversary in the hair-pulling episode. 'Her performance of the part,' said the *New York Globe* (14 February 1912), 'is far and away the most interesting the Metropolitan stage has witnessed in a long time.'

Within the next few weeks Mary signed a contract with the Columbia Phonograph Company of New York. In mid-May she recorded the favourite aria from *Louise*. 'Of greatest historical interest in the operatic group is the first of her two recordings of "Depuis le jour",' wrote Richard D. Fletcher:

> This number also was standard in her concert programmes because of the genuine affection she felt for the work in which she had made her spectacular debut. Like the early Debussy discs, the Columbia 'Depuis le jour' does not yet show the rich coloring which her later recordings reveal. It is in the original key (D) and is taken somewhat more slowly than her Victor recording of 1926. The tone is reserved but well-supported. Her more dramatic recordings are characterised by abrupt attacks and releases which critics have sometimes mistaken for poor breath control.[5]

Hugues Cuénod commented that 'the aria from *Louise* is done admirably, the high tessitura magnificently managed, with the purest of voices'.[6] And Desmond Shawe-Taylor was to write that 'The "Depuis le jour" is a radiant version of the aria that had launched her career, if one or two notes are slightly suspect in intonation, it shows charming timbre and enunciation, and is crowned by a triumphant high B on "Je suis heureuse"'.[7]

A fascinating glimpse of Mary and her fellow-artists at work around this time is given by Clare Peeler in *Musical America* (18 May 1912) writing of a rehearsal for *Cendrillon*:

> I saw on this and successive occasions a company of well-bred men and women, showing each other all possible encouragement and kindness, taking suggestions from one another with courteous acknowledgement, relaxing into utter 'fooling' at the right times, but always holding one idea before them, and only one – to do their work well. Mary Garden (in her tailor-made frock and little white silk shirt-waist, severely plain, with a big white and black bow at the bare throat, a small toque jammed down on her hair), was a dominating figure every time she walked on the stage to rehearse with a big score under her arm; or, returning, sat with her secretary or maid in the auditorium.
>
> 'Last night,' Miss Garden said once, 'we never finished rehearsing until one. It was a quarter to two when I got to bed.' It was eleven in the morning when she told me this. At one that day she went to her hotel for lunch; at half-past two she

posed [in her costume] for the photographer, continuing until half-past three. Before four she was at rehearsal again, and at seven, when I left, was still at work. She told me: 'It is in each case a question of sacrificing one's bodily comfort for a purpose of absolute concentration for the sake of results.'

But in spite of all this self-denial, her Prince Charming in *Cendrillon* at the Met was far from being an overwhelming success. 'Miss Mary Garden,' wrote *Musical America* (March 1912), 'looked well in knickerbockers, but that was all. Her "singing" – as when she later appeared as Carmen, as Thaïs and in *Le jongleur de Notre-Dame* – failed lamentably to reach even a fair vocal and artistic mark.'

The New York Herald felt that, as Prince Charming, Mary seemed very ill at ease. Her costume fitted her as though she and it had been cast in one mould but she was stodgy in her movements and did not dominate the stage. As for her singing, she had very few happy moments; and when she had little acting to do her singing never sounded at its best. 'Her immobility savored more of stiffness than of dignity,' added the *Brooklyn Eagle* (21 February 1912). 'The resources of facial play which are hers in other parts are not brought into effective recognition in this one.'

Other critics complained that she had an excellent natural voice, but used it badly. She sang with wavering tones, constantly out of tune, and in attacking a note usually scooped the tone, which was begun under the true pitch and lifted up to it. Her 'chest' voice was produced in a manner that gave a hollow and very disagreeable sound. The acting of the former Manhattan star was also thought to be stiff and unnatural. This defect also marred her first attempt to interpret *Carmen*, in which she was considered by some New York critics to have failed completely. Her cigarette-girl was attacked for lacking feminine appeal.

*   *   *

During this period Mary's work-rate was astonishing. From 20 February 1912, she sang eight times in 13 days – a record apparently unprecedented in America. But she continued to baffle, in spite of her defects. 'She can break all the laws of singing,' claimed the *Musical Courier* (5 March 1912), 'she can act like a conventional Italian prima donna, she can look her worst, and still fascinate, magnetize, stimulate. Whether she is doing everything or nothing she can always hold center. Ordinary analysis grows pale before her.'

In Boston she continued to defy description. She and Maurice Renaud violated all the so-called canons of *bel canto*, sang with no voices, or with remnants of voices. 'The sum total of their achievement lay in portraying so truthfully and realistically the struggles of Thaïs and Athanaël that the drama of the Alexandrian period became a palpitating reality.'[8]

In the spring of 1912 rumours began to filter across the Atlantic that members of the Opéra-Comique were about to take over another theatre in Paris and turn it into an opera house. It was said that an American syndicate was backing Mary and that she was likely to join the French enterprise with a view to renting the Vaudeville Theatre in the Boulevard des Italiens to present a modern – especially French – repertoire. It was thought that it might be called the Mary Garden Opera House and that Mary would have the artistic direction of it as well as interpreting star roles. German opera appeared to modern opera-lovers to be looming large and horrid on the horizon and it was believed that Mary, like Debussy, was infinitely bored by the 'insufferable people in helmets and wild-beast skins' who moved ponderously through the music-dramas of Wagner. There were those who would dearly have liked to see some American-generated wealth endow a theatre and let French opera come into its own. Mary, it was felt, would make the ideal manager of such an institution.

However, later that spring, before she left New York for her Paris engagements, Mary would attempt to scotch these rumours by denying any involvement in the scheme. 'Yet such a house as the Opéra-Comique would flourish in New York. I have money enough to build one,' she said.[9] Still there lingered a persistent rumour that she had ambitions to become an impresario and had been negotiating with Oscar Hammerstein for his entire company with a view to giving a rival opera season in New York.

Meanwhile, there were concerts to be given in Montreal (where she was guaranteed $2000 and the impresario, Honoré Bourdin, lost $300) and then in Syracuse, where, in a green velvet gown, with a corsage rope, a dagger of diamonds and a huge green feathery ornament in her hair, she captivated the large audience. They loved to see Mary trip across the stage, smile, bow and wave her hands, to say nothing of the skilled way she handled her long skirt with its zigzag train and a tremendous bouquet of pink roses which she received after the first aria. On the train from Pittsburgh to Syracuse Mary had lost one of her earrings, an immense hoop of diamonds worth $1000. A telegraph was sent to New York and the earring was eventually discovered behind the steam pipes in her compartment. But she had to appear in the concert with only one earring, which caused many in the audience to think she had started a new fad.

Returning to New York, she helped raise $14,000 for the Titanic Fund at the Metropolitan, along with Caruso and Lillian Nordica. Dressed in a wonderful sea-green gown, she received so many encores that she just ran away with 'At parting' and 'Comin thro' the rye'.

Next it was off to Paterson. The concert platform was already prepared in grotesque fashion. To one side of the conductor an attendant placed what looked like a cross-section of a steam-roller with a handle on it; on the other, a white box and some paper flowers. The 'stage' being thus set, Mary appeared to act the Garden Scene from *Faust*. 'She turned the improvised spinning-wheel with perfect composure as she sang the "King of Thule" ballad,' commented *Musical America* (11 May 1912), 'and might have looked like Marguerite, if she hadn't rather suggested a dairy maid churning butter.'

Mary was still receiving plenty of press attention on the non-operatic front. When her chauffeur was fined for speeding and could not afford to pay the $50 bail, Mary grandly pulled a $1200 diamond bracelet from her wrist and put it up as security. And on another occasion it was reported that she was being sued by her milliner in Paris for 13 or 14 hats bought at $150 two years previously. When the milliner won her case, Lina Cavalieri was said to have commented: 'How bourgeois! A bagatelle! I would never wear such cheap hats.'

Now Mary, boasting of a repertoire of fifty operas to which she would shortly be adding *La lépreuse* and *Roma*, the latest of Massenet's compositions,[10] announced that she would sing at the Opéra in Paris that summer and then go on a motor tour before studying in Germany. 'I am going over to sing in Paris and make a vaudeville tour of the continent,' she confided. 'After that I expect to look after a shooting-box that I have taken in Scotland for the summer.' 'Will you invite Oscar Hammerstein?' she was asked. 'Oh, he doesn't need to be shot,' was her instant reply.[11]

*   *   *

Mary sailed late in May on the *Savoie*. The soprano, Lillian Nordica, an ardent supporter of the Suffragette movement, heard that Mary was a fellow passenger. 'She is a wonderful woman and I am going to try and convert her to the cause,' said Nordica enthusiastically. But Mary, throwing up her hands, cried, 'Me a suffragette! Much as I admire and respect Madame Nordica, I am sure she will not succeed in converting me. My love for the home is intense! probably because I have neither husband nor home.'[12] Later that year, pressed on the same subject, she would be even more dismissive: 'The minute a woman works outside of the sex impulse, her work is futile. That is why this suffragette business doesn't appeal to me. The women are not appealing through sex as they should, but have tried to get away from their sex. Their fight is not against men, I take it, after all, but against their Maker.'[13]

Her first public engagement in Paris was at the end of June when she sang in a musical evening given by Fanny Reed at her residence in the Rue de la Pompe in honour of the American ambassador. There, Mary promised she would give a gala performance later for the French Society for the Protection of Animals. She had already given $200 for a retreat for overworked horses.

Part of that summer she spent in the country near Aberdeen, revisiting her roots. 'There was a dance,' she told the *Chicago Record* (15 December 1912),

one of the kind that ends with a breakfast. About fifty friends stayed to the bitter end. When the bacon and porridge were finally served, all the men poured stout instead of milk over their porridge and some of them poured it over their bacon too. In that moment I discovered Scotland all over again. They said it soothed their nerves and made them keen for luncheon later. I think I shuddered for a week.

Mary's debut in *Tosca* at the Opéra-Comique in September 1912 was probably witnessed by Giacomo Puccini himself. The credit for her success in the role was given to her teacher, the Marquis de Trabadelo, who had coached her for most of the summer at San Sebastián. Her Tosca drew opposing storms of praise and condemnation. There was an ovation from the audience but the critics were scathing in their reviews, claiming she had mistaken sensuality for art and imbued the character of Tosca with all the grossness of Salome.

By now, in one year, Mary had sung six times at the Opéra-Comique and six times at the Opéra.

On 11 October, writing to André Caplet, who wanted permission to orchestrate some of the *Ariettes oubliées* for Mary, Claude Debussy warned: 'I should say that I've always refused to orchestrate my songs, and have done so politely, obstinately and fiercely. Several great singers – large ones anyway – have asked me to do so and my view remains the same. But in your case, the position's different. If you think it's a good idea and would like to do it, then choose any of the 'Ariettes' you think worthy of your ingenuity. But I hope you'll agree with me, there can be no question of Mlle Garden making her own choice. That sort of thing is absolutely incompatible with the freedom an artist must have in dealing with his own work'.[14] In the event, Caplet (who was to conduct Mary as Thaïs in Boston later that year) orchestrated Ariette No. 1 'C'est l'extase' and No. 5 'Green'.

* * *

Shortly after returning to America that autumn, Mary appeared in concert at Carnegie Hall, singing the Bach-Gounod 'Ave Maria', accompanied by Ysaÿe on the violin and by a harpist. She ended with Strauss' 'Zueignung' and sang ravishingly. 'She brings into her smallest number,' added the *New York Mail* (27 November 1912), 'a sense of the dramatic context of the song which in itself is the kernel, the soul of it.'

But it was the *New York Sun* (27 November 1912) that captured most vividly the full splendour and eccentricity of her performance. She had made her entrance to gasps, chokes and gurgles in a picture hat, with a corsage of two pink roses, a white lace pannier caught by blue bows and a clinging back train perilously high-geared at the left ankle. 'From the moment the lithe figure swung full around as the star entered the stage, till she left under a zebra robe of chinchilla furs, there's no doubt Miss Garden held her audience in the hollow of her hand'. Watching her every move was the Garden family: father, mother and sisters, who filled a box near the stage.

Mary then set about shaking the Boston audience to its foundations. 'An operatic performance,' wrote the *Boston Globe* critic (3 December 1912) of her Tosca,

> rarely is so pervaded and dominated by an individuality – an operatic role marvellously composed in knowledge of character, in breadth of imagination, in finesse and significance of dramatic detail, in subtlety of illusion, both as actress and as singer and in the fulsome prodigality of her beauty. It was the development of the drama as revealed in the woman's face, her body and her marvellous coloring voice and variety of diction.

As Tosca, Mary wore a red wig, a green dress and a blue scarf:

> Miss Garden's Tosca was expected to be badly sung – and it was not. Her voice kept its usual propulsive power, its rich depths of tone, its warm human coloring. It had, besides, a wholly unanticipated sensuous quality. For once, even her detractors must give her credit for voice, skill and intelligence in Italian song. The new and distinctive note in Miss Garden's Tosca is her solicitude for Cavaradossi. The other new note was the absence of coquetry in the episodes with Cavaradossi.[15]

So effective was the relationship between Tosca and Scarpia (played by Vanni Marcoux), that there were complaints from Mayor Fitzgerald and many members of the public. Henry Russell of the Boston Opera Company denounced Boston's puritanical views, but agreed to modify the seduction scene. It was the realism that was objected to: 'When Vanni-Marcoux pursued Mary Garden around his room on the stage, seized her in a frenzy and threw her upon a couch, a part of cultured Boston gasped'.[16] 'After the second act of this sensational opera, which had been most sensationally acted, half of the audience gave vent to pent-up emotions by furious applause; the other half sat still and stiff – and scandalised'.[17]

When it came to *Thaïs*, Philip Hale, writing in the *Boston Transcript* (8 December 1912), noted that 'the voice of Miss Garden disclosed such warmth and color in set arias; never had she shown such technical skill in the management of her voice. This Thaïs is incomparable, unique.'

Early in December, Mary appeared at the Boston Opera House in concert. With Mme Florence De Courcy she performed Debussy's 'La Demoiselle élue', followed by 'C'est l'extase' and 'Green', arranged and conducted by André Caplet. Later that month, when it came for her to repeat *Tosca* in Boston, both the Mayor and the Police Department had installed a censor in the audience.[18] Mary's parting shot to the press was: 'There is nothing in the way we acted the scene that should shock anyone but a prude'.[19]

She was welcomed back to Chicago where, in the Blackstone Hotel, she posed for photographs and denounced the flashlights, because 'they make you look like the Devil'. She cursed the powder when it missed fire on one occasion.[20] Singing *Le jongleur de Notre-Dame*, 'she was not a prima donna at all, but an ardent, slim-legged boy, with a clear, sexless voice and, though she chose to sacrifice vocal display to the artistic necessities of the part, she triumphed none the less. Only a great singer could exhibit such versatility; could strike all dramatic quality from a voice'.[21]

On 26 December, Mary appeared in *Louise*. 'This singer has improved immeasurably since a year ago,' wrote the *Musical Courier*. 'The chest notes, on which she used to scoop while using her medium range, have been changed into good head notes, thus improving her rendition of the aria "Depuis le jour".'

'Never has Miss Garden sung more beautifully or with greater abandon, passion and feeling,' enthused the *Musical Leader* (January 1913), 'and she rose to some of her greatest moments, especially in the now famous aria of the third Act. Here she proved herself a singer of rare art, that of singing *mezza voce* so as to be distinctly heard throughout the great Auditorium.'

But 1912 ended on a bitter note. Carolina White, Eleonora de Cisneros and Maggie Teyte had lodged vigorous protests with director Andreas Dippel that they were being overworked. To these, Mary added an ultimatum of her own: she would not sing *Tosca* on 3 January unless Vanni-Marcoux sang with her. But Dippel wanted Sammarco to sing Scarpia and was determined not to yield to her.

Notes

1. *Musical Courier*, 17 January 1912.
2. *St Louis Globe*, 6 February 1912.
3. *Cincinnati Times-Star*, 7 February 1912.
4. Unidentified New York newspaper cutting, 14 February 1912, NYPL, Billy Rose Theatre Collection, Robinson Locke Collection of Scrapbooks 1856–1920, vols. 224–234, series 1.
5. Richard D. Fletcher, 'The Mary Garden of Record', *Saturday Review*, 27 February 1954, pp. 49–50.
6. Hugues Cuénod, 'Remembrances of an Enchantress', *High Fidelity Magazine*, July 1964, p. 37.
7. Desmond Shawe-Taylor, 'A Gallery of Great Singers 15 – Mary Garden (1874–1967)', *Opera*, October 1984, p. 1083.
8. *Musical Courier*, March 1912.
9. *Toledo Blade*, 12 June 1912.
10. Ibid. In fact she had about 35 operas in her repertory by the end of her career.
11. *New York Globe*, 18 May 1912.
12. Ira Glackens (1963), *Yankee Diva*, New York: Coleridge Press, p. 258.
13. *Chicago Examiner*, 29 November 1912.

14.   François Lesure, *Lettres 1884–1918, Claude Debussy réunies et présentées par François Lesure*, Paris: Herman.
15.   *Boston Transcript*, 3 December 1912.
16.   *New York Journal*, 14 December 1912.
17.   *Musical America*, 10 December 1912.
18.   *Boston Globe*, 12 December 1912.
19.   *New York Journal*, 12 December 1912.
20.   *Chicago Examiner*, 23 December 1912.
21.   *Chicago Tribune*, 26 December 1912.

9 American Tours and War in Europe: 1913–1914

The year 1913 began with rumours of a new romance. Boston was now certain that Mary's on-stage emotional bonding with Vanni-Marcoux had been carried over into real life. Marcoux, now divorced, was reportedly engaged to Mary. During December 1912, he had often been seen lunching with her at the fashionable Copley Plaza Hotel. However, Mary categorically denied that she had objected to singing *Tosca* unless Marcoux was the Scarpia. 'I have never refused to sing with Mr Sammarco or anyone else in the company,' she told the *Musical Leader* (January 1913), 'except Mr —— and I absolutely refuse to sing with him.' For his part, Marcoux did not deny the imminence of matrimony. 'It is true that I am practically engaged to an American girl, a singer,' but, he added, 'An artist's life is impossible for marriage unless they are both artists.'[1] Mary read his words in the newspapers and smiled, but again denied the story.

Performing *Tosca* in Chicago that winter, Mary's dialogue and singing were in French, except one aria ('Vissi d'arte') sung in the original Italian, the language which all the rest of her colleagues used. Mary explained this aberration by asserting her Continental origins. 'I am really a French artiste, bred in the traditions of that stage, saturated with their feeling and though I sing *Tosca* in Italian, the play is French – I give it the French interpretation.'[2] But her mixture of French and Italian in *Tosca* was deplored by the critics. The *Chicago Record Herald* commented on 'the mystery of Miss Garden's sudden plunge into Italian in "Vissi d'arte"; the grotesque confusion of tongues which Miss Garden introduces into her interpretation of the work'.

Her technique on stage, however, was considered to be illuminated by intuition as well as craft. *The Chicago News* (18 January 1913) reported that she had a strange, almost uncanny understanding of the stage pause. In terms of melodrama, she drove the nail with vigour and clinched it with earnestness. It was said that Mary had developed the power to be missed for every moment she was not on the stage; she was a strange, fascinating force who could master a big situation in stunning and sensational fashion, securing thrilling effects.

When she appeared in Chicago in *Thaïs*, the critics complained of costumes that were scant to the point of vanishing and defied description as to fabric, fashioning and anchorage. 'She shocks, writhes, postures and sensationalizes,' moaned *The Chicago News* (29 January 1913). However, the paper did admit that her study and captivation of character was singularly lucid, complete and convincing; she was the high priestess of rampant realism.

At the Metropolitan, New York, with a kilted Harry Lauder in the audience, Mary sang *Louise*. There, the strange habits of the different social classes in American audiences were plain to see: the occupants of parterre boxes arrived during the second act; high society left after the Montmartre scene but the crowd stayed until the end, just before midnight.

Once again, court proceedings raised their head, this time in Peoria, Illinois. In City Court Robert E. Johnstone was the defendant for breach of contract. Mary had been booked to sing in Cleveland, Indianapolis and in Peoria during a private concert side-tour at a fee of $2500 per concert. Johnstone had promised *Salome* with bare feet and not much else. When she had first arrived, Mary refused to sing from *Salome*. But because there were big houses in Cleveland and Indianapolis, she compromised and promised to do the same in Peoria. Then she changed her mind and cancelled the concert. When she sang in the next town, Johnstone sued the Peoria impresario Burton Collver for the balance due on the contract. Collver filed a counter-suit claiming that because Mary did not sing *Salome* he had lost $4100. But Collver failed to appear and so Johnstone got judgement for the sum claimed.

For *Tosca* in Washington, Mary – despite any inclinations she might have had to persuade the dashing Vanni-Marcoux to be lured to the capital – had to make do with the equally powerful but older, Sammarco. In any case, Marcoux, then engaged in Boston, was shortly to be sidelined when he was injured on stage after a statue of the Commendatore fell on top of him during a performance of *Don Giovanni*. In the second act, Sammarco was sensationally tempestuous. Mary's Tosca overwhelmed Washington: she was sinuous and then tigerish. Her magnificent 'Vissi d'arte' (sung in French), pulsated with feeling, was wonderfully rich in colour and satisfyingly full and clear.

But later, in Philadelphia, her necrophilistic writhing over her dead lover on the parapet was deplored. Her technique was scrutinized: some said she could not sing; others, however, admired her little vocal quirks – her contralto thickenings, her tonal eccentricities, her change to the speaking voice, her curious modulations. 'For it must be acknowledged,' explained the *Boston Traveler* (20 February 1913), 'these fit her for the modern music-drama of Massenet, Charpentier and Debussy. In these works histrionism counts more than vocalism, for most often the orchestra does the vocalising as well as performs some of the drama; hence *bel canto* would be amiss, while *coloratura* would be sacrilege.'

It was one night in mid-February 1913 in Philadelphia that saw one of the most tragic episodes in Mary's career. Nineteen-year-old Helen Newby, the only daughter of John Newby, a wealthy iron manufacturer of Hector's Mills, Pennsylvania, committed suicide because she was unable to see Mary, whom she worshipped as an idol. The young girl had become obsessed with the idea that Mary was Queen Cleopatra and that she was her slave. She had never spoken to Mary; hers was one of those long-distance infatuations in which photographs become fetishes.

Helen Newby's imagined romance had had its beginning two years previously. She had seen pictures of Mary and fallen in love with them; she then read all she could find on her heroine's stage triumphs and her life as a woman of the world. The extravagant language she employed in praise of her divinity – the language of religious ecstasy – convinced some of her friends that her brain had been turned by long brooding upon her fancied attachment.

Miss Newby's pitiful tragedy neared its climax when she came to Philadelphia to see and hear Mary at the opera house for the first time. She attended two performances, and, not content with merely being a member of the audience, asked some newspaper critics for help in obtaining letters of introduction to Mary. On the second night she made her final attempt to see the object of her adoration. She went to the Ritz-Carlton Hotel, where Mary was staying; but Mary, who was worried over the illness of her mother, refused to give her an interview, and the girl left the hotel in tears.

'I have done everything to make myself useful to "my Mary",' she had told one of her friends. Miss Newby was not seen by any of her friends after she left Mary's hotel until her dead body was found in the morning on the lawn of her home at Hector's Mills. There was a bullet-hole through her head; beside her body was the revolver. Hidden in the bosom of her dress was a picture of her adored Mary Garden.

In the morning, Mary received a reporter for the *Evening Sun* who asked if the story in the morning papers was true. 'If it is true,' Mary replied, 'it is terrible. I really never have seen the girl in my life and I don't recall ever having spoken to any girl in my dressing-room in Philadelphia to whom an interview was refused. I would have given her a good common-sense talk.'[3] Later, speaking in Boston, she added: 'I always try and see these poor girls when I can, if only for a minute in the dressing room. Miss Newby never tried to see me, as far as I know. There are so many girls that hang about the stage door. The child never even wrote me.' The reporter pressed her: 'You receive many letters from men and women?' 'By the hundred. And more

from women than from men. Some are in love with me – or think they are –
and others are stage-struck.'[4]

Meanwhile, Mary's busy schedule rolled on remorselessly. In Boston her
very individual reading of *Carmen* provoked the comment that 'she clips
phrases or she prolongs them; she sprinkles strange but telling accents over
the music. By the coloring of her tones, by sheer distortion of pace, rhythm
and phrase, she makes the role do her will'.[5]

*   *   *

Early in March, equipped with 42 trunks, Mary arrived to perform in Los
Angeles as part of the Chicago Grand Opera Company tour. She had
reserved nine rooms for herself, her mother and her maids – frugally Scottish
in comparison to the eleven-room suite set aside for Luisa Tetrazzini.

Between the second and third acts of *Natoma*, Mary sang the
Silverwood-Frankenstein Ballad of the Stars: 'I love you, California'.
Maestro Campanini had had the music orchestrated and his musicians
played it as if they were native sons. According to the *Los Angeles Examiner*
(12 March 1913), at the end of the last verse, a battalion of Shriners (a
quasi-Masonic order of men) marched to the stage with their arms full of
flowers which they gave to Mary. She took the brightest of them all and
tossed it to Campanini.

After appearing in *Natoma*, Mary was invited to supper by the Shriners.
The table was banked with flowers. In the centre, fountains played; around
the board, in their white robes, were seated the Nobles of the Mystic Shrine.
In a throne at the head of the table, like the chair last occupied by the
Emperor of China, sat Mary, the focus of their worship.

Mary made eight appearances in San Francisco where she proceeded to
torment the press unmercifully. As the reporters hung on her every word,
Mary languidly ate grapes and baited her prey with smiles and shrugs. 'I
adore my art and my God,' she told the *Louisville Herald* (30 March 1913)

> I am profoundly religious. Nothing would be easier for me to do than what Thaïs
> did – become a nun and a religious zealot. Most probably I shall end my days in a
> convent. In fact, I already have my nunnery picked out; it is in Turin. How can I
> tell in what my imagination will find final satisfaction? But I will not weary of
> giving. I find my utmost satisfaction in spending myself for what I love.

She fully expected to become a Roman Catholic: 'Two years ago I decided to
give myself to the Catholic faith. But my mother begged me not to do it while
she was alive. When she dies, I shall become a member of the Church.' And,
explaining her motives:

> What draws me to the Catholic religion? First of all, the artistic beauty of the
> services, the beauty of the robes and lights and the gorgeous decorations and

architecture and painting of the churches. Then, I like the constantly open church. And I love the majesty, dignity and beauty of the marriage and burial services.[6]

Waiting to have her picture taken in the Brown Palace Hotel, Denver, she presented a restless figure. Her eyes glowed and danced and her mouth constantly changed expression. Her hands – expressive hands that twisted and flashed with every change in her mood – were nevertheless surprisingly bony and angular, the hands of an old person. The heavy rings flashed on them as she gesticulated and fluttered around the room singing scraps of Italian and French and chatting. The papers were already full of the kiss she had given head porter John Barry, which had come about after Mary dropped a $10,000 brooch when entering the hotel at midnight after her performance. Several hours later, Barry found it on the pavement.

Arriving in Minneapolis she declared herself nine pounds lighter than two weeks before. 'Luisa Tetrazzini and I have the same trouble,' explained Mary, 'we dare not eat. Every night after the performance when we are together we do a little trotting. It is wonderful how it brings one's weight down.'

Her Thaïs in Minneapolis presented two very different aspects. 'Mary Garden dazzled the eye and pained the ear,' commented the *Minneapolis Journal* reviewer (23 April 1913). 'Her mediocre voice, which never appears to have been rightly placed, has in *forte* a disagreeable metallic timbre. But when applying *mezzo* or *pianissimo* effects her work is fine – at times.'

The tour ended and as it did so, the Chicago Grand Opera Company was rocked by the resignation of Andreas Dippel as general director. Dippel had been battling with Campanini for over almost three years. His departure was widely interpreted as a victory for the Italian repertoire over the German.

Mary returned to Chicago at the end of April, suffering from bronchitis. Then, two days later, along with Farrar and Caruso, she boarded ship for Europe. Caruso had been entertained by his Italian friends to a banquet and was rather the worse for wear; his friends carried him aboard and put him to bed. When Mary invited the reporters to her stateroom, she discovered smoke coming from under her bed. 'A man under my bed?' she enquired innocently. 'Oh, what an ardent admirer. He has stowed himself to be near me. Isn't it beautiful? All my life I have dreamt of such a moment and now it has come true.'[7] As she spoke, the man was being dragged out. He was a portly man with a red face; his hair was tousled and his clothing creased. It transpired that he had gone aboard with the Caruso party. Caruso's stateroom was only two doors beyond Mary's and, her door being open, the banqueter strolled in. The ship had a list to port and he simply rolled under the bed, perfectly happy. Mary took one look at him and cried: 'Take him away. Feed him to the sharks!'

Mary was to sing only once in Paris that year, and that was very nearly a disaster. 'When I reached Paris, there was a *Salome* waiting to be sung. I didn't know I was so fatigued, but I went on. I was just through the dance when I felt something within me give way. It was the first time in my life I had dreaded collapse on the stage. Everything swam before me. But I just rallied my grit together and got through the performance. Nobody knew. But I knew. I knew too well.'[8]

Despite a plea from the composer, Wolf-Ferrari, who had written from Munich,[9] the June dress-rehearsals of *The Jewels of the Madonna* at the Opéra (in which Mary was to have played the role of Maliella) were postponed until September because of Mary's breakdown. She was tired by her long American season and was said to have lost her voice. Hearing that she was being sued by a ladies' tailor for $1000 (a long-standing bill for costumes provided during previous engagements at the Opéra and Opéra-Comique), Mary simply packed her trunks and departed, leaving no telephone number behind.

> They took me to Scotland. My Mother was there and Daddy and my sister. There, among the Scotch hills and the heather, I rested and got again to be a human being. For weeks they made me live simply, just as a child does. Then they put me on horseback. Every morning at seven o'clock I rose and bathed and breakfasted, and by eight my horse was around and then I was out and off for two good hours. No luncheon at all, but a ripping good dinner. I played tennis; I started my autobiography up in Scotland. I'll do more work on it next summer.[10]

By the end of August, Mary had definitely decided not to create *The Jewels of the Madonna*. One French critic retaliated that she had no idea of French style and taste, nor comprehension of French works. Inevitably, America was blamed as Mary claimed she had to pull out of *The Jewels of the Madonna* because she had previous engagements in the USA.

Late that October, Mary sailed into New York. Vanni-Marcoux was also on board. She had a sun-tan, a rope of pearls, a little blue three-cornered Napoleon hat, a gold-topped snakewood cane and a Belgian Griffon dog called Brussel Sprouts. In the cane was a miniature clock which told her when it was time to feed her dog. Before setting off for Philadelphia, she told the press that she had been playing tennis and riding horses every day and never felt better in her life – although she had read reports during the summer that she was supposed to be dying.

A few days later, Philadelphia was agog with the suspected romance between Vanni-Marcoux and Mary. Their apartments conveniently faced each other across Broad Street and every morning Vanni-Marcoux would step to the window of his hotel drawing-room and wave a good morning kiss to Mary in her apartments across the way. 'Oh, oh,' enthused Mary, 'he is wonderful, he is splendid. He is not afflicted with a protruding stomach. So many men are, you know.' Later the placid Vanni-Marcoux, a former Milan barrister (whose given names were Jean Emile Diogène), spoke tantalizingly of Mary in profound, rumbling tones. 'Mary Garden. Ah, Mary Garden is the best.'[11]

On 2 November 1913 came news that fascinated Mary – the discovery in Egypt of the tomb of the early Christian saints, the hermit Serapion and Thaïs. Thaïs had been found with a chaplet of wood and ivory, a basket and a bottle, a cross, palm branches and a rose of Jericho in her bony hand. Mary kept the newspaper cutting to prepare for her next performance of *Thaïs* in mid-December.

The following day, during a performance of *Tosca*, events on stage became more than usually dramatic. Vanni-Marcoux had thrown the Spoletta (Venturini) so violently across the stage that he struck the sofa with an audible thud. The sofa wobbled. There was a crack and then Venturini sprawled over on his head and back. The audience tittered as, while still pursuing his song, he thrust the broken leg of the sofa into place. When Tosca entered for her hectic interview with Scarpia, the audience hung in sniggering suspense upon the question which was obviously in everyone's mind. What would happen to Mary? But the resourceful Mary was equal to the occasion. After shaking it twice to test its load-bearing properties, she balanced herself carefully upon the edge of the sofa, and burst into song.

In spite of the stage mishaps, Mary's Tosca, opposite Vanni-Marcoux and Giovanni Martinelli, was acclaimed. 'The role enables her to display a vocal power not disclosed by any other singer on the stage of the day', wrote Agnes Gordon Hogan. 'To a critical eye, it is plain that the best singers are forever conscious of their tones, forever limited by musical notation, one of the most painful and noticeable defects in opera. It is not so with Miss Garden in *Tosca*. The explanation is that Miss Garden so far lives the actual Tosca that her entire personality is lost in the role.'[12]

Out of the blue, Mary announced her intention of making Southern California her permanent home. An architect's plan had already been produced. The house, on a four-acre site in Beverly Hills, was to cost around $80,000 and would incorporate a small concert theatre.

On 15 November in Philadelphia, Mary sang Dulcinée in Massenet's *Don Quichotte*. 'The Dulcinea of our favorite Mary Garden was delightful in more ways than one,' wrote the correspondent for the *Los Angeles Examiner* (23 November 1913). 'It surprised many in the audience, who have been told and told again by serious critics, that Miss Garden cannot sing, to hear her reel off florid passages with ease and skill.'

The following day Mary returned to Chicago. At the station, she was greeted by ten Blackfoot Indians, acknowledging her espousal of the role of Natoma. 'Next year', she proclaimed, 'I shall have a D'Annunzio opera to work on, *Phèdre*, and I shall create the part.' She added that she had acquired the sole American rights for *Monna Vanna* and *Don Quichotte*. 'I'm also going to dabble a bit in Wagner,' she threatened. This was a reference to her long hankering to sing Wagner – for which she had studied German diligently. She had claimed in the past, however, that despite an unconquerable desire to sing his compositions she simply could not face singing opposite a fat German tenor. 'Most German tenors are fat, aren't they?'[13]

Chicago marvelled at her Dulcinee. 'Miss Mary Garden revealed herself as a bravura vocalist,' said *The Chicago Record Herald* (28 November 1913) with some surprise. 'She warbled scales and other coloratura brilliancies.'

In Boston, Mary was challenged over her alleged love-affair with Vanni-Marcoux. 'I have never been in love with anybody on the stage,' she retorted. 'I don't believe in stage marriages. I don't love any actor off the stage. If I married I would leave the stage at once. But I wouldn't marry an actor.'[14]

Appearing as *Monna Vanna* in Boston, she 'scored one of the great successes of her life, with her careful conception and admirable interpretation,' wrote the previously hostile Charles Henry Meltzer. 'Her first entrance was in a wonderful red costume. Her self-repression and economy of gesture were remarkable.'[15] But a diametrically opposite view was taken by 'HKM', who breathed fire and brimstone about what he saw as Mary's cynical abuse of art for her own self-promotion:

> The great beauty of play and performance was once again besmirched by Miss Garden's playing. Her costume, more naked than nudity itself, was a shade of light red rose that hits the eye with a painfully strident tone. Nothing but Miss Garden's selfish and debased desire to display herself could have made her so defile Maeterlinck's fine drama. No responsible artist at the Opera House had the least authority over her. A singer as idolized and as highly paid as Miss Garden is diva indeed, for she can issue orders and follow whimsies which the most able conductor or most famous régisseur in the world is powerless to combat.[16]

In mid-December she again sang *Thaïs* in Boston. The *Boston Transcript*'s 'HTP' (18 December 1913) was delighted and at the same time, like his colleague 'HKM', scandalized: 'Her voice was smoother of texture, brighter of timbre, fresher of quality and more supple to her every purpose. To have such resources as singer and as actress and yet time and again to make debased and perverting use of them is the endless riddle of Miss Garden.'

Back in Chicago, Mary played *Le jongleur de Notre Dame* in front of an audience that included Ruggiero Leoncavallo. Glenn Dillard Gunn, writing in the *Chicago Tribune* (24 December 1913), was astounded by Mary's ability to change her voice for the role. 'She sacrifices vocal display to truth and assumes the bold clarity of tone that belongs to a boy's voice. This illusion she sustains throughout the performance. Not even in the moments of religious ecstasy does she permit her voice to be touched by sensuous warmth of tone.'

After a performance of *Thaïs* played opposite Titta Ruffo, Felix Borowski berated Mary in the *Chicago Record Herald* (27 December 1913) for vocal vulgarity and inconsistency. 'She scoops often, and often speaks as well as sings. That is her conception of the manner in which Massenet's music should be given.' Despite the ambivalence of the critics, the recent performances of *Thaïs* finally raised $35,000. It was one of the greatest box-office draws of the Chicago Grand Opera Company.

* * *

In the middle of January 1914, Mary failed to appear for a Columbus Women's Musical Concert, giving the impression that she took little account of the feelings of her public. After the audience had assembled in the hall in great anticipation, Mary wired to say she could not come as she had to appear in *Le jongleur de Notre-Dame* in Chicago. She offered an alternative Columbus date four days later. She then appeared with Muratore in *Manon* at the Auditorium but it was said that her tone lacked freshness and seemed forced and worn, the high notes particularly sounding as if they were placed far back in the mouth, which gave a colourless effect. Her acting seemed greatly exaggerated.

Meanwhile, back in Columbus, antipathy was building a good head of steam. The *Columbus Citizen* ran a cartoon of Mary hoeing a garden planted with dollar signs with the jibe: 'Mary, Mary quite contrary, how does your garden grow? An opera date will surely bring more kale in the spring, y'know.' But on 19 January, in spite of such jibes, Mary again failed to turn up at Columbus.

The following day, Mary saved *Manon* from curtailment and the management from embarrassment by going on with her part in spite of an attack of vertigo which seized her during the last scene of the fourth act. She had tottered to a divan just before the end of the scene. The chorus gathered around and a glass of water was passed to her from the wings. Then, in the last act she appeared and completed the opera, apparently without ill effect. Mary declared that she was completely recovered. It emerged later that 56 pages of music had been cut out of the first act, 22 pages out of the second, while the third scene was omitted entirely so that musical difficulties might not tax Mary's voice.

By the time *Louise* was given two days later, she was in excellent shape once again. In 'Depuis le jour', the *Chicago Tribune* noted the beautifully shaded and sustained melodic phrase, the rhythmic impulse, the illuminating gesture which confirmed and amplified the dramatic and musical significance. Each step in her remarkable unfolding of the character was given accurate vocal expression.

From time to time, Mary again gave people the impression that she did not entirely see eye to eye with her fellow-sopranos. Early in January 1914, a keen-eyed journalist in the Auditorium had noticed that, during Frieda

Hempel's guest performance in *La traviata*, Mary sat with her back to the stage. And when Melba gave a concert at the Auditorium, Mary irritated many of the audience because she carried on an audible conversation with the others in her box during Melba's numbers. However, Mary later commented with awe: 'My God! If I could sing like that woman!'

Returning in early February to the Metropolitan, New York, Mary played Dulcinée to Marcoux's Don Quichotte but failed to please. She was miscast, it was said, the music was set too low (having been written for a contralto) and the role gave her few opportunities to be dramatic. Stung by this bad press, she announced that she did not like New York and that she was seriously thinking about retirement.

> New York has no artistic courage. It is so used to accepting everything from Europe that it never dares to decide for itself. My ambition as regards my career is to leave it, and perhaps I shall do so within the next two years. I have done my share and I have set my standards. Let others go on. I want people to remember me as I am now, not as a hobbling old woman.[17]

Her Louise was better received. 'It is to the credit of the great dramatic power of this woman that, although her singing has long been a bad joke, her personation of Louise is still able to command the intense interest of great audiences by the sincerity and power with which she throws herself into it.'[18] And in *Monna Vanna*, Mary was an enormous success. 'The audience was more wildly enthusiastic than we have seen it on any occasion this year,' wrote *Town and Country* (28 February 1914).

There now seemed to be good news on the matrimonial front. At last wedding bells were to chime for Mary and Vanni-Marcoux, according to members of the Philadelphia-Chicago Opera Company. Vanni-Marcoux's devotion to Mary had been a matter of common knowledge among their friends and in operatic circles, ever since he first came to America two years before; Mary's partiality for his society had been no less remarked on. The recent announcement that the previous July Lina Cavalieri had secretly wed her tenor adorer, Lucien Muratore, in Paris, was said to have had much to do with bringing Mary and Vanni-Marcoux to the point of marriage. It was said that the ceremony might take place in New York. In fact, in Paris that June Vanni-Marcoux did indeed get married, but not to Mary. Instead his bride was the very wealthy Madeleine Morlay.

Meanwhile, Mary had just lost $2000 through her broken concert engagement at Columbus, Ohio. And in mid-March there came news from Paris of yet another lawsuit brought by a Madame Garrigue against Mary for $1325 for a cloak, stole and muff she had supplied. Mary claimed in defence that only $667 was due, as the balance had been garnished out of her salary at the Opéra. In its judgement, the court ordered her to pay $719 with half the costs. But these incidents did not appear to tax the Garden finances. Mary was said to be already making generous provision through

1 Mary Garden as Louise in Charpentier's opera (Paris: Opéra-Comique, April 1900)

2   Mary Garden as Diane in Gabriel Pierné's *La fille de Tabarin* (Paris: Opéra-
Comique, February 1901)

3   Mary Garden as Massenet's Manon (Paris: Opéra-Comique, September 1901). By kind permission of Mrs Jenny Park

4   Mary Garden and André Messager (Monte Carlo, December 1901)

5   Mary Garden as Debussy's Mélisande (Paris: Opéra-Comique, May 1902)

6   Mary Garden as Fiamette in Xavier Leroux's *La Reine Fiamette* (Paris: Opéra-Comique, December 1903)

7   Mary Garden as Massenet's Chérubin (Paris: Opéra-Comique, February 1905)

8   Mary Garden with Claude Debussy and other members of the cast of *Pélleas et Mélisande* (Paris: outside the Opéra-Comique, May 1902)

9　Mary Garden as Fanny Legrand in Massenet's *Sapho* (New York: Manhattan Opera House, November 1909)

10　Mary Garden as Strauss' Salome in the Dance of the Seven Veils (New York: Manhattan Opera House, January 1909)

11   Mary Garden as Strauss' Salome (New York: Manhattan Opera House, January 1909)

12 Mary Garden as Massenet's Grisélidis (New York: Manhattan Opera House,
January 1910)

13 Mary Garden as Massenet's Grisélidis (New York: Manhattan Opera House, January 1910)

14 Mary Garden as Thaïs and Hamilton Revelle as the Baptist in Samuel
Goldwyn's 1918 film *Thaïs* (desert scenes filmed at St Augustine, Florida,
October 1917)

15   Mary Garden as Massenet's Manon (Paris: Opéra-Comique September 1901).
By kind permission of Mrs Jenny Park

16 Mary Garden with the composer Franco Alfano at her villa in Beaulieu-sur-Mer (summer 1922). By kind permission of Mrs Jenny Park

17 The Garden family (Monte Carlo Beach Hotel, 1930). By kind permission of Mr Mario Goetschel

18 Mary Garden at her desk as Director of the Chicago Opera Company (January 1921)

19   Mary Garden on her lecture tour of America (winter 1949). By kind permission of Mr George F Burr

20   Mary Garden in Aberdeen (1949). By kind permission of Mr George F Burr

deposits in Paris banks for the maintenance of talented girls whom she had taken from the chorus and sent abroad to study. It was also rumoured that she now owned two estates in Europe, one near her birthplace at Aberdeen (presumably, Pitmurchie) and the other at Versailles.

Mary now set off on a Philadelphia-Chicago Grand Opera Company tour of the Far West. There were, as ever, the inevitable mishaps on stage. Once, when singing in a Western town, in the penultimate act of *Louise* (where Louise is supposed to kneel on the grass and see the lights of Paris), Mary found no grass and saw no lights. When the curtain fell she called for the stage manager and shouted: 'What kind of a bum management is this? Here I have had to sing with that midget [pointing to the unfortunate tenor]! No grass to kneel on and not a damned light in all Paris!'

She then again succumbed to illness and had to disappoint a $10,000 audience in Des Moines who were expecting to see her in *Thaïs*. She quickly left the tour and slipped off to New York. She had now failed to appear in four cities and there was even talk of a disagreement with the Company. The banker, E. T. Stotesbury, speaking on behalf of the Company, confirmed that Mary would not be re-engaged. He favoured the submission of no new contract to her. For her part, Mary proclaimed that she would never return to America.

On 1 May, it was announced that a radical change in personnel and in the policy of the Chicago Grand Opera Company would take place as a result of its disastrous tour of the Far West. There had been a total loss of $150,000, in addition to the operating deficit of the company. The loss in Kansas City had been $24,000; in Los Angeles, $18,000; in San Francisco $20,000 and in Seattle $15,000. The wealthy stockholders had decided to institute drastic reforms for the following season. A great deal of dissatisfaction was expressed over the business direction of Cleofonte Campanini and regret was expressed that he was being allowed to supersede Andreas Dippel as impresario. There had been great friction in the organization and it had been open talk that Mary Garden virtually ran the company.

As Mary prepared to leave for Europe, papers were served on her by the indignant Women's Music Club of Columbus, Ohio; they were still suing her for $1000. Mary duly filed a notice of appearance through the firm of Gugenheimer, Untermayer & Marshall. By the end of May she had settled the suit, with undisclosed terms.

*   *   *

On 5 May 1914, the *Kaiser Wilhelm II* left New York for Europe with Caruso, Scotti, Farrar, Alda, McCormack, Toscanini and Mary on board. After nursing her sister in Switzerland, Mary returned to Paris to be one of the prominent hostesses of Grand Prix week. Then she was off to Scotland.

But as the political atmosphere in Europe grew increasingly tense, Mary became concerned: 'I was in Scotland,' she later recalled,

> relaxing from a hard season when, in June 1914, I received a telegram from an American couple. It said that they had secured me my seat for *Parsifal* at Bayreuth. I was delighted. Bayreuth, and especially *Parsifal*, attracted me to the degree that I thought I didn't mind breaking up my vacation and joining my friends across Europe. But as the time drew near, I began feeling more and more unwilling to go. I didn't know why. I told my father that something was going to happen and I had an instinctive feeling that I had better stay at home.[19]

But by late September she found it impossible to stay away from Paris any longer. 'Prepared for all sorts of difficulties, I started in my car from Scotland. There weren't any difficulties, it was as simple as an afternoon's motoring. I sat in my car as we crossed the Channel and from Boulogne we raced down to Paris without seeing any signs of war.' She eventually arrived in the capital and was astounded at the change. 'Poor Paris! Every shop shut; not a restaurant, no theatres, the Bois closed off, separated by deep and wide ditches which they had filled with the cut down trees. At once I turned my automobile into an ambulance for bringing back the wounded and set about seeing what I could do to help.'

Mary felt she had found her vocation for the duration of the war; for two years, in an overgrown chateau at Suresnes, she helped to keep open a refuge for women and children. 'Two years passed and I did not sing a note, except a folk song or ballad at the soirées we arranged for our protegés. In Paris they told me that the men coming back on their short furloughs out of the horrors of the trenches needed to be sung to, and I volunteered to sing whenever they asked me at the Opéra-Comique.'

Mary now started work as a Red Cross nurse, with the American actress and interior designer Elsie de Wolfe and her friends, Bessie Marbury and Anne Morgan, whose lesbian ménage at Versailles, in the Villa Trianon, had been placed under American protection and turned over to the Red Cross as a hospital. Shortly afterwards, the three other Americans went back to the United States to start relief work on behalf of the Allies, not returning to France until 1916.

Mary felt an upsurge of renewed motivation in France. 'I may never sing again, but I don't care. I shall help to move the wounded from the battlefields. I am not afraid. I am a fatalist. If it is destiny, what matters? I expect to be at the front with the French troops next week,' she added defiantly, 'the experience will be broadening.'[20]

She seemed to have been seized by a whirlwind of patriotism towards her adopted land. On Monday 16 November, an extraordinary incident is said to have taken place which captured the imagination of the *New York Review* (21 November 1914). At the offices of the commandant of the Paris garrison there appeared a trimly uniformed titian-haired youth, of somewhat effeminate bearing, who presented himself to the recruiting officer for enlistment in the army – a Zouave regiment preferred. The suspicions of the officer were aroused and he reported to his superiors that the candidate did not seem to be exactly what he represented; possibly he might be a German spy in disguise. The general commanding received the report and ordered the would-be 'recruit' to be examined – then came a revelation. The boyish recruit was not a boy, this was plainly evident, and the examination proceeded no further, for the 'boy' tearfully confessed that she was a girl and her name was Mary Garden.

At this point the minister for war and military governor of Paris, General Joseph Simon Gallieni, personally took charge of the case – the general was a great admirer of Mary's. Everyone else was ordered to leave the room and he had a long conversation with the prisoner. Afterwards the whole story leaked out.

'Yes, I tried to enlist in the French army,' said Mary. 'Why not? I owe France more than I can ever repay, even by giving her my life, and I am sure that I could fight as well as any man if they would only let me. I have never failed to subdue every man I have met so far.'

Encouraged by General Gallieni's advice and admiration, Mary returned to her suite at the Hotel des Réservoirs, Versailles. There she continued her war work, also receiving Allied officers on leave and entertaining them with (among other diversions) frivolous games of chance such as roulette.[21]

Early in December, Mary passed through London on her way to New York – 'just to eat Christmas dinner with mother and father and then rush back to Paris to my hospital and refugee home for French soldiers who have lost their eyesight in the trenches.'

'I don't know if a great opera will grow out of this war,' she continued, 'but this is so real and vivid a time that art seems further from me than ever before. It has been crowded away by the pity and horror of the war.'[22] Later she would add: 'I have seen the light of the soul in the faces of the soldiers of France. I sang for them behind the trenches, in uniforms begrimed with clay and the stains of powder and blood.'[23]

To the *Washington Post* (6 December 1914) she also confessed a radical shift in her priorities: 'It's true my operatic plans for the season have been upset by the war. But after the terrible and the big brave things I've seen lately, our poor worldly ambitions seem so small and pitiful. Even Art fades into mere illusion.' This was a reference to the fact that she had been preparing to sing the role of Octavian in Richard Strauss' *Der Rosenkavalier*. It seems that her contract was signed, she had studied the role; but the rehearsals were to be suddenly abandoned at the outbreak of hostilities and the production in Paris was cancelled.[24]

Mary was to find a new meaning to her life by throwing herself energetically into helping those who suffered most from the conflict.

The hospital where I worked is devoted chiefly to wounds of the head and eyes. It was heartbreaking to see some poor fellows with their eyes gouged out by a bullet or a bayonet, or half the face shot away by a shell. How brave and uncomplaining they all were. They were suffering for France, and that helped them to bear the pain. Nursing in such cases is trying work but there is a fascination about it that brings the maternal nature slumbering in every woman to the surface. I love the work.

Speaking in New York in late 1914 Mary revealed that she had had several offers from Vaudeville, but the war had so affected her that she would not be able to sing for at least a year. She had also been offered an engagement that season at Petrograd in Russia to sing *Salome* but, on moral grounds, the city authorities had refused to allow her to perform. She had crossed the Atlantic for three weeks only, in order to appeal for funds for her hospital ('Mary's Garden', as she liked to call it), which she and her two associates had supported out of their private funds. During her short stay in New York she also hoped to persuade her friends to contribute to the French Red Cross fund.

Mary arrived in America dressed in her famous white spats. But her hair no longer had the reddish-blonde hue with golden lights that it had before she went to France. Perhaps to appear in keeping with more sombre times, it was now a rich, deep auburn.

Notes

1.   *Morning Telegraph*, 21 January 1913.
2.   *Musical Leader*, 9 January 1913, quoting Karleton Hackett in the *Chicago Post*.
3.   *Evening Sun*, 18 February 1913.
4.   *Boston Traveler*, 20 February 1913.
5.   *Boston Transcript*, 20 February 1913.
6.   *Denver Times*, 10 April 1913.
7.   *Toledo Blade*, 30 April 1913.
8.   *Chicago Examiner*, 24 November 1913.
9.   Letter from Wolf-Ferrari to Mary Garden, 23 May 1913. Located in the Department of Portraits and Performing History, RCM, London.
10. *Chicago Examiner*, 24 November 1913.
11. *Philadelphia Morning Telegraph*, 1 November 1913.
12. *Philadelphia Record*, 16 November 1913.
13. *Musical America*, 28 June 1913.
14. *Boston Transcript*, November 1913.
15. *New York American*, 6 December 1913.
16. *Boston Transcript*, 11 December 1913.
17. *New York Telegraph*, 9 February 1914.
18. *Brooklyn Eagle*, 11 February 1914.
19. *Sun*, 23 February 1919.
20. *Toledo Blade*, 5 October 1914.

21. Mario Goetschel, letter to author, 3 November 1994.
22. *New York Times*, 4 December 1914.
23. *Columbus Dispatch*, 25 February 1917.
24. Ernest de Weerth, *Opera News*, 5 April 1954.

10 The War Years: 1915–1919

During her brief visit to New York in January 1915, Mary immediately found herself lionized by fashionable society. There was, for example, a memorable dinner at the Faversham residence on East 17th Street with the conductor, Walter Damrosch, Mr and Mrs Otis Skinner, the actress Marie Tempest and the baritone, Antonio Scotti. Mary, however, was anxious to get back to France and her war work. Before she left New York, she just had time to make arrangements for an American concert tour in the autumn.

Steaming back across the Atlantic, Mary's ship was due to pass through prohibited waters only two days before the fateful 18 February when Germany began her undersea warfare against British merchant vessels. Mary was unfazed. When a facetious friend whispered 'submarine' in her ear, Mary's answer was to snap her fingers in defiance. 'I carry a British passport and I don't give a whoop out of Oshkosh whether a submarine interferes with us or not. I know if I'm caught and put in some horrid old detention camp somewhere, I'll make that camp the liveliest one in Europe.'[1]

At the end of April, she travelled to London for a concert in the Queen's Hall and was infuriated by the way the immigration personnel treated her.

> I could not have been subjected to more rigorous surveillance. I've had to stand for hours amongst other suspects at Paris, at Boulogne and even in England. The authorities seemed determined to make me catch cold by giving me the maximum exposure to biting winds. Do you think they would have done it if they had known I was making a special journey at my own expense and without a penny of remuneration to sing for patriotic causes and for the furtherance of British art?[2]

She was determined to leave England for France as soon as she could. 'I have been in the hospitals where our wounded are and I am going back to sing to them,' said Mary proudly. 'I have also had the privilege of seeing my Scotch countrymen in khaki in France.'[3]

Towards the end of May, she performed at the Drury Lane Theatre Royal in a matinée organized by Lady Paget on behalf of the American Women's

War Hospital. In the audience were Queen Mary, Queen Alexandra, Queen Amelia of Portugal, Princess Mary, the Duke of Orleans, Princess Christian, Princess Marie Louise, Grand Duke Michael and the American ambassador. Many years later, when speaking to the conductor Eugene Goossens, Mary gave her recollections of this concert: 'There are only two things I remember about that concert, Eugene. One was a damnably noisy piece of yours and the other was a simply awful hat I wore which cost me fifteen guineas!'[4]

That June, an announcement was made of an American concert tour for the following season, under the direction of her manager, R. E. Johnstone. Mary was rumoured to be about to join the new opera company organized by Max Rabinoff. It was also said that Mary had recently discovered a composer of undoubted genius, by the name of Frederick Delius, to whose compositions she proposed to give a prominent place in her programmes. But there was also news of more startling Garden ventures. Mary had just been engaged at a cost of $125,000 for two photoplays (films) directed by Tom Ince. Shortly afterwards, it was made known that originally she had been made an offer of $100,000 to appear in four moving pictures as heroine of as yet unspecified operas in her repertoire. Johnstone cabled her in France and received no reply. In response, the film company quickly raised its bid to $150,000!

Unexpectedly, Mary was declared to be seriously ill in Paris after an appendicitis operation. Just three weeks previously she had been at Aix-les-Bains, nursing wounded soldiers. Her American tour was due to begin in two weeks but all her engagements were cancelled forthwith. Mary herself strenuously denied that she had had any operation. She was in fact resting near Aberdeen in Scotland, at a Highland lodge (evidently, Pitmurchie), she claimed, recovering from the effects of her strenuous work during the summer for the French Red Cross. She promised that as soon as she regained her health and strength, she would return to France and serve in the ambulance nursing corps. But the stories of an operation persisted. Her father, Robert Garden, arriving in New York from Liverpool, said he had left his daughter in Paris calmly waiting to have an operation for appendicitis. In a long interview given in Paris later that year, Mary would admit that she had recovered sufficiently from her recent attack of appendicitis to sing again.[5]

By the end of 1915 Mary was planning to give six charity performances at the Opéra-Comique, singing two nights each in *Tosca*, *Louise* and *Pelléas et Mélisande*, beginning on 18 December. She promised she would appear in the early spring six times for charity. Although she would go to New York for a short American trip in April, she would prefer not to sing in America that season.

At the Opéra-Comique, Mary had been scheduled to create the leading role in *Gismonda*, a new work by Henri Février. This production had originally been planned for September 1914 but, although Mary had learned the role before the war, hostilities had made the production impossible at the time originally proposed. Finally, towards the end of January 1916, as promised, she began a series of seven performances at the Opéra-Comique – *Tosca* with Jean Périer as Scarpia, followed by *Louise*. Then she began rehearsals for *La traviata*.

A curious and inexplicable entry in the Paris Opéra register lists Mary and Marthe Chenal as having been replaced by Italian artists at an Arts and Charities concert on 5 February 1916. Perhaps the motivation for this was political or diplomatic, rather than absence through illness. It may have been that both women were giving priority to their voluntary nursing duties.

During Mary's mid-February *La traviata* piano-rehearsals with the tenor Léon David and the whole cast at the Opéra-Comique hall, the ever-present Madame Mariquita was in charge of choreography. But Mary sang no more than one performance on this occasion, followed by a single night of *Tosca*.

*   *   *

In mid-March, Mary cabled R. E. Johnstone in New York saying she had been warned that, in view of the scale of hostilities at that time, sailing was highly dangerous; she considered whether her planned April trip would have to be postponed. Mary was still immersed in her charitable activities in connection with the war, one of which consisted in supplying parcels to African Zouaves on the French front. She had even agreed to become god-mother to children of six of her Zouaves. She regularly sent them what they needed to make themselves as comfortable as possible in the trenches. A photograph of one of her soldiers – a typical stalwart, bronzed, six-foot *poilu* – held a place of honour in her room.

Mary's name on the bill of any concert was always the signal for a crowded house. At a recent matinée in the Trocadéro she had sung before a large military audience – an experience which brought her to the verge of tears.

Despite the warnings regarding the advisability of her American trip, Mary was preoccupied with negotiations over contracts for the following season. She had as yet not signed either for New York or Chicago. She had had a handsome offer to appear in Buenos Aires the following winter, but couldn't bear the thought of a sea voyage of 21 days each way. Besides, they only wanted her to sing *Carmen* and *La traviata* and not the more contemporary French repertoire. Then Cleofonte Campanini cabled asking her if she would come and she replied, naming a pretty large figure. Immediately he cabled back with an acceptance. Mary's guarded reaction was: 'We have lots of things to talk over before I sign a contract. I must know what artists I am expected to sing with. I can't bear to have poor artists around me.'

Mary duly sailed for New York. On her arrival, the papers seized upon her 'godmother' role to French soldiers. The *Philadelphia Public Ledger* (16 May 1916) marvelled that when her soldiers needed a watch or a pair of warm boots or a new wooden leg or an artificial arm, they simply had to write to her. In New York, Mary alternated with the New Zealand soprano Frances Alda at a fund-raising entertainment called 'How Britain Prepared', which had its première at the Lyceum Theatre. But she had changed her image – she was now a blonde. 'Mary, Mary, quite contrary, why have you bleached your hair?' wondered *The New York Telegraph* (16 May 1916).

She arrived in Chicago in early June for her meeting with Campanini. To the newspapers there she divulged her admiration for Colonel Roosevelt: 'I have adored him for years. I am in a frenzy because women cannot go to war. I long for the trenches and the long vigils and the hardships and the sacrifices.'[6] The *Chicago Post* commented on Mary's promotional skills:

> It is tradition in the journalistic fraternity that Mary Garden is the greatest press agent in the world. She holds nothing back, admits everything, cheerfully confirms strange reports – 'I am a Greek spirit, born a Scotch woman, reared in Chicago and condemned to wear corsets!'[7]

Four days later she returned to France, but not before she revealed that she would be ready for the filming of *Thaïs* (directed by Herbert Brenon of William Fox) the following February. She also indicated that she had asked Richard Strauss to compose an opera based upon Harre's realistic novel *Behold the Woman*.

Back in France, Mary continued to take an active interest in her work for the war-wounded, in conjunction with her American friends, Elsie de Wolfe and Elisabeth Marbury. Early in 1916 they had purchased a small house adjoining the Villa Trianon where they had established a home for convalescents.[8]

Even in her absence, Mary was the subject of intense discussion in the American press. The *Chicago Herald* revealed that Mary now had a serious rival and warned of an inappropriate importation of stage acting techniques to the silver screen and vice versa.

> Before Geraldine Farrar bit Caruso on the ear and played Carmen in such sensual and feline fashion, Mary was the queen actress of passion. Theatrical love in her hands was always likely to break up a show. Miss Farrar rose to her highest pitch of simulated passion in her first moving picture. In *Carmen* she made love to Don José so that the censors in several states refused to let it be shown unless radical alterations were made. Large strips of the film were cut out. The movies were blamed for the great change in her grand opera *Carmen* when she returned to the stage. In fact, Caruso, whom she had bitten in the scuffle attendant upon her spurning of José for Escamillo, charged her with employing moving-picture methods in the sacred precincts of grand opera.[9]

At the end of October, Mary sang *Le jongleur de Notre-Dame* for the first time at the Opéra-Comique, with receipts of 9265 francs. But public interest was focused on her next role – *Carmen* – the production of which promised to be unusually spectacular. The parade in the fourth act, in the new scenery by Bailly (in front of the arena in Seville), was to be swelled by additional extras, with a double *cuadrilla* and picadors on horseback. Between Acts 3 and 4 a tombola draw was planned for the public foyer. Mary's performance on the night was warmly applauded, *Le Figaro* commending her individuality and dramatic impact. At a subsequent performance, some 42,000 francs were raised for the war-wounded.

*   *   *

On the eve of her departure for her American season that December, Mary was delivered a charming public relations gift by the press – the news was broken that she had just been ordered by the courts to turn over her lingerie, valued at $5000, to a board of experts for appraisal. This related to an action to recover that amount (minus $1500 paid on account) brought against her by a Paris lingerie company.

She continued ahead to New York regardless. There, she was met by her mother and driven to the Ritz-Carlton where she proclaimed that she hated to leave her hospital work in Paris and would return as soon as possible to continue her care of the wounded. But for now she was obliged to fulfil her contract with Campanini and travel on to Chicago.

On the last night of the year, Mary sang *Thaïs* in Chicago for the renamed Chicago Opera Association. 'Mary Garden, whose art boils,' wrote James Whittaker in the *Chicago Tribune* (1 January 1917),

> melted all Massenet's sugary coatings and left nothing but the wormwood content of the drama. The religion of her Thaïs is her senses' ultimate adventure. Her natural movement is seduction. Her voice has an inherent, wanton, fibrous coarseness. Such is the emulsion of art, personality and showmanship which is Mary Garden.

At a later performance of *Thaïs* in the Auditorium, the critic Karleton Hackett reported in the *Chicago Post* (11 January 1917) that Mary had suffered paroxysms of neuralgic pain in the back of her head and neck that at times made it almost impossible for her to continue. Mary herself complained bitterly that her discomfort was caused by the over-use of the colour green in the theatre's footlights.

When reviewing *Grisélidis*, Hackett declared himself to be astonished at her chameleon-like ability to metamorphose on stage. 'Grisélidis is a kind of humanised Mélisande. There was not the slightest trace in carriage, motion or gesture of the Thaïs of two nights ago. Even the tones of her voice had quite a different colour.'[10]

Stanley K. Faye of the *Chicago News* (22 January 1917) wrestled to analyse Mary's dramatic technique after she appeared in *Louise* at the Auditorium:

> Mary Garden's histrionism seems for the most part to arise from a calculating nature. She plays by rote and allows scant opportunity for the intrusion of spontaneity. Such practice is identical with art and in the role of Louise, Miss Garden approaches nearest to perfection. Once she looked into the audience; once she spoke to someone in the left upper entrance; once (in the workshop scene) she capitulated to the grand opera manner and gesticulated meaninglessly.[11]

On one occasion Mary combined her genius for photo-opportunity with genuine social concern when she and the baritone Hector Dufranne gave a midnight concert to Chicago's 'Hobos' College'. In a barren room on the third floor of an aged structure, hundreds of poor folk and migratory workers were crowded in front of a hastily improvised stage while a man swabbed off the piano-keys with kerosene. But when Mary and Dufranne began to sing, the walls rocked and plaster fell from the ceiling!

Meanwhile, her career development continued on other fronts. In the Ritz-Carlton Hotel early in February 1917, Mary signed a contract with the Goldwyn Pictures Corporation for a series of motion-pictures. She was preparing to return to Paris for the summer, where she would supervise the design and making of her costumes for her first screen production. By the beginning of March she had had her first screen test. 'I walked about the room, looked out of a window and acted a few simple scenes. When they asked me how I would act if I should suddenly discover my husband dead at my feet, I said I was sure I didn't know.'[12] The results of the screen test proved satisfactory but Mary realised that greater deliberateness was necessary in acting for film.

Planning for her return to France, Mary made reservations for three secretaries to accompany her. She would use them on the voyages over and back to dictate her autobiography, which was to be serialized in the summer and autumn in more than 200 newspapers. She was to sail via Vigo for an engagement at the Opéra-Comique. She waved goodbye to America and went down to the pier wearing an orchid corsage. 'I am willing to volunteer as a Red Cross nurse', she exclaimed. Sailing with her was Vaslav Nijinsky and 52 other members of the Russian ballet.[13]

Once in Paris, Mary revealed a profoundly generous heart. She told the management of the Opéra-Comique: 'Until there is peace, I wish to give the salary you pay me back to the Comique. Out of it please pay as many salaries of the lesser people in the company as my salary will cover'. That had been done twice and was now about to be done for a third time.[14]

Meanwhile, Samuel Goldfish (later changed to Goldwyn) had been working at his marketing. He published a request for the public to nominate their favourite Garden role to be made into a film. The response was overwhelming. Sixty-four thousand people wrote in three weeks and about 81 per cent of these letters named *Thaïs* as the ruling favourite. Mary, full of enthusiasm for motion pictures, now took title to a valuable site in Paris where work began with her architects in the designing of a 4000-seat motion-picture theatre, to be named 'The Cinema Mary'. 'I want to play to five million persons a week,' she told the world.[15] Then suddenly came one of her unexpected and unexplained absences. She had been due to sing in June at the Trocadéro in a benefit for two and a half million captive children in Belgium and Northern France. She was billed to sing Xavier Leroux's 'Le Nil', with cello obbligato. But she failed to appear.

On 1 August 1917 Mary sent a wireless message to Goldwyn – said to have been the last private message given transmission before the British government discontinued the Marconi company's transatlantic service. 'Have booked passage for last week in August,' it read, 'and for second time since June, intend to show my contempt for the submarine monsters. Am tremendously fit and will immediately begin *Thaïs*.'[16]

*   *   *

Returning to America, Mary's energies were devoted to raising funds for the Serbian Red Cross; with her she had brought a Gold Book from the King of Serbia to fill with subscriptions from her friends. She also wanted to establish a national sewing day for bandages. She proudly flaunted two decorations – the Red Cross of Serbia and the French Wreath of Public Devotion. Her auburn hair was smoothly coifed; her eyes burning blue. She claimed she was much thinner, having lost 29 pounds, and she confessed she was nearly dead after six days of watching for submarines. She had been booked in October to deliver the prologue at *America*, a huge pageant in the Greek Theatre on the estate of Roland Conkling at Huntington, Long Island.[17]

Halfway through September, Mary began filming *Thaïs* in Goldwyn's glass house at Fort Lee across the Hudson. There, throughout most of the night, the studios gleamed with green flood-lamps. Most of Mary's costumes had arrived from France in a steel portable van. Sitting in the Ritz-Carlton Hotel, she gave an interview wearing a garment of green tulle over a white afternoon frock, cut very low. It covered her like a cloud from head to foot. 'I am quite wild to begin,' she confided.[18]

The costumes for the film had been designed by a young American designer, Ernest de Weerth. Hugo Ballin was responsible for all the settings. 'I have seen them,' added Mary, 'and they are wonderful.'[19] As she started work, Mary received a letter of encouragement from Oscar Hammerstein. Early on, however, she experienced some difficulty with a lion cub called Hector, who needed forty minutes and three strips of raw beefsteak to entice him the length of the great floor. 'I've had rough lovers in opera and I didn't mind,' Mary declared, 'but deliver me from a lion when I'm barefoot.'[20]

After some initial blocking, Mary, leading man Hamilton Revelle, director Hugo Ballin and co-director Frank Crane had to spend two days in St Augustine, Florida, to film the desert scenes. There, for six hours in front of the cameras, they shot two and a half thousand feet of film.

Early in November, Geraldine Farrar, who had been signed by the rival Zukor production company, came over to visit Mary and Samuel Goldwyn. The three posed cheerfully and elegantly for the photographers. But soon financial problems made their presence felt. Goldwyn had promised Mary a fee of $150,000. 'This story, although uncopyrighted in America,' wrote Goldwyn,

> obligated the purchase of foreign rights, and I paid M. Anatole France, its author, $10,000 for these. In so doing I felt sure that the French exhibitors alone would do more than return my expenditure.
>
> No sooner had the actual production began than I was beset by grave fears. Miss Garden did not recognise the difference of medium involved, and her first days on the set showed her, as the studio people expressed it, 'acting all over the place'.
>
> Those days when we were producing *Thaïs* remain with me as among the most troubled of my history. Harassed by financial adjustments and by production difficulties, assailed by complaints from my various stars over scenarios and directors, I now had this supreme anxiety regarding the outcome of my enormous investment in Mary Garden.
>
> The death of Thaïs was almost the death of Mary Garden. She had fought bitterly the scenario's departure from the original text here in this scene. When she saw the rushes of this scene which so violated her artistic conception, her rage and grief knew no bounds. 'I knew it!' she cried. 'Imagine me, the great Thaïs, dying like an acrobat!' A moment later she rushed from the projection room down to the office. Here she found the playwright Margaret Mayo. 'Did you see it?' she stormed to this other woman. 'That terrible thing? Did you see the way they made me die? Imagine a saint dying like that!'
>
> The playwright looked her up and down and then responded in a tone of studied insolence: 'You would have a hard time, Miss Garden, proving to anyone that you were a saint.'
>
> Some time later, when I came upon the set, I found Miss Garden weeping hysterically. 'Oh,' said she, 'that terrible woman! Have you heard what she just said to me?'[21]

But Mary had by now fresh fields to conquer. Her lengthy autobiographical articles were beginning to appear, full of exaggeration and contradiction.

> I am one of the few women in the world who can lay claim to being genuinely modern and yet opposed to all the various invasive tendencies which have come upon women in recent years. I consider that suffrage will do women no good. I have never had a confidante. I have three very good women friends, all of them about twenty years older than I. One lives in Chicago, the other two abroad. And they are all women of brains and power and purpose. One of them has a house in Paris, another on the Riviera and a third on the Canal in Venice. She entertains

royalty and the foremost artists. These three women are my friends, but I could hardly call any one of them a confidante. No man in the nineteenth century has so appealed to me as Oscar Wilde.[22]

As for her physical appearance, Mary struggled fiercely to avoid developing into the stereotypical prima donna: 'These ladies are, for the most part, plain, obese and no longer stricken with youth. I myself am not in the business of being beautiful. I set myself three tasks in the line of good looks: to keep the figure, to keep off fat; to get younger every year. I never drink. I haven't tasted candy for years.' And she had this advice for her readers: 'Wash the face with warm water at bedtime, dry and rub with a towel and apply a good cream, lightly scented. In the morning wash first with very hot water, then with plenty of ice water. Use a little good powder. Avoid cosmetics and skin preparations.'[23]

She painted a stark picture of the choice facing women who wanted to succeed in opera.

> A woman must give up night life, gaiety, restaurants and dissipation. I despise restaurants and night life. I never cared for dolls, like other girls. I had no fondness for this early maternal playing. I cannot remember being more than passingly interested in a boy. There will be times when love will intrude his beguiling face and call the artist from his or her task to the instinctive impulse of life. It is now that the artist must make the great choice. It may be that at the close of life we who chase the golden fleece must all look back and bitterly regret the joys we sacrificed, the youth we gave up to our god.[24]

Exotic fashion accessories were part of Mary's image. She had recently acquired a black wooden bracelet for her left arm, made from the sacred tree of Siam and inlaid with diamonds in a geometrical design. She remained a formidable figure for any news-hack who ventured to interview her, as one Chicago reporter who went to her apartment in the Blackstone Hotel soon discovered. 'The door was opened and the scent of the master craftsmanship of the Parisian perfumer mingled with that of armfuls of fresh roses. It was like a gas attack by angels.'[25]

* * *

January 1918 found Mary singing *Pelléas et Mélisande* at the Auditorium in Chicago, where she encountered production difficulties. 'She battled with some bad, old-fashioned scenery,' noted the *Chicago Tribune* (20 January 1918). 'The lighting at times was prosaic shine rather than mystic gloom. *Pelléas et Mélisande*, like sin, should be done in the shadows.'

Next came the New York première of Goldwyn's motion picture, *Thaïs*. The Stanley Orchestra had been enlarged for the presentation as the score was made up largely of excerpts from the Massenet opera.[26] Mary's absence from the box however (usually occupied by the star of a production when it was given its première in the Strand), was commented upon. Other members of the cast were present, including Hamilton Revelle, the leading man and officials of Goldwyn. 'Where was Mary Garden?' In the gallery, of course. Veiled and cloaked in dark fur she entered the theatre and found an un-reserved seat.[27] She feared the worst.

The film was ripped apart by the critics. They were bitter that,

> one of the most purely spiritual stories in all literature, in the hands of Goldwyn comes out as an orgy of unlovely flesh. It is so tawdry, so crude, so vulgar. Mary Garden brings to the screen the tedious and dismal technique of operatic acting, which is not acting at all, but slow motions made while waiting for the music to catch up with the drama. Moreover, Miss Garden is no longer the lovely creature of *Louise*.[28]

But Mary, putting a brave face on the failure of her first film performance, now brought news of a new motion-picture venture. 'My second picture is much better – *The Splendid Sinner*,' she told Louella Parsons. '*Thaïs* was mangled in cutting – fully 4,000 feet was trimmed and I am afraid that it was ruined.'[29] The failure of *Thaïs* was blamed on director Hugo Ballin. 'He has not been able to distract her attention from the camera,' the *Chicago Tribune* complained (31 December 1917). 'With stilted movement, carefully calculated gestures, smiles, a general woodenness and deprived of the immortal words and music, the story cannot live.'

Later that January, Mary appeared at the Lexington, New York, in *Monna Vanna* and immediately moved the balance of operatic power away from the Met. 'The storm centre of operatic interest shifted suddenly last night from Broadway to Lexington Avenue,' wrote one observer, 'in spite of the fact that Enrico Caruso, recognised still as the greatest of all living tenors, was pouring forth, as Samson, tones of liquid gold in the ancient and honourable establishment presided over by Giulio Gatti-Casazza.'[30] There were 30 curtain calls for *Monna Vanna*. 'Melba in a second tier box joined her voice to "The Star-Spangled Banner" played before the opera's second act,' reported *The New York Times*. A novel feature of the production was that the crowds were summoned from the lobbies by army bugle-calls.

The Chicago Opera Association was functioning under considerable diffi-culties caused by the war. There were congested railroads, a fuel famine (which affected the heating of the theatre) and a Government theatre-closing order which had already postponed the opening of *Monna Vanna*. In fact, the opera had been chosen to begin the company's programme because it was the only one in which general manager Campanini could simultane-ously present both Mary and tenor Lucien Muratore.

Two days later Mary showed just how much more successful she was on stage than on camera when she sang *Thaïs*. 'It was the most thrilling imper-sonation she has ever vouchsafed to us,' wrote the *New York World* critic

(26 January 1918). 'She stirred the vast audience to a demonstration that was tumultuous. Nellie Melba was one of the last to cease clapping her hands.' And W. J. Henderson in the *New York Sun* (27 January 1918) summed up public appreciation: 'Mary Garden is one of the finest, most picturesque, most decorative and most intellectual actresses that ever walked the stage. As for brains – she has an equipment quite amazing for an opera singer. When the voice is of small importance, the interpretative skill becomes of inestimable value, and who possesses more of it than this seductive Mary Garden?'

Commenting a few days later on her *Pelléas et Mélisande*, the *New York Journal of Commerce* (2 February 1918) observed that she gave to each of the many episodes a quality of elusive beauty, an aloofness that attracted and appealed by its restraint. And, impressed by Mary's *Carmen*, Sylvester Rawling observed that:

> The vast audience indulged itself in tumult from beginning to end. Action was halted time and time again. Curtain calls were so numerous as to escape count. From twenty minutes past eight to five minutes before twelve the excitement lasted . . . Miss Garden has reconceived her Carmen. Her impersonation is unique. It is of remarkable force and her tonal production was of great beauty.[31]

There were further column-inches of appreciation. 'She does not sing as others do,' ventured the *Brooklyn Eagle* (10 February 1918):

> Hers is not a purely lyric utterance. Garden's pitch is almost always accurate. But she makes it always subservient to the dramatic value of the line. It has the heightening and emotional element of speech. Garden possesses the ability to color line and phrase in accordance with the poetic content. And with it all there is always the most distinct enunciation. Every gesture and every posture has a foundation in the melodic phrase the orchestra is voicing. It will be seen that the emotional basis for her stage conception is in the music itself.

In late February, filming for *The Splendid Sinner* began again in the Goldwyn Studios at Fort Lee. Its storyline was evidently based partly on Mary's experiences as a nurse in France and partly on the life of Edith Cavell. The character Mary played had shot a man and gone off to war as a nurse; but she turned out to be a spy, and the Germans finally captured her and stood her before a firing squad.

One afternoon during the three weeks of shooting particularly impressed Mary. Just before filming the scene in which the Kaiser's marksmen meted out their punishment, Mary looked up and saw Goldwyn there among the props, examining every one of the guns to be sure there were no real bullets in them.[32]

But, like her film of *Thaïs*, this new venture was a fiasco. This further alienated some theatre owners who had thought they were renting a film with a pretty actress of a few years before named Mary Gardener! And again, the critics savaged the film. 'She who is gracious, lovely and full of personality on the stage,' wrote her friend Louella Parsons, 'is minus every one of the qualities on the screen'.[33] The *Chicago Record* (25 March 1918) commented, 'The picture is dressed gaudily and the story has little reason for existing save to exploit Miss Garden'; the *Philadelphia News* complained of her 'incessant posing', adding that 'the world is a bit weary of stories of fallen women'.

Nevertheless, as ever, Mary bounced back with a diversionary smoke-screen of bizarre aspirations and a rag-bag of personal quirks. 'Her favorite ambition is to sing Mephistopheles, transposed to a mezzo-soprano,' revealed the *New York Tribune* (7 April 1918). 'Mary Garden's collection of furs exceeds $150,000 in value. Roulette is a constant temptation. She is very lucky. Last summer she was decorated by the French and Serbian governments but she has always refused to sing in Berlin because she hates Germans.' Then: 'Mary Garden is known to be quite superstitious and never stages a new role without consulting a high-priced astrologer or palmist,' the *Motion* (May 1918) informed its readers. It had been an astrologer down Broadway who had told Mary she would marry in 1919: 'First there will be a husband, a big, strong, beautiful man – the man who has been waiting for me through the years – the man I have been waiting for through the years,' she revealed, then admitted to a shade of regret for a lifestyle she had rejected. 'I sometimes wish that I had never been a professional woman. I would have liked very much to have ten children. Children are so like flowers; I love to see them develop and grow. When you leave the opera house, you are lonesome with your triumphs.'[34]

* * *

June 1918 came and it was time for Mary to enjoy the lotus life of the French Riviera. She had taken an apartment in the Park Palace Hotel, Monte Carlo. Later she recalled being there in the summer, when US troops arrived on the western front. In those days, the Riviera was idyllic. 'I came to Nice for the first time in 1918 during the end of the War. I also went to Juan-les-Pins at that time. A desert. And so pretty. So deliciously silent. I have tried Deauville, Biarritz, all the supposedly chic places. What disillusion!'[35]

Not far from Monte Carlo was Beaulieu-sur-Mer, where Mary would eventually buy a villa. It was also the summer hideaway of men such as James Gordon Bennett, owner of the *New York Herald*, who died there in 1918, and Harold McCormick of the Chicago Harvester Company, who was to play an important role in Mary's career.

After a lazy summer, Mary returned to Paris in September and cabled New York that she intended to remain there for the winter. She cancelled her American movie and musical engagements – much to the dismay of Campanini who was said to be in despair over her.[36] That November, on the night of the signing of the Armistice, Mary was recognized in the Place de la Concorde by some American soldiers who asked her to sing for them. This she did, to the accompaniment of a zither played by a Chasseur Alpin.[37]

She finally returned to New York in mid-December, arriving with Theodore Roosevelt Jr, Mrs Vincent Astor, Mrs W. K. Vanderbilt and the composer, Henri Février. Février, although a serving member of the French army, had been granted leave by his government to come to Chicago with Mary to conduct his opera *Gismonda*. *Gismonda*'s première had been halted by the outbreak of war. 'Before the war all was ready for the première in Paris,' said Février. 'The contracts were signed. Garden, who interpreted *Monna Vanna*, was to sing. And then came August 1914. For four years the opera was laid aside and I was a soldier. Now I am a composer again and I have come to Chicago to direct the first performance.'[38]

When Mary sang Février's *Gismonda* before a record-breaking Auditorium audience, she dominated the entire proceedings on the stage and contributed the major share in the success of the work.[39] According to *Musical America* (30 January 1919) she made Gismonda a pulsing, passionate and thoroughly enticing lady.

> As to her singing, she colors her vocal delivery and phrases artistically. Her singing is highly intelligent, exquisitely sophisticated. But she 'scoops'. She seems to have not much middle register. She does frequent lyric intoning of irrepressible charm. She 'explodes' often on high notes. Yet the audience showed her warmly how much it liked her. The critics were sceptical but fascinated.

Other successes followed. Mary's *Cléopâtre*, compared to that of Maria Kuznetsova two years before, said Maurice Rosenfeld of the *Chicago News* (24 January 1919), was 'so immeasurably superior as to dramatic lines, as to musical coloring and as to costuming that the other conception of the role was completely obliterated'. But there were still hostile opinions being aired. The *New York Sun* (26 January 1919) commented: 'You are the tuneless singer of the world, the Queen of Parlando'; 'Why whitewash the face, paint the mouth with carmine and circle the eyes with green chalk?' asked the *Boston Transcript* (14 February 1919).

In her usual fashion, Mary unburdened herself of some privately held opinions. She admired Amelita Galli-Curci – 'Her voice I consider the most beautiful, the most wonderful I have ever heard.' About Oscar Hammerstein – 'Who indeed, if not he, was responsible for the wave of reform in the Metropolitan Opera House? Would that institution ever have engaged the services of Arturo Toscanini, (for whose genius I have the profoundest admiration), save under the goading of Oscar's activities at the Manhattan?'

One of Mary's first acts in 1919 was to donate a handbag of platinum and pearls to La Maison des Touts Petits (which she had discovered during her most recent visit to France). La Maison was run by American women in Paris for poor French children aged up to 18 months. The handbag was to be displayed in the window of Tiffany & Co. Already 5000 tickets had been distributed to be sold at $10 each – practically all sold. The winning ticket would be drawn at the Hippodrome by Mary surrounded by the Chicago Opera Company.[40]

Mary still had some large ideas. She hankered after her own company. She proposed to build an opera house in New York, a temple of music with no bel canto. It would feature staging using the ideas of Gordon Craig, without a gilded proscenium arch and using veils and lights for modern music drama. 'I have two scores complete,' she revealed in an aside, 'which I am studying now and shall create in Paris. I have two others on the way. I am going to Rome to study the new roles.'[41]

Mary appeared at the Metropolitan Opera on 25 March in a French benefit conducted by Campanini to raise funds for the reconstruction of French farms. She sang the death scene from *Cléopâtre* and the first act of *Louise*. Artur Rubinstein played; Oscar Hammerstein was in the audience. The concert itself netted over $20,000.

In late March, Mary, now at the Ritz-Carlton Hotel in New York, received a letter from the journalist and critic, James Huneker, asking for permission to interview her. She replied that it would give her real pleasure to know him and talk with him. She apologized for not having written sooner, saying she had been in bed for several days fighting a nasty *grippe* and suggested he come on 4 April.[42] Huneker duly conducted what must have been a very stimulating interview, giving Mary a copy of his book, *Overtones*. ' "Parsifal" charmed me and "Nietzsche" was divine,' Mary wrote back later, enclosing some photographs he had asked for. With the rise of fascism in Europe, Mary would later become fascinated by leaders such as Hitler and Mussolini whose photographs she assiduously pasted into her scrapbooks, as well as those of European royalty. In Huneker, Mary was to find a uniquely sympathetic critic with whom she could conduct a fruitful interchange of ideas and emotions.

A week after her interview, Mary shared the bill with Caruso, Mischa Elman and Rubinstein at a Commodore Hotel Musicale in New York, but was still suffering 'terrible agony', as she wrote to Huneker.[43] Then a surprised world woke up to read in *The New York Times* a volcanic appreciation of Mary Garden – 'Mary Garden: Superwoman' by James G. Huneker, full of the most extravagant animal metaphors. While it is generally thought that the language and imagery in Huneker's appreciation were his own, there seems little doubt, judging from Mary's own words in *The Forum* (April 1919), that he was heavily influenced by her arresting ways of expression and her own dynamic sentiments. Taking a lead from Freud and Nietzsche and calling upon the Buddhist concept of Karma, Huneker explored what he saw as Mary's superwoman status, her irresistible metamorphoses, her multiple personalities and her complexes. He penned the most memorable of all interpretations of the phenomenon known as Mary Garden, all of it based not only on his long familiarity with her art – from her earliest performances in Paris – but also from his intensive interview with Mary the week before.

'Even maternal intuition could not have forseen such a swan swimming triumphantly through the troubled waters of life,' wrote Huneker.

> A swan, do I say? A condor, an eagle, a peacock, a nightingale, a panther. She has studied Sarah Bernhardt and Yvette Guilbert – the perfect flowering of the *diseuse* – but she pins her faith to the effortless art of Eleonora Duse. Should an actor leave nothing to chance or should he improvise on the spur of high emotions? I still believe that she sided with Coquelin. She is eminently cerebral. Miss Garden may not weigh her American side but it is the very skeleton of her artistic organism.[44]

Shortly before leaving for Paris that summer, Mary wrote to Huneker, who was seriously ill: 'I hope that your health is better – and that you will enjoy everything that is beautiful until we meet again.'[45]

* * *

'I am a woman,' announced Mary in April 1919, 'and I accept the responsibility and the glittering opportunities. If I had been a man, I might have been a hunter. Music performs this miracle in the imagination, it restores the emotions of the ages. The word 'opera' is really obsolete. It is like the hand-organ, a name for worn-out music. I sometimes go to the theatre, and I find the play emotionally insufficient, because its substance is robbed of the supreme emotional language of the world. Music electrifies the dramatic pulse of life.'[46]

Yet again Mary came to public attention over a legal matter, when she was sued by dressmakers for various sums which she had omitted to pay, including a boy's costume of red broadcloth at $221 (*Le jongleur de Notre Dame*) and a white Grecian gown (*Thaïs*) at $262. A suit had been brought against her in the Supreme Court of the State of New York by Lucille Limited of New York and Paris (otherwise known as Lady Duff Gordon) for gowns and accessories to the value of $2,708 plus $400 for Lady Duff Gordon's personal designer's fee.[47]

But soon it was summer and Mary was again in Europe. By October she was preparing to appear at Paris's new Théâtre Lyrique (the former Vaudeville) in Massenet's *Cléopâtre*. Robert Kemp from *La Liberté* (22 October 1919) was present at one of the rehearsals of *Cléopâtre* directed by P.B. Gheusi, and he described the scene with great immediacy. Gheusi was wearing a flat felt hat and a voluminous cape against the cold. Maurice Renaud was playing the emperor Marc Antoine in a jacket, with a soft hat over his silver hair, his gestures larger than life, his voice resonant. Cléopâtre had her head hidden in a little cherry-red bonnet, with a shimmering grey cloak dropping down as far as her small white gaiters. She carried a walking-stick in her hand and played with it like a toy. From time to time she twirled the stick.

'When she is Garden,' said Kemp,

> she is agitated; she spins around; she squashes her handkerchief into her face; she drums out a Spanish dance with her heels. She is the most vibrant, the most ener-vated personality in the world. But as soon as she returns to being Cléopâtre again, she draws herself up perfectly still, defying Marc Antoine as he circles her like a wild beast. Suddenly, he snatches her brutally into his arms and kisses her.

'Mary Garden was a marvellous Cléopâtre,' enthused Antoine Banès in *Le Figaro* (30 October 1919):

> She conceived and played the role as a great tragedienne, often recalling her unforgettable interpretation of *La traviata*. However, the tessitura did not sit well with her voice. It was too low, although ingeniously transposed in certain delicate passages. In this role her voice suffers from a lack of volume. When the vocal line goes down below the treble clef, all at once we can't hear Miss Garden any more – it seems as if she has lost her voice. Happily, this was only a momentary phenom-enon.

After the performance, Louis Payen, the elderly librettist of *Cléopâtre*, published a letter in *Le Figaro* (1 November 1919), thanking the director and the cast for a worthy realization of Massenet's opera.

*   *   *

Mary returned to America in mid-November, direct from Roquebrune-Cap-Martin near Monte Carlo. With her, she brought a gown of 1000 mirrors on a background of gold and silver cloth. She had designed it herself, based on an East Indian model. Alighting from the train at Chicago station, she uncharacteristically hit out at the assembled reporters and photographers with her cane. She commented that the fact that Chicago was dry wouldn't bother her at all if it weren't for her French maid, who had had to drink water for the first time in her life. On the subject of jazz, she added: 'I like it. I've got all the jazz band records in my music box. Maybe, some day, some one will write a jazz opera.'[48]

Appearing at the Auditorium in *Le jongleur de Notre-Dame*, Mary once more showed her ability to submerge her personality in the role she played. 'Her walk is so different from that in any other character,' wrote W. L. Hubbard in the *Chicago Tribune* (4 December 1919), 'the awkward boyish movement of hands peculiarly sensitive and expressive; the touching together of palms or tips of fingers as though psychically grasping thought which the mind was doubtfully seeking; the eloquence of eyes voicing forth every process of the mind; the parting of lips and the sudden act of swallow-ing when deeply interested.'

Off-stage, in her personal life, Mary occasionally revealed her naivety, even an immaturity. Merle Armitage, an associate of her tour manager, Charles L. Wagner, wrote that:

> evidence of her inexperience was her fascination with erotics as a subject of conversation. These discussions, which I encouraged as monologues, are very cherished memories. Her questions were often embarrassing until I realised with some astonishment that this sophisticated woman was actually as ignorant of most facts of life as a little girl. If this disclosure is protested by those who claim to have a different version, I am prepared to stand my ground.[49]

At a concert in Columbus, Ohio, Mary first wore her gown of 1000 mirrors, made in Paris out of huge rhinestones. Tossing her head back, she walked straight into the centre of the footlights, flashed her celebrated smile and announced: 'Well, here I am!' The applause was deafening.[50] Mary's differences with Columbus in the past had clearly been forgotten.

But 1919 ended on a note of great sadness, both for Mary and for opera in Chicago. Six days before Christmas, Cleofonte Campanini died from pneumonia. His coffin was brought to the Auditorium, placed centre-stage, surrounded by flowers and flanked by the scenery of the Transformation Scene from *Parsifal*. After a moving musical service, the public filed past the coffin for three hours and then the curtain was brought slowly down. At his funeral in Holy Name Cathedral, Galli-Curci and Rosa Raisa sang with the entire Chicago Opera chorus. His death was to usher in a period of turmoil and agitation for those he left behind.

Notes

1.   *New York World* quoted in *Musical Courier*, 17 February 1915.
2.   Interviewed by the *Daily Telegraph* and quoted in *The New York Times*, 27 April 1915.
3.   *Rochester Times*, 1 May 1915.
4.   Eugene Goosens (1951), *Overtures and Beginners*, London: Methuen and Co.
5.   *New York Sun*, 9 December 1915.
6.   *Chicago Tribune*, 6 June 1916.
7.   *Chicago Post*, 23 July 1916.
8.   Elisabeth Marbury (1923), *My Crystal Ball*, New York: Boni and Liveright, p. 287.
9.   *Chicago Herald*, 20 August 1916.
10. *Chicago Post*, 13 January 1917.
11. See Appendix 3.
12. *New York Telegraph*, 4 March 1917.
13. *Cleveland Plain Dealer*, 2 March 1917.
14. *New York Telegraph*, Billy Rose Theatre Collection, Robinson Locke Collection of Dramatic Scrapbooks, NYPL.
15. *New York Sun*, 8 April 1917.
16. *Dramatic Mirror*, 18 August 1917.

17. *New York Telegraph*, 11 September 1917.
18. *New York Tribune*, 16 September 1917.
19. *Philadelphia Public Ledger*, 23 September 1917.
20. *Photoplay Journal* for January 1918, p. 20.
21. *Brooklyn Eagle*, 20 September 1924.
22. Third of series of six articles for *The World Magazine*, 11 November 1917.
23. *The World Magazine*, 9 December 1917.
24. Ibid.
25. *New York Telegraph*, December 1917, NYPL.
26. *Philadelphia Leader*, 19 January 1918.
27. *New York Telegraph*, 19 January 1918.
28. *New York Telegraph*, April 1918, NYPL.
29. *Chicago Herald*, 31 December 1917.
30. Unidentified clipping, NYPL, Billy Rose Theatre Collection, Robison Locke Collection of Scrapbooks 1856–1920, vols. 224–234, Series 1.
31. *New York World*, 9 February 1918.
32. Scott Berg (1990), *Goldwyn – A Biography*, London: Sphere, p. 75.
33. *Chicago Record*, 26 March 1918.
34. *Philadelphia Journal*, 10 February 1918.
35. *L'Éclaireur*, 15 August 1926.
36. *Trim Topics*, 26 September 1918, NYPL.
37. *The New York Times*, 17 December 1918.
38. *Chicago News*, 20 December 1918.
39. *Chicago News*, 15 January 1919.
40. *Trim Topics*, 2 January 1919.
41. *The Sun*, 23 February 1919.
42. Letter 30, March 1919, Dartmouth College Library, Hanover, New Hampshire.
43. Letter 11, April 1919, Dartmouth College Library, Hanover, New Hampshire.
44. *The New York Times*, 13 April 1919.
45. Letter 22, April 1919, Dartmouth College Library, Hanover, New Hampshire.
46. A Mary Garden Mood, *The Forum*, April 1919.
47. *Musical Courier*, 29 May 1919.
48. *Chicago Tribune*, 20 November 1919.
49. Merle Armitage (1964), *Accent on Life*, Ames: The Iowa State University Press, p. 60.
50. Charles L. Wagner (1940), *Seeing Stars*, New York: G.P. Putnam's Sons, p. 205.

11 Directa: 1920–1922

The chief problem facing the Chicago Opera Association at the beginning of 1920 was in the administration of the company. Mary Garden herself was initially not forthcoming on the subject; in reply to the question 'Are you going to be head of the Chicago Opera Association to succeed Cleofonte Campanini?', Mary raged at her interlocutor: 'What do you care?' The *Chicago Tribune* (9 January 1920) scented blood.

> There were three explosions in operatic circles yesterday. First, the announcement in a New York paper that Mary Garden would succeed Campanini. Second, the oil magnate, Bernard Ulrich, formerly connected with the Chicago Grand Opera, expressed support for her, saying: 'That woman could run a pickle factory, a narrow-gauge railroad, a corporation counsel's office, and a steel strike with more success than any ten men in the country.' Third, 'Bang – crash!' It was our Mary. She denied all possibility.

Mary had the advantage of a powerful backer and close friend waiting in the wings. It was reported that she enjoyed an exceptional friendship with J. Ogden Armour, director of the meat-packing house of Armour & Company and financial power-behind-the-throne of the Chicago Opera Association'.[1] Merle Armitage, concert administrator who grew to know her well, would echo the sentiment: 'Only one man, J. Ogden Armour, ever really intrigued her, and, insofar as she could love any person other than her immediate family, she certainly loved him.'[2] In her autobiography, Mary would allude to her love-affair with a married businessman whose name she would not disclose. The personal details she reveals, however, all point indisputably to Armour, a man whom she tried to encourage to appreciate the arts but who, finally, succumbed to the secret misery of alcoholism.[3]

It would have been understandable if an affinity of sorts existed between them. Armour was a handsome, warm-hearted man who, at that time, enjoyed a great hard-earned fortune. He, in turn, might well have admired in Mary a woman who had risen to the heights by her own efforts. Armour, whose wealth was once estimated at $100 million, had first met Mary during her second year in Chicago (1911–12). On one occasion, according to Mary, he followed her to Kansas City where he also had a large interest in the Kansas City Traction Company. In Louis Biancolli's biography, Mary recalls that her secret admirer invited her to lunch at one of his clubs, to his house many miles out of Chicago and to his London apartment. Armour belonged to eight Chicago clubs, including the Arts Club; he had a house in the country – Mellody Farm at Lake Forest and an apartment in the Carlton Hotel, London. He had no great appreciation of music; work was his recreation and he was shortly to lose much of his fortune in the Crash.

The matter of the directorship unresolved, Mary and the rest of the Company transferred to the Lexington for their annual New York season. When she appeared in *L'amore dei tre re* the *New York Evening Sun* (27 January 1920) was dumbfounded by the anomalies in her performance.

> Her voice remains in constant error – and is yet a constant wonder. She is always aware of the picturization she makes – but what pictures they are! She is harsh, she is hard in her vitality and beauty of conception – but the conception cuts the deeper thereby into the memory. She clothed her Fiora in an orange scarlet which, when she stood upon the battlements, seared the open sky behind her with a swaying fire. Her love expressed itself in prostrations to the ground, in such suppleness of the back that her lover crushed her into contortions and almost topsy-turvy bliss. The oracle confined its message to the dashes, dots, cabalistic curves and heliographic flashes which spell Mary Garden.

An historic reconciliation took place on 27 January. Mary sang *Pelléas et Mélisande* to an audience which included the librettist Maurice Maeterlinck, once the sworn enemy of Mary and Claude Debussy. The critic Katharine Lane wrote of Mary's having 'the delicate haunting perfection of moonlight. It is as if you watched her, with Debussy's music woven into her long pale-gold hair and her fluttering draperies, seeing her always through the mist of a cobweb.'[4] She watched Maeterlinck sitting in a stage box listening for the first time to his beautiful lines being sung before an audience. At each curtain call Mary waved the applause toward the author until he finally rose and bowed, looking a little as if he shared the uncertainty of his characters about happiness.

The film producer Samuel Goldwyn also remembered the occasion. Maeterlinck had been signed for the Goldwyn Company and one of Goldwyn's publicity men sat near him in his box. He reported that 'from the large placid face those ethereal strains which Debussy wove about his own play drew not a sign of response'.[5] After the performance, Mary, Maeterlinck and his young wife were photographed together in a pose of strained civility. But two days later Mary received a warm letter of congratulation from Maeterlinck. 'I saw many things which I had never perceived or which I had forgotten. Like every great artist, more than any other perhaps, you have the genius to add to a work or to bring to life in it those things which I omitted or had left in a state of sleep.'[6]

After singing in Boston and a number of other cities, Mary left for Europe and spent the summer and early autumn in the south of France, returning to Paris in mid-October. Early November saw Mary in concert at Des Moines. She again dazzled the capacity audience with her now famous gown of 1000 mirrors. Accompanied by Isaac Van Grove, she sang 'Triste ritorno', written by her Monte Carlo coach, Richard Barthélemy.

For her forthcoming American season, Mary revealed, she would sing nothing but French works. She pledged to give the receipts of her first performance in Chicago to the French charitable tubercular children movement. Merle Armitage described the impact that Mary could now make on her audience, recalling an evening at Louisville when:

> we packed in a cheering, enthusiastic crowd of seven thousand. Garden, sensing the importance of that event, staged a coruscating show. All the finesse, the nuance of her artistry was employed, but so was the showmanship in ample measure. She made her entrance in a gown of crystal mirrors, designed without a back, and carrying the largest ostrich feather fan ever seen this side of the Atlantic. Before the concert started, she strode across the stage, giving that eager, expectant audience a lesson in the sinuous charm of plastic form – literally shocking them to attention.[7]

But there was a psychological price for her straining for success. Also on the programme was the young cellist, Gutia Casini. 'There was something perverse in her amazing energy,' recalled Armitage, 'and in her fierce jealousy (only partly concealed) of new and younger performers. It was fantastic that a career of unparalleled brilliance, of accomplishment seldom achieved by a performer – a career singular in its creativeness – had resulted in so little satisfaction and serenity. Only applause continued to have the power of even momentary satisfaction.'[8]

From her eyrie at the Blackstone in Chicago, Mary wrote in December 1920 to James Huneker in New York, now in bad health and living in reduced circumstances. Huneker had just sent her his novel, *Painted Veils*, which had been published that spring. 'It is immeasurably nice of you to have thought of me and I appreciate it more than I can tell you', she told him.[9] *Painted Veils*, along with a short story by Willa Cather, entitled 'Scandal',[10] drew obliquely on Garden's supposed double-life of sexual experimentation which had gained wide currency in America. Both works helped fuel the belief that Mary led a life of secret depravity; Mary's reputation off-stage was inadvertently tarnished by both the novel and the short story. However, from the friendly tone of the letters between Mary and Huneker it is obvious that it cannot have been Huneker's intention to implicate Mary in anything of a scandalous nature and Mary took no umbrage at anything Huneker had written.

Both literary works could be called 'faction' – constructs which weave true incidents taken from a number of biographical sources (other than

Mary Garden) into a fictional whole. Cather's Scottish heroine, Kitty Ayrshire, for example, is probably loosely based on Garden, while others in the same collection of short stories make use of the careers of Lillian Nordica, Olive Fremstad and Geraldine Farrar.

Huneker's protagonist, Istar, is also based on the public image of Mary Garden. Many of the incidents and personality traits in the book are factual, but they are yoked together in new combinations to create characters that are wholly composite. The identification of Istar with Mary may have come about because readers may have associated *Painted Veils* with Huneker's overblown and slightly decadent *New York Times* 'Superwoman' review the previous year. It was also widely believed that Mary and James Huneker were both involved in the scandalous dinner party with naked women depicted in *Painted Veils*.

This notorious event, known as the 'Girl-in-the-Pie' party, was given by the Wall Street millionaire, Henry W. Poor, in honour of the sculptor Augustus Saint-Gaudens in a photographer's studio on Sixteenth Street in New York. Huneker admitted to the critic Burton Rascoe that he had suppressed one detail – a monstrous phallus modelled in clay by Saint-Gaudens.[11] The chronology of events detailed in the book exonerates Mary completely. While *Painted Veils* had been written in 1919, the real-life 'Girl-in-the-Pie' dinner took place twenty years before in 1899. But Mary had left America in late May 1896 and did not return again until 26 October 1907. She cannot therefore have been present at a dinner in New York at the same time as she was in Paris struggling to overcome the withdrawal of the Mayers' financial support. Moreover, it is clear that Mary had only met Huneker for the first time on 4 April 1919.[12] The subsequent correspondence also throws serious doubts on the suggestion that Garden had ever interrupted Sibyl Sanderson and Huneker *in flagrante delicto* in Paris in September 1899. Huneker's most recent biographer, Arnold T. Schwab, thinks it unlikely that Huneker was even in Paris at that time.[13]

*   *   *

As the bells pealed in the new year of 1921, a thunderbolt struck Chicago. Gino Marinuzzi resigned as musical director of the Chicago Opera Association. Mary, who was suffering from fatigue and illness, was immediately sucked into the resulting conflict. 'Too ill to fight back', as one correspondent put it,[14] Mary, who had been mentioned frequently for the position of artistic director of the Company, was made the target of yet another personal attack.

Dorothy Jardon, an American soprano in the company two years previously and now engaged for vaudeville, was the latest member of the 'anvil chorus'. She gave an interview in New York, in which she declared that

Mary Garden's jealousy had forced her to quit the Chicago company. She insisted Mary was not only jealous of the role assigned to her, but even resented her clothes.

Then a second opponent stepped into the ring in the form of the soprano Ganna Walska, wife of millionaire Alexander Smith Cochran of New York. She had quit Chicago suddenly just as she was about to appear in the title role of *Zazà*. The Polish dilettante was said to have been engaged for the part by Harold F. McCormick, chairman of the board of directors and principal financial backer of the opera. McCormick was known to be a close personal friend of Alexander Cochran. Walska, after a preliminary rehearsal with the company, left Chicago hurriedly. She made no explanations. Her departure left room for the wildest speculations, among them, that her husband was jealous because of the story that she preferred stage kisses to his. Her fellow-artists, however, were reported to have said that the real reason for her hasty flight was that her voice was not large enough to fill the opera house. Gino Marinuzzi, then the artistic director, was said to have asked her to let out her voice, and when she could not do so, refused to let her appear. Still other reports had it that Miss Walska's flight from Chicago was due to differences with Mary. Unsurprisingly, Walska's friends insisted that Mary's 'jealousies' were to blame.

For some time there had been other troubles in the Chicago Grand Opera Association. Ben H. Atwell, former journalist, now tour manager, and currently the dean of theatrical publicity-men, had left Chicago almost a physical wreck because of overwork produced by disputes within the Company. Dorothy Jardon, seizing her moment, fired off a volley of accusation. 'I had a five year contract with the Opera Association, and I cancelled the three remaining years this season because when Campanini, the director, died last year (when I was a member of the company), I realised my future with that organisation was dead also. I've got no angel or multimillionaire to buy my costumes,' she said in a guarded reference to Walska's husband, Alexander Smith Cochran and, perhaps, Mary's friendship with T. Ogden Armour.[15]

When Walska's departure was rapidly followed by the sudden resignation of Gino Marinuzzi as artistic director, gossiping tongues worked rapidly and the 'outlanders' were particularly vigorous in their mutterings about Mary and her influence in the affairs of the Company. Marinuzzi was said to have grown tired of 'temperamentalism' and to be suffering from insomnia as a result of the constant bickering. The story whispered around the Auditorium that gained the greatest credence was that the Walska incident was the last straw.

After Marinuzzi's resignation, suggestions were once again made that Mary Garden should become director of the company. Suddenly her appointment as director of the Chicago Opera Association was made public on 14 January. Telegrams and cablegrams wishing Mary success began pouring into the offices of the Opera Association. Mary denied herself to would-be interviewers and, when demands for statements became more numerous, stationed two bulky guards at the doors of her suite in the Blackstone. The main question being asked among the artists was 'Can she be both the artist and the impresario?'[16]

In response, Mary made a statement to the press outlining her future plans:

> I will surround myself with the greatest people. I will pay my singers at their real value. With such artists as Galli-Curci, Muratore, Titta Ruffo, Baklanoff and Vanni-Marcoux I would have no discussion as to the fee they demanded, as artists who draw are the cheapest in the long run. Then I would fill in with good people but I would not pay them fancy salaries. I do not believe in a star regime but in good ensembles. I would have an understudy for every role. Then if a singer were ill there would be no change of opera.
>
> I will give 50 per cent of operas in Italian, 35 per cent in French and 15 per cent in English for the present, until Wagner and other big German composers' works will be presented in the language intended, when I will treat them all alike – 33 per cent Italian, French and German. When good opera comes to be written by American and English composers I will have their work performed in English.[17]

The day that she was appointed director, Mary sang *Monna Vanna*; after the second act she gave an interview in her dressing-room.

> All this new power was placed in my hands this morning and I feel I am greatly honoured. The first telegram I opened was from Madame Galli-Curci conveying her congratulations. I replied that we hoped we would have her glorious voice and charming personality with us a long time. Then I came here and found a letter signed by every person in the company, assuring me that I had their undivided and loyal support. I am taking this big work on for one year and if they like me, we shall go ahead and I shall be happy. If they don't like me, I shall have to say good-bye.
>
> In the business offices I shall put nothing but American business men. Foreign voices, of course, on the stage, but the only voice in business affairs will be an American voice.[18]

It was widely expected that Charles L. Wagner, concert manager for John McCormack, Frances Alda, Mary, and many others, would take charge of the company's business affairs.

Chicago welcomed their new *directa-directrix* with open arms: 'Well! It's our Mary now with a vengeance,' enthused Karleton Hackett. 'Miss Garden knows Chicago and she knows our operatic situation, for she has been identified with it since the beginning. Everybody knows her. It is not like the importation of a stranger, for she belongs to us.'[19] But there was private apprehension in the dark corridors of the Auditorium; the theatre had the aspect of a morgue. Singers, passing each other, glanced up questioningly, each wondering if the other had some inside news. Especially fearful were the Italian singers: 'Ah, I fear it will mean French domination,' they whispered. 'The table is turned – no more the Italian.' But for public consumption they expressed their support for Mary. 'I think the appointment of Mary Garden is a splendid one,' confirmed Mary's intimate friend, J. Ogden Armour. 'It should be a good thing for the opera.'[20]

'Opera is opera,' announced Mary, 'but not with a $300,000 deficit – that's what we must wipe out. I shall give more repetitions and not attempt offering a different opera every night of the season. We have just given thirty-five operas in ten weeks and as a singer, I know what a strain that means for those who sing so many different roles.'[21]

Mary announced that the appointment of an executive director for the Chicago Opera Association had been indefinitely postponed. The position had been offered to Charles L. Wagner, who had refused it. Herbert Johnson denied he was to be reappointed as business manager: 'I have had magnificent support from the artists all the way through, but I am not going to remain here as executive director.'[22] It was said by insiders that the sudden departure of Mr Wagner followed soon after the arrival of a stranger from El Paso, Texas, who came to Chicago to prevent the appointment.

For the record, *The Musical Courier* (20 January 1921) was quick to point out that Mary was not the first female director of an opera company. Emma Carelli (the singer and wife of Walter Mocchi, a leading Italian impresario), had been in charge of Il Teatro Costanzi in Rome for a number of years. What was unique was for a singer to become director while still in mid-career.

Already, another season in Chicago had been guaranteed by H. F. McCormick and his wife. Mary had agreed to direct the artistic course of this period, the 1921–22 season, receiving only her usual fee when she sang. She confirmed the appointment of George M. Spangler as her new business manager. It had been hinted in the West that Spangler's selection was an indication that business men generally would take a hand in continuing the Chicago Opera Association after the McCormick guarantee expired.

* * *

The Chicago Opera Association's season at the Manhattan Opera House in New York followed. The Manhattan had been having a gloomy time; Mrs Oscar Hammerstein had been quoted as saying that the unjust demands of stage-hands for overtime pay were making opera impossible and unless these demands ceased, she was prepared to turn the Manhattan into a soap factory. Only the annual six-week Chicago Opera Association's season and the dancing of Pavlova would ensure the survival of the Manhattan until the spring.

At the Manhattan, Mary was a still centre in a turning world. Frederick N. Sard captured the phenomenon in print.

Around her there may seethe men, women, letters, telephone calls, instructions, countermands and engagements; in all the fret of activity intensified by her dynamic force, she remains the center of control, with the cerebral calm of the Brahmin. She is crisp, soft, harsh, terse, staccato, tense, managerial – but always the woman. Her stage presence is magnetic; behind her desk she is phenomenal. In the rear of the boxes at the Manhattan Opera House in a converted dressing-room, is her improvised little office, furnished simply.

It is 1:15, and at 2:00 she is scheduled to rehearse *Monna Vanna*, in which she sings the name part. In the interval she answers a dozen questions, decides on the bill for the ensuing week, makes up her appointment calendar, and is being interviewed. Enter the stage-director, noiselessly, with score in hand. She motions to me. I follow. We walk out onto the stage. There are Muratore and Baklanoff, in severe civilian clothes, primed for action. Polacco, the new conductor-in-chief, in work-jacket, gesticulates and analyses a phrase. She takes in the whole psychology of a scene with one line of her body, the line of her walk. When she dominates a situation through intellect, she walks from a line drawn from the head; if she is to be 'spirituelle', the line of the walk starts from the top plane of the chest; when it is love, she walks straight from the heart; when it is passion, she sinks the line lower than the hip and prowls destructively.[23]

As general director, Mary had charge of the affairs of the Chicago Opera Association (both artistic and executive), under the executive committee.[24] How did she cope? 'I keep my work well-organised so that my artistic powers will not be impaired,' was her answer. 'I rise at nine, devote an hour to breathing exercises, then an hour to vocal study, but only exercises. Then down to the theatre for three hours for business, including rehearsals. Then home about five o'clock and rest till seven. I dine well and then go down to the opera house to see how things are going – that is, on nights when I do not sing. Here I have been singing three times a week and by strict regimen I am able to get through with all my work.'[25]

Again, her *Monna Vanna* was a triumph. 'Miss Garden sang in fabulous voice last night,' wrote Pitts Sanborn. 'She poured forth tones that were unalloyed gold and her art of song might be set down in capitals.'[26] But already there was speculation. 'Can Mary Garden hold both ends of her job?' wondered Benjamin De Casseres. 'Will her mind, her beauty and her voice stand the double pounding? She can even up some old scores – there are rumors about Miss Walska and Dorothy Jardon. For Mary Garden is Will incarnate – Maestro Mary.'[27] All was not necessarily under Mary's control, however; one of Mary's first acts as directa (a title she chose herself) was to lose Galli-Curci to the Metropolitan.

A few weeks later, during a performance of *Manon*, she received word of the French government's decision to create her a Knight of the Légion d'Honneur.

* * *

By March 1921, Mary was executive head of five opera companies. This development was made known when she announced that, under manager George Spangler, four new incorporated opera companies had evolved from the parent organization: the Othello Opera Company, the Lohengrin, the Traviata and the Monna Vanna. Travelling as five distinct companies for transportation convenience, the Chicago Opera Association now started from New York on a transcontinental tour that would be among the most expensive ever undertaken in America. The financial backers of the company would be called upon to make payments of $130,000 to artists in the event of non-appearances in roles to which they were entitled under their contracts.

Spangler was unhappy. 'On Washington's Birthday alone we turned away business amounting to $10,000,' he complained. 'And the tremendous cost of giving opera makes it impossible to break even, even with packed houses.'[28] And there was more trouble at the Manhattan. A dispute over trivia (payment of $125 for paper cups and paper towels) between Mary and Mrs Hammerstein nearly led to the lease for the following year not being renewed. Then the greatest baritone in the world, Titta Ruffo, had not announced whether or not he would sing the following year. It was suspected he was flirting with the Met. There was a quarrel with Rosa Raisa over a story in *The New York Tribune* which claimed that Mary had said Raisa was one of her worst problems because the Polish prima donna was ruining her splendid voice by singing not wisely but too well. Mary was supposed to have remarked: 'This season Raisa's voice already has begun to go back and I cannot accurately foresee its failings of next year and I dread them.'[29] However, Raisa's lawyer, whom she had retained to demand a retraction, announced that Mary had denied she ever said anything of the kind about his client. To prove that the incident was closed, it was made known that Rosa Raisa's engagement with the company had been continued for another season at the same salary.[30]

Just how much nationality played a part in opera was revealed when Mary explained her motives for taking over the company. She observed:

> Italians are gobbling up the Chicago Opera, and I decided to become director. They were trying to make an Italian company out of it. In 54 nights they sang only four operas in French. All the rest were Italian. They were trying to establish an Italian musical monarchy in my company. I took the directorship to save the Chicago Opera Association for America. Look at the Metropolitan Opera House. Absolutely Italian from roof to cellar. Why shouldn't it be American? She concluded: America must have a conservatoire of opera.[31]

With Harold McCormick's help, Mary had fixed on a plan to democratize membership of the Association's investors by finding 500 guarantors at $1000 each for five years. This would 'transfer the sponsorship of grand opera in Chicago from the social register to the telephone book.'[32]

During her tour with the Chicago Opera, Mary kept up her creature comforts; she retained a nucleus of personal staff: her secretary, Muriel Draper, her sister, Mrs Edward Walsh, and her personal representative, H. E. Potter, formerly of the secret service. When she arrived in El Paso, she asked to be chauffeured from the station in her favourite car – a Peerless.

Just how much planning went into erecting the stage for a touring company was described in El Paso by H. W. Beatty, technical director for the Chicago Opera Association. 'We practically rebuild every stage upon which our company appears. We carry with us everything we need, our own scenery, ropes and rigging for scene shifting, our own stage-lighting system. We ask nothing but the theater and a bare, unlighted stage.'[33]

Mary still disclosed moments of wild ambition and imagination. To El Paso newsmen she declared: 'I am going to get four horses, three good friends, ride through Texas, New Mexico, Arizona and up to Wyoming and make love to every sheriff that I meet on the way!'[34] In early April she left El Paso to cross the river to Juarez in Mexico. Mary was thrilled to see the old bull-ring, where she had herself photographed. 'Oh, if I could only be Carmen in such surroundings as these,' she exclaimed. She viewed with passionate interest the bullet-holes in the adobe houses left as a relic of Pancho Villa's entry into the city. Next, the touring party stopped at a gambling-hall. The band played a selection from *Carmen* as Mary took her seat at the roulette-table. One of the souvenirs that she carried away from Juarez was black Mexican cigarettes. 'Won't these be wonderful for *Carmen*? I must use them tonight in the opera.' She said she had never had as good a time since she left her villa at Monte Carlo.[35]

Mary was back in Chicago in late May, where she was presented with the Cross of the Légion d'Honneur by the French vice-consul in acknowledgement of her services to French music.

*   *   *

Her summer was spent as usual on the Riviera. She met with the Cole Porters whom she had previously advised to holiday there. The Porters entertained in a large, vine-covered villa they had rented at La Garoupe near the still-undefiled beach area of Antibes.

Part of July was spent in Paris seeking voices for the Chicago Opera Company. She told the press that although she expected to create the title role in *La ville morte*, she had also chosen the work of a Hungarian composer. French opera-lovers, somewhat xenophobically, were especially critical of this latter decision as they complained that the excellent French score (by Nadia Boulanger and Raoul Pugno) surely deserved all her attention.[36]

As she left Cherbourg for New York in mid-October, a Papal Blessing sped on its way to meet her.[37] Stepping off the *Aquitania* at New York, she declared somewhat controversially: 'If I am married, I shall certainly not live with my husband. We shall live apart.'[38] Told that the McCormicks, supporters of the Chicago Opera Association, were living under separate roofs, she reiterated: 'That doesn't mean anything. Why, if I had a husband, I'd live under a separate roof, and only let him come around when I wanted him. My horoscope says I am to be married in 1924. I'm always looking over my men acquaintances and wondering if he is to be the one.'[39] She continued: 'By the way, who has been divorced since I sailed?'

On 11 November, Mary made Chicago history by speaking some of the first words ever broadcast from the Auditorium on Chicago radio. 'My God, but it's dark in here!' she said on radio station KYW. With others, she had been asked to participate in a test of the transmitter and was standing on the stage of the Auditorium inside a tent, linked to the transmitter by a telephone line; the area was lit only by a single bare light bulb.

Preparing to sing *Salome* in late December, Mary showed that her old mastery of public relations had not left her. 'One brilliant, stimulating morning we arrived in Chicago,' wrote her assistant tour manager, Merle Armitage.

> Garden decided on a walk before taking a taxi to her hotel. Two policemen, handsome fellows mounted on sorrel mares, recognized Garden, saluted, dismounted and walked over to shake hands. 'We're glad you're back in town, Miss Garden,' they said. She gave them a very friendly greeting.
>
> That noon, when the inevitable reporters arrived for interviews, Garden made next day's headlines with the following statement: 'This morning I saw two of the finest-looking men I've ever seen. Is there anything handsomer than a Chicago policeman? I might marry one some day. One could do a lot worse.' Only those who knew the inside story guessed the double motive of those remarks. Ten years before, agitation from the blue-noses had forced the police to ban a performance of *Salome*. It was, they said, too frank, much too erotic. But this season when *Salome* returned to the Chicago Opera repertoire, the police changed their minds.[40]

Around this time, the Russian composer Sergei Prokofiev had also arrived to conduct rehearsals of his opera, *The Love of Three Oranges*. He had been delighted that an artist of Mary's standing had agreed to put on the work but rehearsals proved to be difficult. He recalled that 'Mary Garden turned out to be a director who liked to make generous gestures but who was chiefly concerned with her own roles and was never available when wanted.'[41]

Additional trouble was brewing for Mary from a new and unexpected direction. The French Consul in Chicago wrote a long letter of complaint to the President of the Council at the Ministry of Foreign Affairs in Paris:

> The question of the Chicago Opera is too important for me to neglect informing the Ministry about what is happening. There have only been five French artists here this year, one of which is M. Grovlez, the conductor. M. Grovlez is a

composer who is well-known and held in esteem. He has been a conductor at the Paris Opéra for seven years. An outstanding artist, Miss Garden engaged him during the summer, ostensibly to conduct French works. Yet, I had to intervene to make the Directa of the Chicago Opera give him a work to conduct. For six weeks out of ten, he has not held the baton; the Italian conductor, Sr Polacco taking everything with the undisguised consent of the Directa.

With Mary Garden, from whom we had the right to expect better, the interests of French music are in bad hands. During this season not a single new French work has been performed. The only one would have been M. Grovlez' ballet. People say to me: 'There is no theatre in the world with a repertoire such as ours.'

I agree, there is quantity. They multiply the premières of works which never appear again. There are not enough rehearsals and the gaps in performances are often lamentable.

How I regret that we decorated Mary Garden, whose name I put forward. We should have asked, as soon as she was appointed Directa, that the decoration was postponed until she gave us proof of her goodwill! There have been no such proofs. I do not know if she will still be Directa next year or even if there will still be a Chicago Opera. All the subscriptions needed have not been collected.

What I want, in any case, is that our French artists and the Beaux-Arts directorate make it known at the Chicago Opera, by the means they have at their disposal, that French Art and French music is something infinitely respectable and that the situation of the latter is such that we cannot accept that it is relegated to the second division and treated as it has been in the season which is about to close.[42]

At the same time a writer of poison-pen letters, who had terrorized a number of wealthy society women in Chicago, threatened Mary's life. Mary received a box containing a revolver and six cartridges. The letter writer said that she retained three cartridges for use on Mary and 'hoped soon to see her body floating down the Chicago river'. The only comment Mary would make when asked about the incident was, 'Why, the pig'. She personally reported the case to the Chief of Police Morris. The police had already been working for several weeks on the letters, about a dozen in all, and were convinced they had been written by a woman. Some repeated gossip, others carried threats. When reporters called, Mary was resting from rehearsals of *Salome*. 'Some wretched person sent me a horrid box with a pistol and bullets,' she said. 'I don't know why they picked on me.' The bullets, according to Chief Morris, were cut dum-dum fashion.[43]

The first performance of *Salome* that year was branded by the critics as 'unclean', 'obscene', 'immoral', 'vulgar' and 'an exhibition of a girl demented by passion'.[44] Storms of protest from scores of people, headed by Edith Rockefeller McCormick, led to Mary cancelling all future performances of *Salome* for the season in Chicago.

Replying to questions over whether Mary would continue as director, Samuel Insull, head of the new Civic Opera Association, declared in a statement that she positively would direct the Chicago Opera the following year and 'no foreigner will be allowed to interfere with the company's welfare'.

He was commenting on the recent resignation of the tenor Lucien Muratore and reports that other singers might revolt against Mary's management. Insull explained that Mary had already been elected director of the company for the next year, but intimated that her contract covered her singing only.

Mary sang the season's farewell on 21 January 1922 without her chief conductor, Polacco, who had refused to conduct. The story was that Polacco, whom Muratore claimed at that time to be his comrade in revolt against Mary Garden, tossed a score of *Louise*, the day's production, into her lap and shouted: 'Lead your own orchestra. You don't sing with me!' 'I would not have you,' replied Mary. The incident was reported to be the aftermath of a row over the 16 January performance, when Mary, infuriated by his conducting of *Pelléas et Mélisande*, was said to have pummelled the Italian maestro with her fists and told him to get out. Polacco's place was now taken by the Frenchman Gabriel Grovlez, who had been brought in three days previously perhaps in response to the French Consul's letter to Paris.

*   *   *

Mary arrived in New York full of hope for the future. 'The enthusiasm for opera in Chicago and the West has given the Chicago Opera Association a field sufficient in itself and the organisation has no need to come to New York any more,' she explained. She said that hostility between the Chicago Opera Association and the Metropolitan always developed when the Western company invaded this territory. She denied problems with Muratore or Polacco and said she would continue as head of the company. 'I have no trouble with anybody – not even with Mr Muratore. The only time that I have the pleasure of looking on his face is when I am on stage with him.' She said she would be delighted if Farrar joined the company to play Thaïs. And Mary confirmed that the company had been supported by the enormous gifts of the McCormicks. Now they had stepped out and left the people of Chicago to back it and more than $300,000 had already been raised. Mary hoped to obtain $500,000 a year for five years in endowments, in other words, a total of $2,500,000, which she wanted for a reserve but planned never to touch. Spokesperson Marguerite Namara denied the charge that Mary had been partial to foreign artists and named fourteen prominent singers with the company who were American.

As guest of honour at a New York Lotos Club dinner, Mary was addressed in conciliatory tones by Otto Kahn, chairman of the Board of the Metropolitan Opera Company.

> In an unusual degree you exemplify those qualities which in their combination we like to look upon as typically American – vision, daring, capacity, dynamic energy, shrewd common sense and idealism. I have always said that an annual

season of limited duration by a rival worthy of our steel, is a useful and desirable thing. The greater supply of opera through your organisation's visits to New York has created a greater number of opera-goers. The attendance at the Metropolitan Opera has not decreased since the Chicago Company's invasion. On behalf of the Metropolitan Opera let me assure you: we wish well to you, Miss Garden. When the record of the development of American art in our generation comes to be written, a page of honor and gratitude will be inscribed with the name of Mary Garden.[45]

But there still persisted a rumour that Mary was about to give up managing the Company. 'She will give her decision in a fortnight. Miss Garden declares that she has just had the most exhausting time of her career. Being Director didn't leave her a free moment and forced her to turn down many foreign engagements. She also had many problems with members of the company.'[46]

In March, during her annual tour with the Chicago Opera Association, there was a new source of conflict between the demands of the opera company and those of the concert venues. 'These clashes produced her excessive quota of cancelled dates,' wrote Charles L. Wagner.

> For instance, I had booked Garden for a concert in Pittsburgh under one management. The rival outfit immediately signed the Opera Company. These conflicts became serious enough to persuade us we needed someone in the Opera camp to avert similar situations. Miss Garden obtained a post there for Howard Potter, and when things continued to be wearisome, I had him go straight to Samuel Insull. Garden supported this move with a personal appeal to Insull. It was an effective manoeuvre. Insull set about putting an end to the unfair tactics. Yet, even with Insull's timely help, we lost many dates because of the necessity of sandwiching Garden's concert appearances in between her opera engagements.[47]

After the tour, Mary returned to Chicago and on Sunday, 23 April 1922, regretfully announced her retirement as director-general of the Chicago Opera Association.

> I am an artist and I have decided my place is with the artists, not over them. It was understood that I would hold the position for a year, which meant the end of the reign of grand opera in Chicago under Mr and Mrs McCormick. When the new civic organisation through its president, Mr Samuel Insull, elected me again general director – which honor I now decline – my fighting spirit tells me to stay, but my reason bids me to go.

During the year of the Garden administration the organization's losses were estimated at nearly $1,000,000 – the largest in its history. Mary explained the size of the deficit as due to the fact that Mr McCormick had instructed her to make his last year as backer of the company a gala season. Many new singers were imported and the attendances for the season, both in Chicago and while the company was on tour, broke all records. She herself received no salary as Director, her only compensation being the fee she received as an artist, said to have been about $2500 a performance. Mary confessed that 'I never had respect for the poor, charming, tired businessman until I became directress of the Chicago Opera Association. Now I know what it is to go through a busy day and then dress and sit through an opera at night. I sympathize with them now, poor dears.'[48]

Hearing of her resignation, Lucien Muratore said that if she had been a man, he would have 'killed her to defend my honor. Because she is a woman, I can and will do nothing'. Discussing the aftermath of the hostility between them in mid-season, Muratore said: 'To me, when we sing together, she hisses "pretty boy" and when I am on the stage, she talks to other members of the company about me. She calls me "pig"!' When asked whether he would sing with the company the following year, Muratore answered that he 'didn't know if there would be any company'.

But Samuel Insull, president of the Civic Opera Association, shortly to be renamed the Chicago Civic Opera Company, defended and praised Mary, and said her conduct of the company that year had been 'manly – that is the only word that describes it'.[49] One of the most disappointed at her resignation was the composer, Sergei Prokofiev, who had hoped she would put on his *The Fiery Angel* and sing the title role. 'I was left with a thousand dollars in my pocket and an aching head,' commented Prokofiev bitterly.[50]

*   *   *

While her career had reached its stormy climax, Mary still found time to nurture young singers. The soprano Grace Moore, who had once written fan letters to Mary, recalled a Sunday evening supper at the Coffee House Club on West Forty-Fifth Street: 'When they were introduced, her idol wanted to know if she was that funny little creature who had been writing her all those letters'.[51] At a later meeting Mary advised her to study Charpentier's *Louise* and promised to arrange an audition for her at the Opéra-Comique when she had mastered the role. Later, in Paris, Grace found herself welcomed into the studio of the famous teacher, Trabadelo, 'as a young friend of three of his former pupils: Garden, Gluck and Farrar. After she had sung for him, Trabadelo, who was thin, old, wore a toupee, high heels and rouge, and spoke in an effeminate voice, asked her to push his baby grand piano across the polished floor while singing "ah".'[52]

Mary reached Paris in mid-May 1922. That summer was spent on the Riviera with brief sorties into Switzerland to see her sister. Elsa Maxwell recalled:

> When I first went to the Riviera in 1922 to visit Mary Garden, she was considered something of an eccentric for spending her summer there. Mary practically was the sole occupant of the Park Palace Hotel in Monte Carlo and the only diversion during the day was fishing. We went out every morning, but I suspected Mary was interested mainly in catching the young handsome pilot of the boat. In the drowsy

afternoons we drove through the lovely, deserted countryside for want of something better to do.[53]

Mary still dreamed of breaking the bank at Monte Carlo. She had perfected a wonderful system which, although it did not enable her to break the bank, had some success, 'I broke tables. Once I won 80,000 francs. Another time 60,000.'[54]

At the end of October she prepared to return from Monte Carlo to Paris and then on to New York. Before she did so, she sang through a new opera, *La leggenda di Sakuntala*, with its composer, Franco Alfano, director of the Conservatoire at Bologna, who wanted her to play the leading role in the French première of the work.

Upon reaching New York, Mary announced characteristically that she was a new woman. She had lost nine pounds 'clambering up and down the mountains of Switzerland' and was now feeling 'less weighed down with responsibility'.[55]

Notes

1. Unidentified Chicago newspaper, 15 January 1920, Uncatalogued Scrapbooks, Music Information Center, Chicago Public Library.
2. Merle Armitage (1965), *Accent on Life*, Ames: Iowa State University Press, p. 60. See also J. Ardoin (1983), 'Namara: A Remembrance', *Opera Quarterly*, vol. 1/4, pp. 76–77, where he is described as 'her generous lover Ogden Armour'.
3. Mary Garden and Louis Biancolli (1951), *Mary Garden's Story*, New York: Simon and Schuster, pp. 181–93.
4. *New York Evening Mail*, 28 January 1920.
5. Goldwyn, Samuel (1924), *Behind the Screen*, London: Grant Richards Ltd, London, pp. 255–6.
6. Garden and Biancolli, op. cit., p. 111.
7. Merle Armitage, op. cit., p. 63.
8. Ibid., pp. 63–4.
9. Letter from Garden to James Huneker, 26 December 1920, Dartmouth College Library, Hanover, New Hampshire.
10. Willa Cather (1920), *Youth and the Bright Medusa*, New York: Alfred A. Knopf.
11. James Huneker (1932), *Painted Veils*, New York: Liveright Publishing Corp., 1932 edn, Preface by Benjamin de Casseres, p. 277.
12. Letter from Garden to James Huneker, 30 March 1919, New York, Dartmouth College Library.
13. Arnold Schwab (1963), *James Gibbons Huneker – Critic of the Seven Arts*, California: Stanford University Press, p. 256.
14. Unidentified Chicago newspaper, Départment de la Musique, Bibliothèque Nationale, Paris.
15. *Chicago Daily News*, January 1921.
16. *New York Times*, 14 January 1921.

17. *New York Times*, 15 January 1921.
18. Ibid.
19. *Chicago Evening Post*, 14 January 1921.
20. *Chicago Herald*, 15 January 1921.
21. *New York Times*, 19 January 1921.
22. *New York Times*, 24 January 1921.
23. *Musical Observer*, New York, March 1921.
24. Unidentified Chicago newspaper, 25 January 1921, Uncatalogued Scrapbooks, Music Information Center, Chicago Public Library.
25. *Musical Observer*, New York, March 1921.
26. *Globe*, 26 January 1921.
27. *New York Times*, 6 February 1921.
28. *New York Herald*, 2 March 1921.
29. *New York Tribune*, 6 March 1921.
30. Ibid.
31. *Baltimore Morning Sun*, 8 March 1921.
32. *New York Herald*, 23 March 1921.
33. *El Paso Herald*, 31 March 1921.
34. Ibid.
35. *El Paso Herald*, 2–3 April 1921.
36. *Trim Topics*, 21 July 1921, quoting from *Cri de Paris*.
37. Mary Garden scrapbook, vol. 13, RCM.
38. *Baltimore Sun*, 22 October 1921.
39. *Toledo Blade*, 24 October 1921.
40. Merle Armitage, op. cit., p. 65.
41. Sergei Prokofiev (n.d.), *Autobiography, Artistes, Reminiscences*, Moscow: Foreign Language Publishing House, p. 59.
42. Letter, 19 February 1922, from Ministry of Foreign Affairs to the Beaux Arts directorate, enclosing letter from French Consul in Chicago, 6 January 1922. Bibliothèque Nationale, Paris.
43. *Toledo Blade*, 7 January 1922.
44. *Toledo Blade*, 14 January 1922.
45. Otto H. Kahn (1926), *Of Many Things*, London: Cape, pp. 39–41.
46. *Paris Hier*, 22 February 1922.
47. Charles L. Wagner (1940), *Seeing Stars*, New York: Putnam's Sons, pp. 207–8.
48. *Kansas City Times*, 11 January 1967.
49. *Toledo Blade*, 25 April 1922.
50. Prokofiev, op. cit., p. 60.
51. Rowena Farrar (1982), *Grace Moore and Her Many Worlds*, New York: Cornwall Books, p. 82.
52. Ibid., p. 87.
53. Elsa Maxwell (1955), *I Married the World*, London: Heinemann, p. 153.
54. *New York Times*, 13 November 1922.
55. *Toledo Blade*, 11 November 1922.

12 Last Years with the Chicago Civic Opera Company: 1923–1931

The year 1923 began for Mary with a concert in Detroit. Yet not everything appeared to be quite as it should be. A glittering headband of jewels clasped the dull glow of her fluffed auburn hair. 'She moves from studied pose to careless silhouette, a gorgeous Mary Garden coiled with ropes of barbaric pearls', wrote the reviewer for the *Detroit News* (17 January 1923). But the Detroit critic felt she was not generously endowed with beautiful tone. She seemed handicapped by a slight huskiness; there were frequent false intonations and the performance was lessened by the visible annoyance she felt at the rather subdued demeanour of her listeners. Despite these uncertainties, Mary was encored after every group and appeared four times.

Mary left for France at the end of February, accompanied by her protégée, the young soprano Mary McCormic, who was returning to resume her musical studies, financed by Mary. A month later, tanned by a 14-day cruise in Mediterranean sunshine, looking ten years younger and acting as sprightly as a girl of 16, Mary arrived in Monte Carlo on the *Adriatic*; she was followed by a maid with two gorgeous Madeira parrots, 10 trunks and 27 porters, each clutching a crate of Florida grapefruit. She said that she would remain only a few days because she had to rush to Nancy to study for three weeks under the pharmacist and hypno-therapist, Emile Coué, whose formula was 'Day by day in every way I am getting better'. Coué also told his patients: 'You can become masters of yourself, physically and morally. It is our subconscious that shapes our lives. When we learn to lead it, we learn to lead our lives.' After four weeks of his treatment, she declared her voice improved 100 per cent. 'He restored my health, made me feel years younger and improved my singing.'[1]

Part of the summer was spent in Venice as a guest of the newly-affluent Cole and Linda Porter at their Palazzo Barbaro. The Cole Porters had brought brawling costume-parties to the gilded ballrooms and floating jazz-bands to the Grand Canal. Among their other guests were Tallulah Bankhead, the art historian Bernard Berenson and the interior designer Elsie de Wolfe.[2]

But it was on the Côte d'Azur that, dining at François Montagne's Hotel-Restaurant, she met the future mayor of Peille, a small village perched on a rockface an hour's drive from the coast. When it was explained to Mary how much the people of Peille would like to erect a monument to their war dead, she decided to donate 9500 Frs Or, adding the request that the words 'Thou shalt not kill' should be engraved on the monument.

It was that same summer that Grace Moore met Mary again, this time at a dinner given by Dudley Field Malone. 'Under the chestnut trees in the gardens of Armenonville, where we watched the enchanting Irene Castle and Billy Reardon dance, I had my first opportunity to talk to her about my dreams and ambitions. She was so alive-looking, with bright red hair and a face that could never be old because the eyes dominated it with such an intense and enormous intelligence. She told me I ought to study *Louise*, inquired about my plans and promised to arrange an audition at the Opéra-Comique for me. She also gave me a letter of introduction to a friend of hers, Edward Herman, a man of solid critical judgement and friend of many musicians.'[3]

Returning to North America in October, Mary toured in concert: Seattle, Vancouver and then to Toronto, which found her past her prime.

> Mary Garden has an excellent figure. Her profile is perfect. She moves with studied grace. She wears a beautiful sheath gown. Her smile is intentionally bland. Her stage presence is good but her vocalism is peculiar. Her voice, originally beautiful and still highly expressive, is becoming a remnant, though still a very effective instrument of passion, of narrative, of occasional ideas and sometimes of true sentiment. It has been marred by too much usage. The flower of that voice is gone. The voice was tight in the top notes, hard and ungracious except in the middle and lower register, yet her dramatic phrasing and articulation were perfect.[4]

Early in January 1924, Mary sang *Thaïs* in Chicago. The city was gripped that winter by the worst cold in years; eight people died as the temperature fell to 16 degrees below zero. She met a mixed critical reaction. '*Thaïs* has always been and still is one of Miss Garden's most colorful and vivid parts,' wrote Edward Moore,

> though as the seasons go on the high notes are dropping like autumn leaves out of her part of the score. Her entrance in the second scene is one of the superb moments of opera. Her sinuous attempt to vamp Athanaël is another; a third is the hysterical outburst with which she closes the following scene. These are flashing moments and they leave their imprint upon the memory. I am less enthusiastic over their vocal or musical value, but they sum up as uncommonly good *theatre*.[5]

In March she was in Seattle, ready to present *Salome*. The local police, who had been detailed to attend the performance, reported bluffly that '*Salome* is OK. The show was better than the movies and the costumes were up to snuff. Regarding Miss Garden in her veil dance, we have seen worse right on Second Avenue. It was a nifty dance, but it was kind of sad – John the Baptist being beheaded.'[6]

After finishing a six-month tour (covering 25,000 miles – twice from coast to coast in concert and 30 performances with the Chicago Civic Opera Company), Mary prepared to sail for Europe. She had radical plans; 'No more red ladies. Next season I create Charlotte in *Werther* – and Charlotte is a good woman. I'm working right now cn Kundry in *Parsifal* which I expect to do a year from now. And I consider that in this role I will reach the highest point of my operatic career. It is the most beautiful thing ever written and has been my ambition for years.'[7] Mary had also agreed to enter the cast of *The Miracle* in the wordless role of the Madonna in the Morris Gest-Reinhardt spectacle then running at the Century. The engagement would be in the summer for 10 or 12 weeks at the most. She would give five performances, sharing the role with Lady Diana Manners. Mary was scheduled to spend four weeks rehearsing with Max Reinhardt in Salzburg; however, no contract had yet been signed for *The Miracle*, nor would there be one. No salary had been fixed but Norman Bel Geddes had already been asked to design her costume.

On 8 April 1924, Mary (according to the papers, 5 feet 5 inches tall and weighing 120 lbs), applied for American citizenship. In the oaths administered by Chief Wiesner of the Naturalization Bureau, she declared it was her intention to become a citizen and to renounce her British allegiance. She would have to wait the statutory period of two years before applying for final citizenship papers. Her father, described as president of an automobile concern in New York, claimed she was already American because he had become a citizen over 30 years ago before she was 18.[8]

Mary spent the summer of 1924 in Switzerland and then holidayed around Monte Carlo. 'Every morning in my bathing suit I'd jump into my motor boat at the Casino. I'd go out a mile and a half and then take off everything.'[9] At night she would drive with her father to nearby Monte Carlo and they would gamble.

In September, Mary was in the village of Peille for the initial construction work on La Place Mary Garden and the Avenue Miss Mary Garden. At the ceremony, she was declared godmother of the village. As well as paying for the war memorial, Mary had made considerable contributions to better sewerage and lighting.

Three weeks later, she suddenly fell ill with what she described in a letter to the impresario Morris Gest as a second attack of appendicitis. The illness prevented her from performing in *The Miracle* before it closed early in

November. She returned to America in November and moved into the Drake Hotel on Chicago's Lake Shore Drive. 'For Garden we had reserved a large apartment overlooking Lake Michigan,' remembered Earl Kardux. 'There was a very large living room, several bedrooms, a room for her costumes and a maid's room. Her personal representative came to inspect everything. She ordered lilies-of-the-valley to be put all about the suite. Her French maid and a French chauffeur came with her and, later, thirty pieces of luggage. A Pierce-Arrow car arrived a few days later from New York, sent by her father.'[10]

Every box and every seat in the Auditorium's dress circle and diamond horseshoe was filled for *Thaïs*. The theatre presented as brilliant an appearance as it did for the opening night of the opera season. Her consultations with Emile Coué seemed to have done the trick. She was born anew and age fell away from her. 'Mary returns and puts new life in opera,' wrote Edward Moore:

> Her voice as well as body are rejuvenated. It would seem as if the stage illumination went up as soon as she became visible with her magnificent gesture of tossing a great armful of roses to the crowd. And whether by personal example or by precept during rehearsals, her performances always seem to go more smoothly than the rest. Evidently Miss Garden did more this summer than take long swims in the Mediterranean, for her voice last night was positively rejuvenated. It would take considerable imagination to allege that even now all of her tones are entirely pleasant or that all the high notes of this opera are within her easy reach, but she was superb. Her tense panther stride in the scene of her unregeneracy, her reposeful poise after her conversion, were pictures to remember.[11]

Mary then sang Charlotte in the Chicago performance of Massenet's *Werther*. 'Her voice went through the notes of the mezzo-soprano score as though Massenet had composed it for her use this season.'[12] Next came *Carmen*. 'Her Carmen was a better sung performance than it had been the previous year,' wrote Moore, 'but it still falls far short of her best role. It is piquant, stormy and energetic but it is not entirely bewitching. More sheer weight of tone is needed to project the notes. However, her wig with its absurd bang is another matter.'[13] Finally, her triumph reached its climax. 'Garden is at her best as the Juggler,' was Moore's judgement early in December. 'Mary Garden's Jean has always been just about her finest accomplishment. It is not one of her flashing roles and it has no purple patches but its gentle pathos is unfailingly deft.'[14]

At the Auditorium performance of Montemezzi's *L'amore dei tre re*, however, Moore felt she had not entirely caught the character of Fiora. 'Miss Garden's Fiora is not quite the ideal Fiora, but it is first class Garden. Wistfulness, the unconscious fate that sweeps herself and the rest to destruction, is the one quality that she chooses not to employ. Her Fiora is a little hard, and more than a little sophisticated.'[15] But her Louise on Christmas Eve was again a triumph. 'Miss Garden was its rejuvenator. She is just about the ideal Louise, so much better in the part than she was last season that one suspects her of having restudied it from its first principles on.'[16]

In February 1925 she performed *Thaïs* in Washington where her performance was praised, with some reservations. 'Now and then in her upper ranges there is a hardness or metallic quality but the emotion and expression she put into it made one forget its technical defects.'[17]

*   *   *

In March 1925 Mary sailed for Europe. Already Paris had word of a new Mary Garden venture – an American grand opera company including many singers who had appeared with the Metropolitan and Chicago organizations during the past winter. Among the company were sopranos Elvira de Hidalgo and Rosa Raisa and tenor Giacomo Lauri-Volpi. The American-Italian-French Grand Opera Company was scheduled to open a five-week Paris season in May, announced managing director Paolo Longone.[18]

At the end of April, Mary was back in the village of Peille with her long-time confidant and adopted brother, Captain William ('Uncle Bill' to the family) Chauncey, who had once been no more than her personal assistant. Together, they were godparents at the baptism of the latest child born in Peille, Marie Barelli. Mary also took advantage of the occasion to award a Croix de Guerre to one of the citizens, former sergeant Laugier, for bravery in the Great War. But this led to considerable public criticism in France. It was suspected that an American singer decorating a former soldier 'in the name of the Government of the République' was little more than an ingenious publicity stunt.

Mary returned to Paris to rehearse on the stage of the Gaité-Lyrique. When she appeared in *L'amore dei tre re*, she was given countless curtain calls. The composer, Montemezzi sat in a box. 'Miss Mary Garden's name evokes one of the most glorious periods of French opera,' began Jean Gandrey-Rety. 'Hers is an admirable interpretative artistry. How long was it since she last appeared in front of a Parisian audience? One had forgotten the very individual resonances of her voice; the myriad skills of her incisive acting technique; the grace of her movements, the fire of her gestures. All these held us under her spell every moment she was on stage'.[19] Mary had equal success in *Tosca*, sung with Lauri-Volpi and her partner of old, Vanni-Marcoux. At a reception given to the company by the paper *Comœdia* (10 June 1925), Mary announced: 'Wait till October! I will come back to Paris and I will create for you, in your gem of a theatre, an unpublished work of Debussy's'.

In August 1925 Bill Chauncey died at the Deauville residence of the oil magnate, 'King' Macomber. His foot, injured at Beaulieu while bathing, had become infected. He died far from Mary, as she noted sadly, for she was in the South of France at the time. She was very disappointed by the refusal by the authorities of Peille to bury Chauncey at the foot of the war memorial, as he had not fallen in action. Instead, they decided to name a street after him: the Avenue Capitaine Chauncey. Nevertheless, despite this rejection, Mary gave the village 35,000 francs to create La Place Mary Garden. It had required much flattening and securing of the uneven ground where it plunged sharply into the valley far below. The inauguration took place with famous lute player, Louis Blanchi, presiding.

Despite sadness over Chauncey's death, Mary continued to enjoy life at the Park Palace Hotel in Monte Carlo. Lionel Fielden recalled Dina d'Alvarez saying: 'Look, I've got a party for Maurice Maeterlinck's birthday [29 August] the day after tomorrow, and I'm having the whole restaurant decorated with blue birds. There'll be the King and Queen of Montenegro and the Grand Duke Andrew and the Phillipps Oppenheims and Lily Langtry and Mary Garden'.[20]

Mary returned to America in December. The press marvelled that all her costumes had apparently been designed and made in Paris by Russian exiles. Her boots, Mary said, were once the pride of a Russian general and her wrap was made by Prince Felix Youssoupoff, once the wealthiest man in Russia. In Chicago, from her apartments at the Blackstone Hotel, Mary sang the praises of Benito Mussolini, whose biography she had been reading. 'A wonderful man. So aggressive, so clear-cut in his wishes and the execution of those wishes. He might be a descendant or even a reincarnation of Napoleon. Would you believe it, Mussolini, (I am told by friends of his), knows every time I sing and the roles I take'.[21] She added, wistfully: 'I do not admire this age. I should like to return to the age of Napoleon – he is my dream sweetheart.'

On the last day of the year, Mary appeared in the American première of Alfano's *Résurrection*. The libretto was by César Hanau with a French translation by Paul Ferrier. 'It is good theatre, consequently a valid basis for opera,' said the *New York Times* (1 January 1926). 'To it, Alfano has composed some highly effective music of the theatre. Katiusha is as good a part as Miss Garden has had in years. She is on the stage through most of the opera and it gives full play to many diverse moods from jocund youth to the semi-hysterical fervor with which she projects an emotional outburst.'

Edward Moore was equally unstinting.

It is the greatest lyric drama of its kind, perhaps the only good one of its kind. It has been slowly growing in its popularity. Probably only Miss Garden's insistence has kept it alive at all. Never was an artist on the operatic stage able to project wistfulness as she does it. A great performance all the way through, with Miss Garden in her most distant and remote manner in acknowledging applause before the curtain.[22]

But there was disquieting news to come. Samuel Insull, president of the Chicago Civic Opera Company, now revealed that the Company had suffered a loss of $400,000. There was, however, the welcome possibility of a new guaranty fund for the next five years and even a new opera house. During the first few weeks of that season attendances were relatively disappointing, but the situation rapidly changed as the season went on, 'until during the last two weeks we have had the greatest attendance at opera that this grand old house ever entertained'.[23]

Insull described the impending closure of the much-loved Auditorium as regrettable but inevitable. His solution was to build a 42-storey office building with the Chicago Civic Opera at street level. It would be financed by selling $10,000,000 of first mortgage bonds to the Metropolitan Life Insurance Company and $10,000,000 of preferred stock to the public. Rentals from the office building would support the interest and dividends on the bonds and preferred stock and leave enough to finance the opera house.[24] Today, architect Bart Swindall, on the staff of the restored Auditorium, explains why in 1929 the Auditorium had been doomed:

> They knew they couldn't fill the Auditorium every night, so they built a hotel on the Michigan Avenue side and an office building on Wabash and the money was supposed to subsidise the opera house. But it didn't work out, because the hotel was the last big, luxury, European-plan hotel. And so, right after this they built American-plan hotels all over the city for the World's Fair. Nobody wanted to stay in a place where you had the bathroom right at the end of the hall. So we had no business here. They had built the Elevated railway right here on Wabash in 1897 for the best offices. But the money didn't come in and the building was in financial trouble. Insull, who was in charge of the opera company, wanted to get out of the Auditorium, not because he wanted to build a monument to himself – although he certainly had a big enough ego – he didn't want his opera company to go down the drain with the Auditorium. He could see quite clearly that the Auditorium was going to go bankrupt. Since all their sets and other theatrical equipment were here – they could all be seized and that would be the end of the Chicago Opera Company.[25]

In February, Mary was on air for the third time in her career on New York's Station WJZ. She discovered that she had a perfect broadcasting voice.[26] She discussed the struggle by opera companies to survive. 'It has nothing to do with New York audiences. I belong to an opera company. And opera companies are worse than prima donnas'. She locked her fingers to indicate the rivalry of competing opera companies, explaining that the Chicago Opera Company stayed away from New York because of the Metropolitan.[27]

On tour with the Chicago Opera Company in the spring of 1926, travelling with Mary was Howard E. Potter, her personal representative. The well-known theatrical photographer, Ben H. Atwell was publicity manager, the critic Edward H. Moore chief electrician and baritone Désiré Defrère acted as stage manager. In Miami, the company appeared in a tent for the first time ever. Mary's Florida début was in *Thaïs*. 'In the shadowy blackness of a darkened stage, the figure took shape under the rays of a faint blue light,' reported a surprised *Miami Daily News* correspondent (10 March 1926). 'The vision (Mary Garden herself) unwound a veil from her body, allowing it to wave from her outflung arms until it fell discarded at her feet.'

*   *   *

Mary returned to Paris in April to sing *Pelléas et Mélisande* at the Opéra-Comique. The audience was bewitched. 'The first of the gala performances was a triumphal success,' reported *La Volonté* (30 May 1926). 'Mary Garden, who remains the unrivalled interpreter of the role of Mélisande, was justly acclaimed. Trembling with sensitivity, with deeply moving humanity, she was finer even than the memory of her legendary past performance.' She was asked by the journal *Candide* (1 April 1926) which was most important: the quality of the voice; the method of singing or the style of expressing what is sung? Her answer was that:

> In the era of Patti and Melba, both admirable singers, the quality of voice was all-important. But Jean de Reszke made public taste develop. At present, audiences are more discriminating. It is first of all the personality, the style of playing to which they attach the greatest importance; then it is intelligence and only after that, the quality of voice. The public no longer admires cooing or long-held notes. They ask for truth to nature.
>
> It is no longer the era of singers who, before going on stage cough, gargle and who, once they are in front of the audience take up poses which show them off to best advantage. Today, artists are needed who above all live their stage characters before thinking about their voice or their appearance. That is huge progress in my opinion.

Pierre Maudru, writing in *Comœdia* (2 April 1926), urged readers to remember the debt French music owed to Mary for her promotion of it abroad. He urged the Paris Opéra to engage her as *Salome*, a performance of which the Opéra was then preparing.

In July, Mary McCormic, Mary's protégée, made her début at the Opéra as Gounod's Juliette. Mary herself attended the performance, sitting in the centre of the first row of the balcony. But the young soprano's great opportunity in the balcony scene failed utterly, apparently through sheer nervousness. The beginner was too conscious of acting and forced her voice as well. In the lower registers, she lacked warmth and was hardly audible, and on the highest notes her voice was colourful but insufficiently trained. It was considered yet another clear example of too early an appearance.[28]

Around this period another protégée, the young Grace Moore, again wrote to Mary asking for advice. Mary's cabled reply moved Grace to tears; she was to go immediately to Monte Carlo and live for the next six months in the apartment Mary kept there. She was to study with Mary's favourite accompanist and operatic coach, Richard Barthelémy, who had formerly worked in that capacity for Caruso. Grace duly arrived in Monte Carlo and entered the salon of Mary's fourteen-room apartment.

> The draperies, paintings and furnishings, rich color and texture were a charming extension of her idol's dramatic personality. The windows framed exciting vistas of the promenade, the opera house and the casino and a row of colorful shops. The dining room could seat thirty. Grace promptly fell in love with the bed she chose to sleep in, of green and gold leaf with a gold eagle perched on the crest of the headboard above a cover of green and gold taffeta brocade.[29]

Later, Grace called on Mary soon after she had opened her new villa at Beaulieu-sur-Mer. 'She received a gracious welcome and was shown through the villa, which was even more lavish than the apartment in Monte Carlo. At length, Mary led her to the piano and asked her with business-like briskness, to sing.' After hearing arias from *La bohème*, *Roméo et Juliette* and *Louise*, Mary again advised Grace to concentrate on *Louise* and arranged an audition with Masson and Ricou, directors of the Opéra-Comique, who suggested further training in acting technique. Accordingly Grace promptly arranged to take acting lessons from Albert Carré, then artistic director of the Opéra-Comique.[30]

In addition to her apartment at Monte Carlo and the villa at Beaulieu, Mary had also recently bought a house at Vevey in Switzerland as a home for her retirement. She lent the house to her sister Helen who came to live there with her two boys. Hugues Cuénod, the tenor, recalled that Mary visited them often, receiving friends and giving many parties.

> I first met her at a party. She came with two of her sisters. They were all three very smart, amusing and unpredictable. Mary was kind enough to take an interest in my studies. Sometimes we all went to nearby Montreux, and we sat at a large table at the local cabaret, where her striking appearance always created a sensation. At other times we went out on the lake in a houseboat belonging to her friends.
>
> Most often, however, she let her sister act as hostess and received us in the house. There was a beautiful piano, but, alas, Mary never sang, as she was resting from her work and travels. It was there that she insisted on sending me to see Noël Coward in London, which resulted in my engagement for one of his musicals.[31]

After singing *Pelléas et Mélisande* at Strasbourg, Mary prepared to return to America where she was to create the role of Judith in Honegger's opera of that name; there were also plans for her to appear in Honegger's *Antigone*, based on a play by Cocteau derived from Sophocles. She played Mélisande again at the Opéra-Comique, and the directors fêted her at a farewell supper in the Café de Paris. The tables were covered with flowers. Directors, artists, members of the corps de ballet, of the orchestra, and chorus; electricians and stage-hands were present. At the end, Georges Ricou, on behalf of all, expressed the admiration they felt for Mary's magnificent career. 'She has been a precious example to our younger artists who worked beside her and these performances of *Pelléas et Mélisande* have forged a bond between the younger generation and their glorious predecessors'. Albert Carré then toasted her. Mary, very moved, replied: 'Dear M. Carré, I cannot forget that if I am here and if I have had the career that I have had, it is thanks to you who, in days gone by, opened the gates of the Opéra-Comique to me'.[32]

*   *   *

Arriving in America in October 1926, Mary was wearing a double strand of pearls, five bracelets on her left wrist and a slave bangle on her left ankle, but she had mislaid her medallion of the Virgin which she had worn for many years. She then embarked on what were her first recordings since 1912, at the studios of the Victor Talking Machine Company in Camden, New Jersey, with her young Canadian accompanist Jean Dansereau. Recordings with an orchestra under Rosario Bourdon continued sporadically till the end of the year.

'Dieu de grâce' from Alfano's *Résurrection* did not find universal favour. Desmond Shawe-Taylor refers to 'The dramatically sung, but musically rather dull, aria from Alfano's *Risurrezzione* (sung, of course, in French) – an opera which had by then become a favourite item in her repertory'.[33]

'There is also a recorded excerpt from the bad joke which is Alfano's *Résurrection*,' wrote Hugues Cuénod, 'quite one of the worst operas I have ever heard, but one to suit Garden's histrionic possibilities, offering a role in which she could send a chill down your spine... When she made this recording, she was at the end of her singing time; though you can guess at her artistry, she exaggerates effects too often and her diction is not always perfect.'[34]

Her performance of Cadman's 'At Dawning' was, according to her published biography and Desmond Shawe-Taylor, 'the only one of her records that she said she could bear to hear played'.[35] Richard D. Fletcher enjoyed her new version of 'Depuis le jour': 'The later Victor version of the aria, though taken down a full tone to F, and sung at a slightly brisker pace, is more rewarding in timbre. The rounder, fuller vocal quality and the more skilled portamento give this recording greater musical interest. The Victor version, too, shows top tones which achieve a floating quality, adding much to the general effect'.[36]

Other critics concurred. 'A warmly glowing, seductive account of "Depuis le jour", now transposed down by a tone to the key of F,' wrote Shawe-Taylor, who was intrigued, however, by the number of 'takes' made.

'An odd feature of these 1926–29 Victors is the large number of takes that were involved for some of the titles. 'Depuis le jour', to cite the most extreme case, had no fewer than sixteen takes during four distinct 1926 sessions – of which the fourteenth was passed for issue. I have sometimes wondered whether some of the unsuccessful ones were attempts to sing the music at score pitch. Stranger still, a year later she made three further attempts at the same aria, but this time with piano accompaniment, one of which (likewise transposed down) achieved LP publication by RCA long afterwards.[37]

When Edward Moore saw Mary in *Résurrection* at Chicago's Auditorium that November, he felt it to be an excellent vehicle for her: 'The part of Katusha gives Miss Garden the chance to do a good many of the things that she does supremely well, all the way from love-making to hysterics'.[38] When it came to *L'amore dei tre re*, Moore found Mary's Fiora 'striking, eye-filling, stirring. Of wistfulness, tenderness there is scarcely a trace in voice or action, most of her energies being reserved for the love scene with Avito and the death scene with Archibaldo.'[39] Among the concerts she gave at this time were two with the distinguished pianist Rudolph Ganz, one in the Medina Temple and one in the Auditorium.

Not long into 1927, there were more rumours of conflict between Mary and Giorgio Polacco. Whether illness or an attack of temperament kept Mary out of a performance of *Carmen* was a mystery but there were stories of a spectacular run-in between the two. It was guardedly admitted that there had been a 'little tiff'.

Her *Carmen* at the Eastman School of Music, Rochester, New York, came in February. The conductor was a still youthful Eugene Goossens, who recalled embarking on the School's 1926–27 season with the usual run of symphony concerts and performances by the Opera Department, which had made great strides towards its goal of becoming a professional opera company. Mary Garden happened to be in Rochester at one of their performances of *The Marriage of Figaro* and was astonished and delighted by what she saw; in her enthusiasm at the end of the evening, she told Goossens that she almost felt like taking part in it herself. In a moment of daring, Goossens asked her if she would consider singing *Carmen* with them, and then later lobbied George Eastman to ask her:

> So it came about that in February, with a mere couple of orchestral rehearsals, Mary Garden sang with all her old fire and still quite a lot of her former vocal artistry, the role of Carmen with the members of Eastman School of Music's Opera Department. The diva overpowered us by her electrical vitality and the fire of her performance. All the intensity and vigour at her command were thrown into that characterisation as though she were determined to show that she had lost none of her cunning. The fact that she sang in French, while the rest of the opera took place with the English translation, passed comparatively unnoticed. Charles Hedley, the Don José, was completely shaken by the whole thing, and related that in the last act he felt as though Carmen might conceivably put the knife into his heart, rather than he into hers! I have never seen that crusty old bachelor [George Eastman] so openly fascinated by anyone as he was by the alluring Mary that night. Some indeed whispered that he had, for the first time in his life, fallen in love.[40]

* * *

In late March 1927, Mary sailed for Cherbourg along with the sopranos Maria Jeritza and Claudia Muzio. She joined her sister Helen in Paris and then left for two weeks in Switzerland. She later scored a triumph in Geneva, with two performances of *Pelléas et Mélisande*, given as part of an international festival of music. Returning to the Opéra-Comique in mid-May, she appeared in *Résurrection* and renewed an old acquaintance. 'I was profoundly moved to see M. Carré again. It's an immense joy to work with him. I have known the artist and the man for many years but I can't describe the emotion I felt to be rehearsing *Résurrection* with him'.[41]

The Paris performance of *Résurrection* on 21 May was also notable for a dramatic public announcement made from the stage that the American aviator Lindbergh had just achieved the single-handed crossing of the Atlantic from New York to Le Bourget. He had landed that evening at 10.21 pm. The register of the Opéra-Comique records that artists and audience joined in singing American hymns and the Marseillaise. Mary was invited to sing the Star-Spangled Banner but had forgotten the words. 'At a formal reception the following day, I asked Ben Tilden to give me the words to the song and he went as far as "O say can you see" and then la-la-ed the rest of the lines. I had to get a Frenchman to have the words looked up in the library'.[42]

A year after the sudden death of her beloved Bill Chauncey, sadness once again entered Mary's life. On 16 August at the Carlton Hotel, London (in his suite where he and Mary had often met), her intimate friend, the once fabulously rich J. Ogden Armour, former head of the great Chicago meat-packing company, died. Mary took his death very badly but had to mask her grief, as Armour had a wife and family.

In January 1928, Mary sang in *Monna Vanna*, *Le Jongleur*, *Louise*, *Résurrection*, *Carmen* and *Sapho* in Chicago. Her impersonation of Fanny Legrand was much appreciated. 'If it had not been for the flaming performance of Mary Garden,' observed Edward Moore,

> the chief memories of the revival of Massenet's *Sapho* at the Auditorium last night would have been of lots of trouble taken on a piece that was not worth it. In and out Miss Garden flashed in gorgeous red hues, bare-legged in the first, bare-armed in the second act, which classifies as a distinct tactical error. She was forceful and agile, perhaps nervous in manner, but with a lot of pep, all of which went to make the character of Fanny Legrand more nearly a living character than would otherwise have been the case. In fact, she came close to making the hit of her Chicago career with it.[43]

As that 1927–28 season ended, it turned out that the most popular works had been *La traviata*, *Faust* and *Tannhäuser*. But around 107 performances had been given during the last home season, with 34 different operas in four languages. It was now time for the Chicago Civic Opera Company to leave on tour. Three special trains carried the whole organization to Boston, the first of 19 cities to be visited. There were 40 trunks of music and the scenery was moved in 29 special baggage cars, each 72 feet in length. In addition to this, each train carried four drawing-room compartment cars, a diner and an observation car.

At the Eastman Theatre in Rochester, the critic Stewart Sabin was able to observe Mary at work in *Résurrection* with only the most meagre production facilities. 'It is her capacity to project a personality, to hold the stage with little to aid her and to rise above musical lapses in the score, that makes the performance. Miss Garden's voice was fuller and freer in dramatic color than it was when she sang here in *Carmen*.'[44] Mary's non-verbal communication skills were much in evidence a month later in Fresno: 'Even from across the room one feels the spark of ceaseless vibration. Her hands express what no words on earth could say.'[45]

In San Francisco, she once again entertained the press with her unbridled imagination and exaggeration:

> In two years my contract with the Chicago Civic Opera Company will be up. Then I am going abroad, to sing in Paris, in Madrid, in Berlin. Afterwards, I'm going to take a trip around the world – China, Japan, India. And on that trip I shall find a high mountain some place, Abyssinia maybe and live there all by myself. . . . Women are worse than men. We're the sly sex, the dishonest sex. The only worthwhile women are the women who are trying to be good sports and play fifty-fifty with men.

And she boasted that she had recently acquired an airplane and was looking for a pilot. 'He must be young,' she announced, 'not more than 21 or 22 – and very very good looking'.[46]

* * *

In the summer of 1928, once again safely ensconced in Paris, Mary gave away some of her secrets to Harold Horan of the *Los Angeles Examiner*. She was wearing a gold and platinum anklet given her by Gabriele d'Annunzio after her first performance in *Pelléas et Mélisande*. 'That is a man who possesses sex appeal to the fullest degree,' said Mary. 'I am going to show them up in my memoirs – but they will only be published after my death. I have always kept a diary and that will be the source for my book.' (But, of course, no diary has survived.) She dyed her hair with her own special solution of red ink. She took 'strawberry baths', claiming that crushed fruit in the bath treated her skin, but denied rumours of a facelift. She only took one meal a day – fish or chicken with lots of vegetables at noon. She drank coffee in the morning, tea at night.[47]

That August there were again reports that Mary was soon to be married. This time the man in question was said to be Pierre Plessis, a young French writer, but Mary denied the rumours. Later that year she was reported as saying: 'Some day I may marry but to date I have been unable to find the perfect balance between love and work. Work always comes first with me, and besides, men are selfish animals.'[48] 'An operatic career is everything – life, love, happiness. It is everything.'[49]

Mary stayed in Paris until Grace Moore had made her Opéra-Comique début as Manon and then returned to America. Although she had listed herself as 'foreign resident' to avoid customs duties, she was required to pay several hundred dollars duty on foreign purchases. The customs official maintained that when she had applied for citizenship four years previously, she had declared herself a resident.

In Chicago she told the press that she loved sport. She was president of a sports club on the Riviera and an incurable boxing fan. 'Recently we have been putting on boxing show champions. You know, I think there is nothing so good as to see two beautiful men get in the ring and fight. And I like the fights to be rough – the rougher the better.'[50] Then, quizzed about her resources as a singer, Mary proclaimed that 'My voice is no more important than my shoulders. Everything about me is a vital part of the scheme of things. My voice is a means to an end. I use it to express the emotions, just as I use my hands or my eyes or my shoulders.'[51]

Mary recommended performing and touring with the Chicago Civic Opera Company. The discipline under which artists worked at that time can be gauged from the Company's detailed stage regulations.

> When appearing on the stage for rehearsals artists should not carry walking-sticks, hats, coats or other articles of apparel. During a performance, artists are requested not to acknowledge applause until after the curtain has fallen at the end of the act. Should the applause actually interrupt the performance, the artist should remain in position and in the character of his or her part and acknowledge by a slight inclination of the head.[52]

Her return to Boston in *Pelléas et Mélisande* brought fresh plaudits. 'Miss Garden's Mélisande justified the reams of rhapsody and of more discriminating praise which have been bestowed upon it in many climes,' wrote Olin Downes. 'Her voice is better today, more beautiful and under finer control than it was in certain former years. Throughout, it was by voice as well as gesture that Miss Garden affected her hearers.'[53]

In Los Angeles, Mary met up with a colleague of earlier times, a fellow-student of Trabadelo.

> The two most vivid figures in grand opera paid tribute to one another. Geraldine Farrar sat in a stage box and applauded Mary Garden's portrayal of Thaïs. And Mary, stepping before the curtain to acknowledge the adulation of a packed house, tossed a red rose to Geraldine. Now Farrar, white of hair, has retired from the operatic field. While Garden, incredibly youthful and lithe, still queens it before the footlights. She sang in a manner to silence those who cast aspersions upon her vocal prowess. It was clear, brilliant, poignant tone.[54]

One of those to cast aspersions on Mary's abilities was Gene Howe, editor of the Texas paper the *Amarillo News-Globe*. Howe wrote that Mary was so old that she actually tottered. When she read this, Mary (now aged 55) retorted: 'When Mr Howe is tottering, I'll still be singing opera!'[55]

April 1929 was notable for a concert at the Metropolitan Opera House with Beniamino Gigli on behalf of Fordham University's School of Sociology and Social Service. It was the first and only time they appeared together and they were much applauded for the duet from *Manon*.

Later that year the young American composer, Hamilton Forrest, travelled to France to meet Mary, now ensconced in her summer retreat of Beaulieu. They were working on his opera *Camille* which was planned to be given in January at the Civic Opera. She had received a fan letter from Forrest asking for an interview. The frankness and brevity of the letter impressed her and she granted the interview, so discovering Forrest to be the youngest American composer to have an opera produced by a leading company. Every day a long line of automobiles was parked in front of the Garden villa where composer, musicians and assistants were working on the new opera. For recreation, Mary was often seen at night in the Casino, having a fling at the green tables, always playing her favourite number thirteen. Whenever possible, she chose the thirteenth of the month to open a new opera. In fact, *Camille* did not receive its première until 11 December 1930 when it was performed before an encouraging but unenthusiastic Chicago audience. The applause was weak, although Mary and Forrest were both cordially received.

* * *

At the Philadelphia Academy of Music in October 1929, Mary appeared in *Le jongleur de Notre-Dame*. 'She triumphed over Time,' wrote Linton Martin,

> in appearance and art of acting and there was actually greater subtlety in her singing, while the voice itself was essentially the same – so utterly spontaneous, so impulsive and unstudied seemed her compelling characterization. She has a radiant personality, a magnetic quality, the faculty of vocal characterization rather than singing; the voice, neither commanding nor colourful, was made eloquent in the interpretation of mood and emotion.[56]

On 4 November 1929, only eleven days after the stock market collapse (which had spared Mary's finances but ruined those of her father and sisters, who would henceforth be completely reliant on her), the old Chicago Auditorium closed its doors. The new riverside Chicago Civic Opera towering over Wacker Drive opened with *Aida*; for the wealthy Chicago patrons, the new opera house was a culture-shock. The 'Golden Horseshoe', where the society ladies loved to see and be seen, had been done away with – the seating had been effectively democratized.

How did the two houses compare in theatrical terms? Bart Swindall of the Auditorium holds the opinion that the Civic Opera House is far inferior to the Auditorium where sight-lines or acoustics are concerned,[57] while Alfred Glasser of today's Chicago Lyric Opera (based at the Wacker Drive opera house) takes a contrary view:

> At the time they put the opera house here, it was nothing but a bunch of factories with no public transportation. It was a strange place to build it.
>
> It's a throne with its back to New York. An office tower with two wings. Our loft ends on the 16th floor but the building itself goes up to the 42nd. Among the differences between the two houses is that here we have hot and cold running water. The Auditorium didn't. There are various other technical effects which only this theatre is capable of. Probably the acoustics at the Auditorium are too good. You can hear the commissionaires counting the money in the hall while you're trying to listen to the opera.
>
> The capacity is practically the same. Ours seats 3600 and the Auditorium 3600 plus. But that's only if they use a gallery which has been closed off for a generation.
>
> We have a lot more space for hanging scenery. In the old days the scenery was painted on flats. They could be raised and lowered. The stage here is not raked but there is a hydraulic system which is used to raise and lower parts of the stage. We've had 120 players in the orchestra (for *Der Rosenkavalier*), but some of them were actually on the stage.[58]

As for Mary, she found the new house made empathy with the audience almost impossible: 'When I looked into that long black hole I said, "Oh, no!" It was no real opera house at all, more like a convention hall. We had absolutely no communication with the public.'[59] Bolstering her dislike of the new house was Mary's mutually uneasy relationship with Samuel Insull, who had succeeded her as director.

In July 1930 the recordings she had made the previous year in New York were released. 'It is a pity to have Mary Garden as Victor has seen fit to present her this month,' wrote the reporter for the *New York Times* (6 July 1930). 'Wanamaker's Auditorium rigged up as a recording laboratory, and Wanamaker's pipe organ in accompaniment, cannot make "In the Gloaming" or "Jock o' Hazeldean" the fare we can welcome from Miss Garden. There is so much that she could and should do for us that after receiving this latest disk, the temptation to give advice where it should not be needed, is strong.'

Richard D. Fletcher, writing twenty years later, provides a more positive assessment:

> The later Victor contains three verses, telling more of the dramatic tale, and employs the large organ of the Wanamaker Auditorium in New York which comes through with tones remotely resembling the bag-pipe effect Garden wanted. On the Victor the singing is good and well-supported. In this recording we find examples of Garden's frequent and intentional tendency to break rhythm with the accompaniment. Her approach to music was horizontal in relation to the

orchestral line. The notes were sung vertically in time with the accompanying score. Each phrase was interpreted with full attention to its dramatic intent and drive, leading it where it must go, not as a mathematically determined exercise in time values.[60]

Mary spent the summer of 1930 at Monte Carlo. Barre Hill, a young American baritone, had come over to study the role of Pelléas with Mary:

> When I first arrived in Monte Carlo, she told me: 'Now, we will see what you can do with the role of Pelléas. You have the voice that both Debussy and I have looked for in this role. The part ought to suit you like the proverbial glove. I am going to coach you, but you must use your brains.' Throughout the summer I studied with Miss Garden and after my appearance in Chicago [22 January 1931], she said to me 'Barre Hill, you are the best Pelléas I have ever had to my Mélisande'.[61]

By October, Mary was in Paris where she explored some of her immediate ambitions: 'On 1 November I am supposed to film something in Hollywood. If the results are encouraging, perhaps I will realise a dream – to film *Pelléas et Mélisande* in French, with a French cast and director. In March I am due to sing in Monte Carlo. But it is in Paris that I have my only true artistic emotions, in front of this terrible but so dear public.'[62]

Later that month she gave a concert with Walter Gieseking in Carnegie Hall. Olin Downes wrote:

> Miss Garden, when she was thoroughly mistress of her voice and breath, sang Debussy with an extraordinary wealth of color, nuance and mood. The voice, which never was one of distinguished beauty, had tones of haunting loveliness. She is an artist of the rarest intelligence and sensibility, even more evident in song than on the operatic stage. It is true that some of the singing last night was short-phrased and innaccurate of intonation but we prefer Miss Garden with all her tricks of vocalism and adorable stage presence.[63]

Shortly afterwards, in Amarillo, Mary had tea with Gene Howe who, despite his past criticisms of Mary's age, had recently commended her for her attitude. A truce had been agreed – the tea party was given by Howe in her honour. Mary denied that she couldn't sing, that she was too old or that she tottered. To prove the point, she sang before an Amarillo audience of 7000!

*   *   *

On 22 January 1931 Mary was performing *Pelléas et Mélisande* in Chicago, with Vanni-Marcoux as Golaud, in front of an appreciative audience that included the distinguished discographer, the late Harold Barnes: 'It was a stunning performance, something that I don't think I will forget if I live to be a hundred or more.'[64] Two days later, on 24 January, she made what was to prove her last appearance on Chicago's operatic stage, in *Le jongleur de Notre-Dame*. Her final appearance in America as Mélisande came on 29

January in Boston, where she sang *Pelléas et Mélisande* with Barre Hill and Vanni-Marcoux. 'The curtain must have gone down at least 30 times,' remembered Margot Gibbon. 'She came off the stage and threw her arms around Marcoux, and we heard her say, "Chéri, chéri, never, never have we given such a performance".'[65]

Mary's final evening with the Chicago Civic Opera Company was in Boston on 6 February where she sang *Camille* with tenor Charles Hackett. It was not the ideal vehicle for a farewell performance. *The Musical Leader* (12 February 1931) noted that: 'never within memory has Boston been so cold and an occasion so disastrous! True, applause did bring Miss Garden before the curtain alone, just once, but it was a gesture of the admiration that Boston has for her and certainly in no way expressive of the audience's feeling for the opera itself.'

Bentley Stone, then a ballet soloist, had sour memories of the occasion: 'The ballet dancers, including the soloists, volunteered to be supernumeraries in the opera. When it was all over, as she stood at the door, having sung her last performance, only the ballet and chorus people were there. Mary Garden thanked us and remarked, "After 20 years, not one official of the Chicago Opera to say thank you or good-bye".'[66]

Notes

1. *Toledo Blade*, 14 March 1923.
2. Jane S. Smith (1982), *Elsie de Wolfe*, New York: Atheneum, p. 219.
3. Grace Moore (1947), *You're Only Human Once*, London: Latimer House, p. 82.
4. *Toronto Daily Star*, 23 November 1923.
5. *Chicago Daily Tribune*, 2 January 1924.
6. *Seattle Times*, 15 March 1924.
7. *New York Times*, 24 March 1924.
8. *New York Times*, 9 April 1924.
9. *Bulletin*, 13 November 1924.
10. Earl Kardux (c. 1950), 'Lilies for Miss Garden', journal unknown.
11. *Chicago Daily Tribune*, 25 November 1924.
12. Ibid., 29 November 1924.
13. Ibid., 4 December 1924.
14. Ibid., 15 December 1924.
15. Ibid., 17 December 1924.
16. Ibid., 25 December 1924.
17. *Washington Post*, 15 February 1925.
18. *New York Times*, 21 March 1925.
19. *Comœdia*, 22 May 1925.
20. Lionel Fielden (1960), *The Natural Bent*, London: André Deutsch, pp. 93–4.
21. *Chicago Daily Tribune*, 12 December 1925.
22. Ibid., 6 January 1926.
23. Ibid., 23 January 1926.

24. Forrest McDonald (1962), *Insull*, Chicago: University of Chicago Press, pp. 243–4.
25. Interview by author 12 July 1993 with Bart Swindall, architect and public relations manager, Auditorium Theatre, Chicago.
26. *Chicago Daily Tribune*, 10 December 1925.
27. *New York Times*, 2 February 1926.
28. *New York Times*, 4 July 1926.
29. Rowena Farrar (1982), *Grace Moore and Her Many Worlds*, New York: Cornwall Books, pp. 101–2.
30. Ibid., p. 104.
31. Hugues Cuénod, 'Remembrances of an Enchantress', *High Fidelity Magazine*, July 1964, p. 36.
32. *Comœdia*, 17 October 1926.
33. Desmond Shawe-Taylor, 'A Gallery of Great Singers, 15 – Mary Garden (1874–1967)', *Opera*, October 1984, p. 1083.
34. Hugues Cuénod, op. cit., p. 37.
35. Desmond Shawe-Taylor, op. cit., p. 1083.
36. Richard D. Fletcher, 'The Mary Garden of Record', *Saturday Review*, 27 February 1954, p. 50.
37. Desmond Shawe-Taylor, op. cit., p. 1084.
38. *Chicago Daily Tribune*, 12 November 1926.
39. *Chicago Daily Tribune*, 18 November 1926.
40. Eugene Goossens (1951), *Overture and Beginners*, London: Methuen and Co., pp. 239–40.
41. *L'Intransigeant*, 15 May 1927.
42. *The New York Times*, 12 November 1927.
43. *Chicago Daily Tribune*, 13 January 1927.
44. *Rochester Democrat*, 4 February 1928.
45. *Fresno Bee*, 12 March 1928.
46. *San Francisco Bulletin*, 14 March 1928.
47. *Los Angeles Examiner*, 21 June 1928.
48. Ibid., 26 December 1928.
49. Ibid., 7 January 1929.
50. *New York Times*, 24 December 1928.
51. *Los Angeles Examiner*, 10 January 1929.
52. Vanni-Marcoux's press cuttings, Bibliothèque-Musée de l'Opéra, Paris.
53. *New York Times*, 10 February 1929.
54. *Los Angeles Examiner*, 10 March 1929.
55. *Los Angeles Examiner*, 21 March 1929.
56. *Philadelphia Inquirer*, 1 November 1929.
57. Interview by author 12 July 1993 with Bart Swindall.
58. Interview by author 18 July 1993 with Alfred Glasser, Chicago Lyric Opera.
59. Mary Garden and Louis Biancolli (1951), *Mary Garden's Story*, New York: Simon and Schuster.
60. Richard D. Fletcher, op. cit., p. 50.
61. Rene Devries, *Musical Courier*, 4 April 1931.
62. Pierre Lazaeff, *Paris-Midi*, 2 October 1930.
63. *New York Times*, 26 October 1930.
64. Interview by author 4 July 1993 with Harold Barnes.
65. Margot Gibbon, 'Memories of Garden', January 1962.
66. Ann Barcel, *American*, 5 January 1967.

13 Lectures, Master Classes and Hollywood: 1931–1937

In 1931, reports that Mary would not be appearing with the Chicago Civic Opera Company during the coming season were given added confirmation by the fact that Mary's picture was absent from a group of photographs in the Company's advertising display. When questioned, opera officials merely said that interested persons should draw their own conclusions. Speaking from Monte Carlo, Mary's secretary issued a denial of her impending retirement. Then a Chicago critic and friend of Mary said that she was considering an offer from a New York opera patron to recruit her own company in opposition to the Metropolitan. He added that offers for vaudeville and moving-picture contracts had also been made to her.

Finally, Mary herself announced that she was leaving the Chicago Civic Opera Company, gaily adding, that she would retire and ride over Corsica on a mule. Simultaneously, the Chicago Civic Opera Company issued a statement that Miss Garden would not return to the Civic Opera the following season. John Clayton, publicity director for the company, acting in the absence of manager Johnson and president Insull, stated that Mary Garden did not desire to come back, but there were no ill feelings at all. For several seasons her contracts had been for one season only. Replacements had already been found; Claudia Muzio playing Fiora and Conchita Supervia playing Carmen. Following this development came an assertion from Charles L. Wagner, Mary's concert manager, that he felt reasonably sure Mary Garden intended to sing opera in New York during the coming season. Wagner declared that, while Miss Garden had terminated her agreement with the Chicago Civic Opera Company, she had no plans for retiring.

Wagner revealed that the following season Mary would divide her time between opera and symphony orchestras in all-Debussy programmes. She intended to return to America in October to appear with the Minneapolis

Symphony Orchestra and to present the same Debussy programme with the Boston Symphony in December. She also planned to learn the role of Kundry in *Parsifal*. Then she would appear in opera in New York.

In February 1931, Mary realized a lifetime's ambition. With her sister Aggie and her ever-watchful manager, Charles L. Wagner, Mary, wrapped in an enormous fur coat, met the thin and pawky John D. Rockefeller at Ormond Beach, Florida and promised to sing a song especially for his benefit in her concert at Daytona Beach that evening. They were all photo-graphed together, Wagner looking sharp in his fedora, Rockefeller with a flat motoring-cap shadowing his hawk-like eyes.

Her next major engagement was in April at Monte Carlo, where, as a res-ident of the Côte d'Azur, she could be sure of a very warm welcome. 'I never think of Monte Carlo Opera House,' wrote Grace Moore,

> without remembering that Mary, who should have been its most brilliant star, had found her own way of refusing that honour. The Monte Carlo impresarios had been after her all her life to sing there. Her villa had brought musical and social prestige to the Riviera and they considered that a season with her would be made. Each year Raoul Gunsbourg would send his telegram asking her to open the season, but each year she had only one answer, 'Merde', an economical enough reply signifying in the one word dismissal, reason and point of view. When she finally did sing *Carmen* there, I am sure that when Gunsbourg came back to kiss her hand, she probably dismissed him with the same 'Merde'.[1]

Mary appeared in a *Carmen* which was directed by Gunsbourg. The maître de ballet was Paul Petroff, with a chorus under Amedeo de Sabata. The décor were by Visconti and Geerts. 'Beauty, grace, seduction,' wrote *l'Éclaireur du Midi* (4 April 1931), 'she unites everything in her personality which communicates with a smile and conquers hearts even before she sings a note. And when she sings, how can one explain the spell under which everyone falls? There is such magical purity in her voice, such volume, such movement of the very soul.'

Mary spent that summer near Aberdeen trout-fishing with her father and then left him to go mule-riding in Corsica as she had threatened. Next she entered into litigation, suing a Paris perfume manufacturer whom she had given permission to use her name for one of the best examples of his wares. She claimed that the perfumier had not stopped at this but had proceeded to name and portray almost everything in the shop after her. She was now seek-ing that the perfumier be prohibited from using her name and that he be ordered to reimburse her for the damages and embarrassment she had been caused. The suit she had filed in the Supreme Court was against Parfumerie Rigaud, Inc., the American branch of Rigaud, Paris; she demanded $100,000 in damages. A similar action was brought in Paris against the parent company. Meanwhile, Parfumerie Rigaud, in a counter-claim, alleged Mary had greatly profited by the advertising and publicity. The whole affair seems to have been sparked off because in 1931 Mary received an offer from another perfumery company for the use of her name (*New York Times*, 11 April 1933). Two years later the matter reached a conclusion. In her suit against Parfumeries Rigaud, Inc. before Supreme Court Justice Schmuck, Mary admitted that in 1909, as a friendly gesture, she had given Dr Mason, an agent for the company, permission to use her name. The company had been marketing Mary Garden perfume ever since. On 20 April 1933 she won an injunction restraining Parfumeries Rigaud, Inc. from selling any cosmetics labelled 'Mary Garden perfume' (*New York Times*, 21 April 1933).

In New York, meanwhile, news was emerging that an opera company to sing *opéra-comique* in English over the following season was being planned for the city by Mary's manager, Charles L. Wagner. This new company would serve as a nucleus to bring Mary back into opera. The company would open in November and their first production would probably be von Suppé's *Boccaccio* which (in German) the Met had added to their repertoire only the previous season.

After holidaying in Corsica at the Hotel Bonaparte, Ile Rousse (where she indulged her celebrated penchant for nude sunbathing), Mary sailed into New York at the beginning of October 1931, her hair a deep golden instead of the customary bright red, and from there set off for a holiday in the West and a series of concerts on the Pacific Coast. She arrived in Rapid City, South Dakota, to sing at a benefit to raise money for the completion of the Mount Rushmore National Memorial. At a banquet given in her honour, where the sculptor Gutzon Borglum acted as host, Mary was advised that a new road over Iron Mountain to the National Memorial had just been named 'The Mary Garden Way'. So overjoyed was she that Mary gave Senator Norbeck, chairman of the Park Board, a smacking kiss.

The concert in Rapid City, recalled Merle Armitage, 'was the most bizarre of Garden's whole career. Coming from a radius of two hundred miles, miners in overalls and cowboys in boots mingled with townsfolk sparkling in full dress.'[2] It was almost as if she had, after all, decided to play Minnie in *La fanciulla del West*. The following day, Mary and Armitage set off to view the mountain itself:

> When we approached the Rushmore Memorial, there, on stone pilasters was a bronze plaque which read 'Mary Garden Highway'. Borglum's men were swinging out on ropes over those huge stone faces, boring holes with pneumatic drills. As we watched, they inserted a charge of dynamite and down the mountainside crashed tons of broken granite, making only a tiny dimple in George Washington's left ear![3]

They drove on, to the famous Homestake Mine at Lead. 'Calamity Jane's grave was pointed out to us as we passed,' continued Armitage:

A band composed of sixty miners, lanterns in their caps, welcomed us to the mine by playing 'Annie Laurie' with enthusiasm, if slightly off-key. The superintendent greeted us and we were dropped via a cage to the twenty-three-hundred-foot level of the mine. Walking through a tunnel for perhaps three hundred feet, we came upon a brilliantly lighted opening where, on rough tables, we were served a miner's luncheon. The superintendent, after a self-conscious speech, presented Garden with a fat, golden nugget.[4]

In spite of such colourful excursions, the tour as a whole was not a success. 'We filled a number of dates through Texas, the Rocky Mountain states, the Black Hills and the Northwest, but with little success,' admitted Wagner. 'So many towns had been cancelled in the past through our continual clashes with the Opera Company that people had lost interest.'[5]

In Boston with the Boston Symphony Orchestra under Koussevitsky, Mary sang Debussy's *La demoiselle élue* with countless recalls. 'We have never heard her sing better or evince greater artistry in opera than in this concert, because of her selection for which sceptics had raised eyebrows,' wrote Moses Smith for the *Musical Courier* (December 1931). 'Here was artistic sincerity on the same plane as her Mélisande – and this is high praise, indeed. Miss Garden was not at all times in thorough agreement with Mr Koussevitsky. Her tendency was to dramatize the text and music, and we were inclined to agree with her changes of pace and dynamics.' As for Koussevitsky, he was overwhelmed, presenting Mary with a signed photograph inscribed: 'A Mary Garden, l'inoubliable *Demoiselle élue*, avec admiration.'[6]

There followed a concert in Oakland, California, but with a very different effect. 'Shorn of the color and warmth and action of the opera,' complained the *Oakland Tribune* (19 December 1931),

> shorn of the atmosphere of high tragedy and of orchestral and choral support, shorn of all the trappings and traditions of the art in which she excelled, Mary Garden stood before a friendly and expectant audience and attempted to give expression to her vivid, vital personality through the single medium of her voice. It was an acid test and the chemist's report said – no.
>
> No one can deny the magnetic charm of the actress, which won the heart of the audience in spite of the operatic mannerisms that seemed bizarre on the concert platform. No one can deny the histrionic genius that was glimpsed in her singing of two or three of the more restrained numbers on the program. But even if allowance is made for the slight cold from which she was obviously suffering, one could not help but conclude that her voice is not for the concert stage. When she essayed volume, her tone was obviously forced. Instead of soaring to high notes, she climbed with effort. In the lower register she was inclined to huskiness. It was only in the middle voice, with subdued volume, that she attained warmth and beauty of tone.

In response, it was later widely reported that Mary was going to write a book about the fool critics who said she couldn't sing. Leaving Oakland, she arrived triumphant in San Francisco where she was photographed with director Gaetano Merola in front of the new War Memorial Opera House (then under construction). Mary prepared to appear for the first time as soloist with the San Francisco Symphony Orchestra under Basil Cameron.

She sang before an 8000-strong audience in the Exposition Auditorium, this time pleasing the critics a good deal more. The *Musical Courier* (January 1932) observed that her singing of the 'Depuis le jour' was admirable; her tones warm, expressive and colourful; her style polished and her interpretation emotionally appealing.

> The Debussy songs were exquisitely treated by Miss Garden who has caught the spirit of the French master as have few of her confrères. Never was there an artist on the Auditorium stage able to create an atmosphere of mystic fascination as did Garden in the lovely 'Beau Soir'. Miss Garden's flaming temperament, her superb histrionic powers and most magnetic personality combine to make her unique among present-day singers.

*   *   *

Before she sailed for Europe on 8 January 1932, Mary announced that she had signed a three-year contract with concert manager Arthur Judson of the Columbia Concerts Corporation. This contract would cover all her future activities in the United States: concert tours, broadcasting, opera and talking pictures. 'I am especially pleased because my new management is affiliated with the Community Concert Service [CCS], a movement which is bringing music to many cities in the United States and Canada which have never had the chance to hear good music. I have always sung, year after year, in the big sophisticated cities. Now I am going to appear before audiences which have never heard me.'

Charles L. Wagner, perhaps from pique, had deep misgivings about the CCS.

> They considered it a triumph to get Garden away from the outstanding independent manager. I urged her to accept their offer, which called for three years of concerts on a promise of $35,000 a year but finally turned out to be a porous plaster contract. As far as I know, she filled only one date the following season and became another victim of machine management. It seems the guarantee was missing when the signatures finally were affixed to the contract.[7]

On 16 February 1932, it was announced to the Friends of the Chicago Civic Opera Company that there would be no 1932–33 season. Samuel Insull, for all his acumen, had been unable to subsidize the company or raise the sum required from alternative sources.

In Paris that summer, a poignant note was sounded for Mary. On 17 June, as part of a Debussy Festival, she represented the United States at the dedication by President Lebrun of a monument to Claude Debussy on the Boulevard Lannes near the Bois de Boulogne. In the evening, at the Théâtre des Champs Elysées, a concert was given under the batons of five different conductors. Mary sang the fourth act of *Pelléas et Mélisande* conducted by Inghelbrecht. She had come full circle.

Ten days later, she was in Cleveland for two performances of *Carmen*. This was Cleveland's second annual season of outdoor opera at the Municipal Stadium, produced by Laurence Productions, Inc., with a supporting cast of 1000. 'It was glorious,' she later told the *Cleveland Plain Dealer* (8 December 1949). 'It was grand. It was magnificent. That great stage and the vast production that was made possible. I'll never forget the third act. I was singing the Card Scene. The campfires were built out over a large area. The smugglers were gathered around them with all their equipment – including their donkeys. Those donkeys! Just as I reached the climax of my aria, they began to bray. The audience just roared and I don't blame them.' She went on, mischievously: 'They did not disturb me. There have always been jackasses in grand opera'.[8]

On 5 July it emerged that Samuel Insull's business empire had collapsed. With him crashed 300,000 stockholders, but Mary was not one of them. For whatever reason (financial acumen, some claim), she had not, unlike a number of her operatic colleagues, invested her hard-earned cash in any of his stock. Insull was in due course forced out of all his companies. Early in October, he and his brother were indicted for embezzlement. On 8 October he fled to Italy and then Greece, where he would stay for a year. Mary arrived back in America a month later, claiming that she regretted not being able to see Insull in Europe and speak her mind to him. She spoke with sorrow of the closing of the Chicago Civic Opera Company. 'Insull destroyed a healthy and beautiful organisation,' she commented.[9] Later she would denounce him as a Frankenstein and a coward:

> Insull killed opera in Chicago. When he became president of the Grand Opera Company four years ago, he set himself up as a czar, he dictated everything. He fired stars because of personal prejudices. He told us what to sing and how to sing it. He couldn't do that. He was a financier – not a musician; an entrepreneur, not an impresario. When he moved us from the old Auditorium to his new Civic Opera Building, he took us from a certain present to a dubious future. And today Chicago has no grand opera.[10]

In mid-January 1933, Mary signed a contract to appear in vaudeville on the Loew circuit, singing classic folk songs. She made her vaudeville début in Washington, in four stage appearances a day, alternating with a Noël Coward film, *Tonight is ours*, with Fredric March and Claudette Colbert, appropriately set in Paris. Appearing at Loew's Fox Theatre, Mary was conducted by Phil Lampkin with Loew's Fox Concert Orchestra and the Radio Rubes (15 minutes of comedy, singing and imitations), Janet May, aerialist, and the O'Connor Sisters.

An indication of Mary's slide down-market came that February in New York. On Broadway, reduced prices for admission reached a new low: 35

cents was now the day and night rate to all parts of the original and once-proud Roxy, with proportionate cuts at all other houses. Another sign of the times was the presence at the Capitol Theatre of Mary Garden sharing headline honours with the Mills Brothers.

Uncharacteristically, Mary left New York on the *Empress of Britain* in the spring of 1933 unrecognized by the press, who were more intent on pursuing George Bernard Shaw. Her immediate plans were to sing *Pelléas et Mélisande* and *Sapho* in Paris. But there were unexpected developments awaiting her at the Opéra-Comique. 'I was deceived when I arrived the other day,' she told Jean Rollot. 'I was not offered the old scenery any longer. No more fountain, no more tower. The room where Mélisande dies is not the same as it was. I don't want to sing on this set.'[11] She decided to go to Beaulieu for a few days, and from there to Corsica.

In September Mary told the press that she was forming an operatic company in Paris to give tabloid versions of *Le jongleur de Notre-Dame* and *Thaïs*. She aimed to bring her company to America and would not be averse to putting these interpretations onto the silver screen. Then from Nice came reports that she was abandoning her villa, 'Les Galets' (the Pebbles). At a quick auction in Villefranche, valuable furniture, books, linens, wines and liqueurs from 'Les Galets' went for almost nothing – a Chinese cabinet; an Empire table; a first edition of *Aphrodite* autographed by its author, Pierre Louÿs; a specially bound set of Sir Walter Scott's novels and fourteen volumes of Voltaire's works in the 1801 edition. It was the sloughing of an old skin.

By April 1934, Samuel Insull was in an Istanbul prison. It was said he was shortly due to return to America. Mary again raged against him: 'I am afraid he abhorred my work because it was too modern. He hated anything modern. I know many fine artists who lost all or most of their money through him.'[12]

That month, Mary sang *Résurrection* at the Opéra-Comique. Parisians found it to be a mixture of Puccini and Mussorgsky. 'The staging was very impressive,' wrote Arnaud, 'thanks above all to Mary Garden who combines her talents as singer and musician with that of great actress.'[13] Paul Le Flem, writing in *Comœdia* (13 April 1934) was even more fulsome in his praise of Mary's performance:

> Her grace, the delicious freshness of her voice, her dramatic speaking overwhelmed more than one member of the audience. Tenderness was followed by strong emotion without warning, a talent that earned her warm applause the other evening.
>
> Katusha in *Résurrection* is not gracious Mélisande, the small figure lost between dreams and amorous passion, but a woman brutally snatched from her illusions and plunged into total physical and moral ruin.
>
> With touching tenderness, Mary Garden personified at the beginning the faith of youth dazzled by love. Then, with sorrowing fire, with unusual power, she

expressed doubt, anguish and abandoned herself to the bitter disillusion which Prince Dimitri's complete indifference produced in her.

Noël Coward was also one of those who went to hear her. After the curtain fell, he rushed into her dressing-room. 'I've never seen anything in my life like that drunken girl, Mary,' he said, to which Mary commented: 'In that drunken daze, I cried hot tears.'[14]

At her final performance of *Résurrection* at the Opéra-Comique on 29 May 1934, in the star's dressing-room – still full of flowers – Mary announced that she was retiring.

*   *   *

During the winter of 1934 Mary appeared in a lecture-recital in Los Angeles. 'Never more beautiful or vibrant,' wrote the *Los Angeles Examiner* (7 December 1934), 'Miss Garden wore a shimmering sheath-like frock of black paillettes with a train. Her golden hair was informal and her manner that of a confident friend.' She limited her vocal work to some Debussy songs – 'Beau Soir', 'Green', 'Chevelure' and 'Mandoline'. All were given with splendid finesse; all were warmly welcomed and applauded.

But then, Mary showed a more brittle side to her nature; having completed the Debussy programme, she stepped to the edge of the footlights to start her lecture on Debussy's works, beginning with an unexpected tirade against Mrs Patrick Campbell's untidy appearance in the London production of *Pelléas et Mélisande* which Mary had attended on 18 July 1904 with Claude Debussy. 'No woman should ever keep her hair black; it always looks filthy,' she commented. 'Mrs Campbell should have discarded her own black hair and worn a blonde wig,' she added.

The audience, speechless for a moment, could not help but laugh at this attack. Mrs Campbell, who had a caustic wit, said later:

> I have great admiration for Miss Garden. Poor thing, maybe she doesn't know that Sir Edward Burne-Jones, who designed my dresses and the scenery for *Pelléas and Mélisande*, preferred my own for dyed hair or a wig. Unfortunately, Debussy didn't like me, but Maeterlinck said: 'You have given me the happiness of seeing my dreams made visible and real.'[15]

Mary returned to Chicago at the end of January 1935, this time to sing in a Debussy concert at the Casino ballroom. She was excited and delighted as she stepped off the train in the La Salle station train-shed that morning.[16] Wearing a printed blouse with a black skirt, a black hat and adorned with lavender orchids, she went directly to the Drake Hotel to rest.

The programme for her concert opened with her accompanist, Jean Dansereau, who played a group of three Debussy numbers. Amusement was provided meanwhile, by Mary, who was practising her songs backstage, little aware that she was being overheard by her audience. Then, after performing the Debussy songs, as a departure from anything that she had ever done before, she proceeded to tell the story of Debussy's life as she had come to know it during her four years' acquaintance with him and his wife in Paris.

The concert drew an audience of 400 society folk. 'Dramatic, vivacious, the blonde-haired prima donna who has a figure that any débutante might envy, captivated her audience, which numbered as many men as women,' wrote the *Chicago Daily Tribune* (26 January 1935). It was her 'intimate talk' on Debussy, however, that drew the longest and loudest applause from the audience. This lecture-recital format was ideal for Mary's failing vocal powers and her flair as a scandalous raconteur. The effect on her audience, however, was not always the one she intended.

Three days later she appeared at the New York's Hotel Plaza ballroom before an audience of many interested and knowledgeable fellow-professionals, including Geraldine Farrar, Marion Telva, Maggie Teyte, Ganna Walska, Frances Alda, Marguerite d'Alvarez and Rosina Galli. Author Paul Horgan happened to be there to launch his first book. He was astonished by Mary:

> Suddenly the stage bloomed with light. There was a bated pause, and with a sudden step, Mary Garden appeared from stage right, halted, raised her arm to rest her hand on the proscenium, and held her pose. She had an affinity of countenance with the great cats here refined exquisitely to retain the tiger's high cheeks above the fixed, meaningless smile; intent gaze; alert focus on all environs; thoughtless confidence of power; all supported by the gift of seeming beautiful at will. Her eyes gleamed with a tigerish light in a little blue cave of shadow. Her voice was without luster – she was past the age of brilliant tone. Perfect in pitch, it had at moments almost a *parlando* quality, in a timbre reminiscent of dried leaves stirred by air. But what expression, now smoky with passion. What musicality; and what sense of meaning.[17]

Speaking in Boston some weeks later, Mary revealed that she had been really and truly in love – just once. But, she added, the man was not free to marry her, so she never married. She wouldn't tell his name, but said that he was not of the theatre or concert world. The unnamed man was J. Ogden Armour. It was also in Boston that she revealed she now had two passions. She was intent on obtaining the entire 2000 volumes written on the life of Napoleon III (she already owned 100). Her other passion was her nephew Mario Goetschel, the good-looking son of the French dramatic tenor, Charles Dalmorès (who had worked extensively with Mary), and Mary's sister Helen. He had been born in Paris at Mary's apartment in the Avenue Malakoff. His natural father would have nothing to do with him so she had taken him into her care.

At a dinner engagement in Hollywood in the spring of 1935, Mary had the pleasure of sitting beside her former protégée, Grace Moore. Mary indulged herself in some wishful thinking: she had been greatly intrigued by

Grace's triumph in the film *One night of love*. If only she could get the right vehicle, Mary said, she herself would be interested in staging a return to the films. Grace, who believed that Mary was one of the greatest actresses of all time, was eager to have her make a sound film and several producers claimed to be interested.

* * *

On 1 May a telegram arrived from Horst Kaiser, Mary's agent. It read:

> Armour Company prospective radio sponsor. Half hour programs, probably combination singing and talking. When do you return to Chicago from California? Desire arrange luncheon conference between yourself, Armour president, his advertising council and myself. Could luncheon be 11 May? Contract will be lucrative if we can land it. Much interest in Chicago master-classes. Regards. Kaiser.[18]

In Chicago, Edward Moore was excited at the prospect of Mary giving master-classes. 'It registers as good news that Mary Garden will come to Chicago this summer to teach an operatic class at the Chicago musical college,' he wrote. 'From the fact that she has been known at one time or another to give private coaching to some of her associates in her active operatic days and from the results thereof, she would seem to have some of the same gifts in teaching operatic lore as she has in transmitting it across the footlights, or in making pungent comments on the subject in private.'[19]

The Chicago Musical College course began in June. The charge for an audition by Mary was $5. The schedule included lessons from 9.00 a.m. to 12.00 noon on Mondays, Wednesdays and Fridays for six weeks. Marie Zendt (later a concert singer) auditioned for Mary with 'Depuis le jour'. The diva's reaction was dramatic. 'She shook me, she stamped her foot, she fairly screamed. "Sing with joy," she said, "Remember you, as Louise, have given up the whole world for this love and it's yours and that song is your whole soul's expression of it".'[20] In that one session with Mary, music took on a new dimension for Marie: never again, she said, would she sing the notes of a composer without understanding the fire of his spirit that had created them.

Another student, Margot Gibbon, recalled that 'Miss Garden was always at the theatre before anyone arrived. At the end of a session the blouses of white silk she always wore would be wringing from the heat of the theatre. Her three don'ts were: smoking, drinking and love-affairs. She always stressed posture, breathing and diction.'[21]

Tenor Robert Long, recently retired as a long-time professor of singing at the Chicago Music College and its successor, Roosevelt University, remembers that:

> I met Mary Garden when I was a student in 1935, first in the summer, probably

June or July. That was her first class of six weeks. I was not a private student. She did not give private lessons as far as I know.

The classes were in the theatre of the old Chicago Music College (from which I graduated), formerly located in Van Buren Street. They were principally acting classes. I was awarded her scholarship for that summer. I think I can say without boasting that I was her favourite that summer, mainly because I knew many of the tenor roles which I could sing with the sopranos and mezzos. What she liked to do was scenes – I did *Carmen*, *La bohème* and *Faust*.

She could be very drastic in her statements. I remember one time that she was ranting around. She said 'None of you knows about the art of singing. None of you – except the tenor!' Perhaps that's why I remember it.

She was very wonderful to me during the summer and I was the star of the class. At the end of the time she had me come down to see her at the Blackstone Hotel, where she always stayed when she was a singer and later also. She said she had great hopes for me, that she was willing to do things for me and perhaps take me to Paris.

Then we had the scholarship trials again for the Fall. In the meantime I was just starting out on a career as a singer. I got a contract to sing the songs of Charles Wakefield Cadman.

Her secretary was a man by the name of Horst Kaiser. I said to him that I was going to be gone for three weeks of the class. He never told her that. The first week she spent mostly hearing voices, so we did very little. When I came back from this tour she didn't even speak to me.

I wrote her a note and told her what had happened and she relented somewhat and I finished the class but it was never the same again. That ended my career with Mary Garden.

I do remember one funny thing about Mary. I was singing a scene from *Carmen*. Somehow, the soprano knocked me down. Mary said 'Are you hurt, darling? I'll sing *Carmen* with you and I won't hurt you!'

Mary approached each role as an actress, rather than as a great singer, to show off her voice. She was interpreting the role. She didn't worry about her voice. She was a great artist. There's no question of that.

I don't recall her singing in the class at all. It was more staging and the acting in it. It was on the stage of the little theatre. I don't recall a great audience, but I think there were visitors. No costume. It was three mornings a week, from 10.00 am to about 1.00 pm. We didn't have air-conditioning in those days, so the theatre would be hot. She would be kinda bedraggled by the end of the morning.

Mary would make remarks. I don't think she thought technically too much when she was singing. She got into the role. She would say when something was wrong, but I don't recall her ever telling anyone how to do it better. She never said anything about the techniques of singing. I don't think she gave private lessons. She wasn't a singing teacher.[22]

The distinguished accompanist, Robert Wallenborn, did, however, recall that several singers had private lessons, among them Helen Jepson. She studied the Garden roles and later sang them – Mélisande, Thaïs and Fiora – in Chicago and New York; also taught by Mary were Jean Tennyson and Joseph Bentonelli (Benton). The latter was shown the door when he protested that he couldn't sing a particular role in Rome. 'Mr Kaiser,' Mary called out, 'give Mr Bentonelli his money back!'[23]

As the Chicago classes neared their end in October, Mary was struck down by an attack of pleurisy. She later resumed her class, but was reportedly under medical care, saving her energy for a concert scheduled for 12 November.

The concert was held in her beloved Auditorium Theatre. She shared the programme with the director of the Chicago Music College, the celebrated pianist Rudolph Ganz who played Debussy. Garden talked, then sang, accompanied by Robert Wallenborn. 'Mary Garden,' wrote the *Musical Leader* (23 November 1935), 'on the sere and yellow side of life, is still naively under her own spell – and she weaves it over others. She told her story, enacted a few situations and sang a few (very few) of the composer's songs.'

In December 1935, Adrian, the costume designer, threw a lavish party for Mary in Hollywood. Her friends Cole and Linda Porter were among the guests. George Eells observed her with fascination: 'Finger-bowls were placed in front of the guests. In each bowl a gardenia floated, beneath which lay an unopened oyster shell. Each guest was given a sharp knife to pry open the shell and discovered a Japanese cultured pearl'.[24]

Then romance unexpectedly entered Mary's life again in April 1936. In New York the radio amateur hour impresario, Major Edward Bowes, an elegant, thickset man, denied he was about to marry Mary: 'Mary Garden is a very lovely lady. I have known her for a long time. The rumour is absolutely ridiculous.'[25] The soprano Beverley Sills recalled that at the time he was dating Mary Garden, Major Bowes had two weekly shows on CBS radio – the Original Amateur Hour, a vaudeville talent contest, and Capitol Family – both broadcast from the Capitol Theater Building.[26] It is not beyond the realms of possibility that Mary was cultivating the Major in the hope that he could help her acquire some kind of contract.

* * *

In mid-April 1936, Mary again travelled to Hollywood, where she had been contracted by Metro-Goldwyn-Mayer (MGM) to act as consultant on all musical picture productions. On the same train were Al Jolson and the comic actor/author, Robert Benchley. In anticipation of her working association with Louis Mayer, Mary declared that he was 'a wonderful man, a great creative soul, a big man, one who knows genius. I know four, only four great voices in Hollywood. Nelson Eddy is the finest artist singing today. I heard him over the air more than a year ago. The others are Grace Moore, Gladys Swarthout and Jeanette MacDonald. Jan Kiepura? I have heard him sing but I do not like his work.'[27]

Mary made her first tour of a modern motion picture studio that July. She was admitted beyond the 'No Visitors' sign and ushered to the sound stage where *Suzy* was being filmed. She accepted a chair beside the camera from director George Fitzmaurice. The scene was the interior of a Montmartre café; Jean Harlow and Inez Courtney were singing 'Under the Bamboo Tree'. They approached a table surrounded by a group of noisy young soldiers and Mary turned her gaze towards them. Involuntarily, a gasp from Mary invaded the sound track. 'Oh, look! Isn't that Stanley Morner?' The scene had to be retaken, of course, and while the cameras were being reloaded Morner recognized Mary and hastened over to her. Wisconsin-born, Morner had been discovered by Mary while singing at the Palmer House Empire Room in Chicago; she had sent him to MGM executives in New York who duly gave him a screen test and a Hollywood contract.

Mary spent the rest of that summer in France and returned to America in October. As she left Le Havre, she discussed her engagement by MGM: 'I am abandoning the stage completely to start a new life, a new career. But the films I will act in will not be simple operas transferred to the screen. They will have a dynamic quality, something new'.[28] On reaching New York, she told the press there about her future plans. She was going to adapt opera for the moving pictures and train singers for them. 'I shall look for talent in the Middle West and the East. Last June, I listened to 750 aspiring singers and there were only two that I would offer to the MGM studio for opera or musical plays. I can tell right away whether they have any talent, even before I hear them sing.'[29] Mary said she already had five young singers in training for operatic productions. They had been studying in Paris since June. All were Americans; all of them were marvellous, although they needed training, and several of the women were beautiful.

In France, her statements on the cinema as a new musical art-form were given a cool reception. The composer Reynaldo Hahn criticized her for saying in an interview that she was turning to the cinema because contemporary composers were writing nothing that was worth staging. 'Mary Garden! Magical name, evocative of proud and triumphant nights; synonymous with grace, poetry, strangeness, seduction – and also fine pluckiness, what amiable impertinence!,' he concluded.[30]

But Mary persisted in her view. To the Los Angeles Association of Advertising Women she proclaimed: 'Opera is doomed to melancholy slumber unless it recaptures glamour. And apparently glamour is in Hollywood.'[31]

In 1937, still acting as a scout for MGM, Mary made yet more discoveries of American singing talent. Margaret Mayer, an 18-year-old Garden protégée, was heard in Chicago by Louis Mayer and as a result was put under contract at the MGM studios.[32] Mary searched Europe: she listened to youthful singers in Italy, France and Belgium and expressed enthusiasm for five 'most gorgeous' tenor voices which she had heard in Rome. The five, all under 25 years of age, were to be given screen tests for MGM in Cinema City, Rome.

Aged 63, yet still blonde and vivacious, Mary was back to spend Christmas 1937 in Chicago, after which she would be returning to Hollywood to resume her talent scouting. 'After 30 years I can smoke the big cigarettes I love. I can go to the movies without being afraid of catching a germ. And I don't practise a minute a day. I'm done. I'm finished. And I'm happy.'[33]

Notes

1. Grace Moore, *You're Only Human Once*, p. 103.
2. Merle Armitage (1965), *Accent on Life*, Ames: The Iowa State University Press, p. 66.
3. Ibid., p. 67.
4. Ibid.
5. Charles L. Wagner (1940), *Seeing Stars*, New York: Putnam's Sons.
6. Mary Garden scrapbook, vol. 13, RCM.
7. Charles L. Wagner, op. cit.
8. David Camelon, 'Legendary ladies', *The American Weekly*, 28 August 1949.
9. *New York Times*, 25 November 1932.
10. *New York Times*, 17 February 1933.
11. *Paris Soir*, 2 June 1933.
12. *New York Times*, 9 April 1934.
13. *Marianne*, 25 April 1934.
14. Bennitt Gardiner, 'Mary Garden', *Musical Events*, February 1967, p. 28.
15. *Los Angeles Examiner*, 10 December 1934.
16. *Chicago Daily Tribune*, 25 January 1935.
17. L'Après-midi de Mary Garden, *The Yale Review*, vol. 76, Spring 1987, pp. 361–73.
18. Telegram from scrapbook in possession of Peter MacPhee.
19. *Chicago Sunday Tribune*, 2 June 1935.
20. *Chicago Sun Times*, 6 January 1967.
21. Margot Gibbon, 'Memories of Garden', unidentified magazine, January 1962, pp. 56–7. New York Public Library, The Fine and Peforming Arts Library, six miscellaneous scrapbooks, ref. *2B-2210 Reel 1.
22. Robert Long interviewed in Chicago by author, 17 July 1993.
23. Letter to author from Joseph Bentonelli, 28 February 1994.
24. George Eells (1967), *The Life That Late He Led*, London: W.H. Allen, p. 132.
25. *Los Angeles Examiner*, 7 April 1936.
26. Beverley Sills and Lawrence Linderman (1987), *Beverley – an Autobiography*, New York: Bantam Books.
27. *Los Angeles Examiner*, 26 April 1936.
28. *Paris Soir*, 22 October 1936.
29. *New York Times*, 24 October 1936.
30. *Le Figaro*, 4 November 1936.
31. *Los Angeles Examiner*, 4 December 1936.
32. Ibid., 4 February 1936.
33. Ibid., 26 December 1937.

14 Retirement Years: 1937–1967

Grace Moore, who managed to negotiate the transition from stage to screen with great success, never failed to acknowledge the debt of gratitude she owed to Mary:

> Garden has had a tremendous influence on my life, my career, my ambitions. Pictures of her come back at random. She was so lovely, so flaming, so much a woman – warm and soft and tender as a woman should be.
>
> When I returned to Paris in 1937 to make the film *Louise*, Mary had been engaged as a European talent scout for Metro-Goldwyn-Mayer. My husband Val and I would often go to her flat on the Rue du Bac for long, laughing chats. The lovely salon was shaded by chestnut trees that bent close to the casement windows, and the light would dapple the myriad mementoes of Mary's great career. It was her room – her whole life.
>
> In one corner was a souvenir painting of Mary as Salome, in another a canvas of her as Mélisande; over there a picture of her in a divine modern dress designed for her by Molyneux.[1]

In November 1938 Mary was photographed with Grace Moore in her dressing-room at the Opéra-Comique. It was the scene of Mary's own great triumphs, where her protégée was about to make her début in Charpentier's *Louise* – in her case, after considerable consultation with the by-now venerable composer who was still as bohemian as ever. Moore had studied the role of Louise with Mary: 'She had a mellow approach to teaching,' she recalled. 'She embued you with such enthusiasm and friendliness and was so uncanny in pointing up strengths as well as weaknesses that her reactions were immediately absorbed in your own interpretation, naturally and spontaneously.'[2]

During the big opening scene in the third act, as Mary had suggested, Grace moved closer to Julien to sing directly to him and, through him, in patriotic fervour to Paris. 'The audience, led by Garden, responded with such prolonged applause that she repeated the aria "Depuis le jour" – and was sharply scolded by some critics for doing so. The prolonged applause was a tribute to Garden as well as to Moore. The elder prima donna stood up, took a bow, unpinned the flowers from her chinchilla wrap, and tossed them on the stage at her protégée's feet.'[3]

After the outbreak of the Second World War, Mary stayed in Paris until in 1940 it became clear that she would have to leave. Her nephew, Mario Goetschel, recalls the events clearly.

> My grandmother, Mrs Garden, was at Juan-les-Pins and I was living with her. She went there during the 'Phoney War'. But, in May 1940, without warning, the Germans broke through. My grandmother quickly went back to Paris, to 44, Rue du Bac, which my Aunt Mary shared with a friend and they took one of the last civilian planes from Le Bourget. They had to make a detour to avoid the war zone.[4]

Mary left all her possessions with her faithful maid, Françoise Donnadieu. This fine woman was devoted to Mary; she had been her personal maid since 1912. She had travelled backwards and forwards to the theatre with Mary in her halcyon days, taking care of her costumes, aiding her in her dressing for the stage, taking a tremendous pride in the adulation Mary received. Françoise was often taken for Chinese – it was said that she had Chinese ancestors, but in fact she came from central France and was completely French. She had a small flat in the 17th arrondisement and at the beginning of the Occupation she gave up one of her rooms to house all Mary's belongings. She looked after everything – books, furniture and pictures, among them drawings by Tiepolo – for four years. She had to watch out for the concierge, who was a Vichy sympathizer, a *collaborateur*. But Françoise had a good family doctor who looked after her; on one occasion the doctor came to Françoise's home, saw one of Mary's paintings hanging on her wall and remarked only: 'You've got a beautiful room there'. After the war Mary learned that the Germans had taken her five automobiles and occupied her house, but Françoise had managed to smuggle out the treasures of her operatic life and had them safely hidden in her doctor's operating-room.

* * *

After fleeing Paris, Mary made her permanent home in Aberdeen, where she continued to work on her autobiography. Once the manuscript was completed, she sent it to her old friend, the New York critic, Carl Van Vechten who took it to a publisher acquaintance, Bill Raney of Rinehart's. Both felt the autobiography was badly written and missed the most important aspects of her career and Van Vechten wrote to her in his most diplomatic terms to tell her so.

During this period, Mary also took an interest in Aberdeen's theatre life, as evinced by an admiring Noël Coward in his autobiography. Coward describes how, in Christmas 1942,

Mary Garden, as dynamic as ever, came to the plays and I saw to it that she was treated as Royalty. There were flowers in her box, and Hugh Kingston-Hardy, our business manager, received her with his usual charm. In my opinion she was one of the greatest operatic actresses in the world. The years left no apparent mark on her and when I asked after her voice she said gaily that she had given up singing for ever and preferred smoking and bridge.[5]

The journalist Gwen Morgan visited Mary at 18 Albert Street, Aberdeen, during the summer of 1946 and was much taken with her home.

This is a severely plain one-and-a-half storey granite row house, with all its beauty saved for the richly furnished interior and the garden at the rear, which is bright with roses and rhododendrons. Mary Garden's hair is bright red. The nails of her slender, expressive hands are polished. Her big rings flash. Her figure still is the trim one of *Salome*. She is in tweeds topped with six strands of choker pearls. Her clothes are almost all pre-War. She usually wears a bright tweed skirt and jacket. And under them – woolies. Her hose are cotton and her shoes are low-heeled brogues.

She favours a jaunty blue beret with the small gold cross of Lorraine given her by General de Gaulle, whose autographed picture stands in a big frame on a drawing-room table. Another autographed photo is of Claude Debussy.[6]

In 1946 Mary was engaged in America to teach French to the young Beverley Sills. Beverley was friendly with Jean Tennyson, both girls pupils of singing teacher, Estelle Liebling. Tennyson's husband, Camille Dreyfus, was chairman of the Celanese Corporation of America. 'When Jean learned that retired soprano Mary Garden was down on her luck,' writes Beverley Sills,

she hired Mary to teach French repertoire to six scholarship students. She paid Mary Garden $1,500 per student.... We spoke only French together, and in our six weeks of study she taught me *Manon* and *Thaïs*. Although I'd already started concentrating on French operas because of my love of Lily Pons, Mary Garden really got me hooked.

That was in spite of her teaching methods. Charming, she wasn't. Mary Garden often struck me as the meanest woman I'd ever met. She was generous when it came to showing me how she performed *Manon*, and absolutely awful about allowing me room for a single creative thought. She received awe and admiration from me; in return, she made me feel like an awkward giant. I used to think of Mary as Mighty Mouse.

Mary urged me to further my study of French repertoire under the guidance of Max De Rieux, artistic director of the Paris Opéra. Mary said I could get to De Rieux through Georges Sébastian, a conductor for the Opéra and a great friend of Jean Tennyson. Jean wrote to Sébastian on my behalf and he called De Rieux, who accepted me into a small class he'd be teaching in July and August.[7]

In 1948 Mary was made an offer by the newly founded American National Arts Foundation to return to the United States to assist in a campaign for a renaissance of the arts. Initially she postponed her acceptance of the offer as she did not want to leave her mother, then 92 and very frail. However, her mother died in December of that year at Mary's home and Mary finally left for New York in September 1949 to start a four-month lecture tour. The idea behind this tour was that Mary would help to spread the gospel of the National Arts Foundation (NAF). She had come to America as a guest of the Conservatory of Music Scholarship Fund. Writing to *The New York Times*, Mary said that the NAF was part of a new and well thought-out programme to bring the arts to more people. She added: 'it is shocking to find that there is no opera house in Washington and no opera company in Chicago.'[8] Few could disagree with her. She announced that opera in America was on the decline and she made several suggestions for improvement. First, each great city should have an opera house that played all year round. Second, American singers should train in Europe, as American singers lacked fundamental training. Third, singers should choose what to do in life – they should either choose a great career or marriage, but not both.

'In my lectures', she announced, 'I am going to talk about the future of music. Music is dying. It has fallen and there are no great composers and no great singers any more.'[9]

Her homecoming to America was epic. Columnists praised her, prize flowers were named after her, hotels blossomed with Mary Garden suites and more than 4000 telegrams and letters welcomed her back. Accompanied by her faithful maid Françoise, Mary disembarked in New York wearing a skirt of Stewart tartan, a white silk blouse, a cherry-red jacket with a five-strand necklace of pearls, a diamond brooch and five ruby, emerald and diamond rings. Her ensemble was topped off with a cherry-red velvet hat with a green feather. On her jacket she wore the Légion d'Honneur and the Croix de Réconnaissance.

Emotionally, she told the press: 'As I saw your buildings with their brilliant lights early this morning, I knew I loved America. It's charming and I'll never forget it, but I want to live and die in Aberdeen.'[10] She declared that she weighed a mere 111 pounds: 'I haven't eaten dinner for thirty years.' She said she was crazy to go to the Metropolitan Opera and hear the singers. She claimed she had given all her music away and had sold her piano – 'I don't believe in farewell performances'. She then announced that she considered Kirsten Flagstad the greatest contemporary singer.

During her first lecture, in Washington, Mary spoke of Debussy. 'One day,' she said, 'standing at a window with Debussy, I killed a couple of flies. He objected to such cruelty. When I looked at him, two tears were rolling down his cheeks.'[11] She delighted her audience by saying, 'The women of America made my career. They took their husbands to see my *Thaïs* or my *Salome*, when men wanted to go to the movies. But when they saw Thaïs was nearly nude, men took the opera glasses away from the ladies and kept them all evening. The men learned that opera could be made interesting.'[12] She had just finished a book, she told New Yorkers. *The New York Times* (9 October 1949) reported that: 'As she talked, her blue eyes flashed and the black feathers on her red velvet cap bobbed with enthusiasm.'

But there were those who were not impressed. Geraldine Farrar, for example. 'I have cancelled my eight seats for any lecture of Miss Garden,' she wrote. 'I was so unhappily affected by her inane and commonplace radio interview; though in earlier days she knew the right kind of sympathetic publicity.'[13] But Geraldine Farrar was by no means hostile to Mary; rather, she pitied her. 'A professional friend,' she wrote, 'tells me she ran into Miss Garden at one of the candy shops in Manhattan, both indulging in a soda. My friend remarked that her face and body were extremely thin.'[14]

America showered Mary with favours. From Monmouth College, Illinois, she received an honorary Doctorate of Music. In Dayton, Ohio (where she was guest of honour at the Dayton Women's Press Club during the National Chrysanthemum Show), she had a chrysanthemum named after her. At a luncheon given by Stanley Woodward, chief of protocol for the State Department and a member of the Public Advisory Committee of the NAF, Mary and her sponsor, J. Carleton Smith, director of the NAF of New York, were guests of honour. This luncheon came immediately after Mary and Mr Smith had been received by President Truman at the White House.

'She is as electric, as provocative a personality today as ever,' noted the *Los Angeles Examiner* (13 November 1949). And, living up to her title of 'Mary Quite Contrary', she told the newspaper that she had never loved anyone of the opposite sex. 'Not one man. Not once was I ever involved in a grande passion. I determined never to fall in love'.

But the tour schedule took its toll on 75-year-old Mary. When she arrived in Cleveland, she was forced to cancel her lecture at Kent State University because of a chipped right elbow. She said she had fallen in Chicago the previous day after tripping on a wire outside a railroad station. She had to carry her arm in a sling but made light of it. 'I'll just have to talk with fewer operatic gestures.'[15]

The final lecture in her tour was on the 26 December in New York Town Hall. It was billed as 'Mary Garden in Person' and presented by the NAF. Appearing with her was the distinguished Metropolitan and Paris Opéra baritone, Martial Singher. The climax of the evening was to be a re-creation of a scene from *Pelléas et Mélisande. The New York Times* (27 December 1949) wrote that 'She swept onto the stage in a coral red lace dress at 9.21 pm and held it firmly for an hour and eleven minutes while she regaled her 1,500 strong audience. After her lengthy speech she returned to the stage with Carleton Smith, who read to her questions that had been put by members of the audience. "Did you ever sing with Caruso?" was one of them. "Yes. In *Manon Lescaut* in Paris [author's note: I can find no evidence of this at all]. He was very afraid of me because he was a gorgeous singer and I was an actress" '.

'It was 10.48 when the questions were completed, so there was no time for an intermission. Martial Singher came back to sing "Le jet d'eau". Then he returned to the wings to bring back Miss Garden. Together they did the Tower scene from *Pelléas et Mélisande*, where Pelléas embraces Mélisande's hair when it falls from the window. Mr Singher sang his part of the scene, but Miss Garden spoke her few brief lines and showed her acting skill by effectively suggesting the distraction and sadness of the young girl.'

The lecture attracted many notables including Cole Porter, Mrs Clarence Mackay (the former Anna Case), Gladys Swarthout, Carl Van Vechten and many other singers. And at the end of the questions session Mary showed she had not forgotten any of her old tricks: she took a red rose from a bouquet on a table on the stage and tossed it to a gentleman in the first row.

Maggie Teyte was also in the audience. Mary's performance served only to sadden her. 'She delivered a huge rambling concoction of supposition, scandal and promiscuous adventure,' Maggie Teyte remembered. 'Garden was mainly an object for pity.'[16] And Geraldine Farrar had already anticipated the embarrassment Mary would cause many of the professional singers in the audience who had known her in her days of greatness: 'Her New York lecture comes on this evening. I can imagine the French singer with her – formerly of the Met – will have the task of "eating time" with his songs. Heaven knows what she will say; so far there have been no properly prepared addresses, just a series of quips.'[17]

*   *   *

At the end of January 1950, Mary sailed for home on the *Queen Mary* after what *The New York Times* described optimistically as her 'triumphant 28 lectures'; the paper noted that Mary was to start work immediately on another series of lectures for the autumn.

Back in Aberdeen, Mary worked on her memoirs with the help of her sister Amy. Her New York publishers had rejected the rough draft she had submitted to them the previous year because it lacked love interest. In writing her memoirs, the publishers told her, she had completely ignored her once-sensational love-life. Now, after a year spent in Aberdeen, embellishing the romances of her golden youth, Mary hoped her autobiography had the right ingredients to be a best-seller.

In the event, her manuscript was still considered to be unpublishable. The music critic, Louis Biancolli was engaged to ghost-write it for her. For six weeks Biancolli and Mary met daily. She poured out her entire story from beginning to end and he took it down in Pitman shorthand, as the anecdotes gushed out of her.

Mary returned to America in October 1950 as planned, for another series of lectures, but this time she was to act as a talent scout for the National Arts Foundation Fellowship, whose Opera Committee chairman she now was.

Winning singers heard on her audition tour would perform for a special fellowship committee, including Rudolf Bing (general manager of the Metropolitan Opera) and the conductor Dr Bruno Walter. A three-year European scholarship followed by a European début was to be the possible award for three of the successful singers.

Arriving in Seattle, where she was to speak on 'Music, Men and Money', she astonished the inhabitants by stepping from her train wearing a leopard-skin turban, a coat of beaver and a veil that could not conceal the enduring beauty of one of the world's most-photographed personalities. At Seattle's Metropolitan Theatre that afternoon she appeared in a sweeping gown of black satin adorned with a great rope of pearls and topped with a dramatic white plumed hat. 'I don't really know much about men,' she began, coyly, 'I didn't need them; when I wanted something and didn't have it, I bought it.' And as for money: '[it] is the pest of the world. It has never been my God – thank heavens.'[18]

Her ghosted autobiography, *Mary Garden's Story*, was published in America in the late summer of 1951. Cecil Smith, editor of *Musical America*, penned a blistering review (September 1951), which captures comprehensively the extensive weaknesses of the book:

> As a documentation of Miss Garden's career this book is highly unsatisfactory. It is difficult, and often impossible, to find dates in the text, or even to infer them. No complete list of her roles is given, and some are never mentioned. When information is given, it is often inaccurate. Miss Garden became director of the Chicago Opera Association (not the Chicago Grand Opera Company) in 1921 (not 1922). She did not sing in Prokofiev's *The Love for Three Oranges*, although she did produce it during a single season in which she managed the Chicago Company.
>
> Gino Marinuzzi did not conduct the Prokofiev opera; both Prokofiev and Alexander Smallens did. Samuel Insull was not the director of the Company when Miss Garden and Edith Rockefeller McCormick had trouble about *Salome*; Miss Garden herself was. Miss Garden was not the first to sing *Salome* in Paris; Olive Fremstad was. She did not create the role of Fiora in Montemezzi's *l'amore dei tre re*; Luisa Villani did. She did not even sing it for the first time in Chicago; Louise Edvina did. Victor Herbert's *Natoma* was not the first American Grand Opera by a long way. Edward Sheldon, author of *Romance* was not the only man in Chicago who admired Hamilton Forrest's opera *Camille* in which Miss Garden sang; Eugene Stinson, critic of the *Daily News*, called it the most important opera since *Pelléas et Mélisande*. Miss Garden <u>did</u> return to America as a singer after her last season (1931–32) with the Chicago Civic Opera Company; though she says she did not, I myself heard her afterward. The Chicago Opera House (correctly known as the Civic Opera House), is described in a caption as 'the place where Mary sang after the failure of the Manhattan'; no mention is made of the fact that for nineteen years she sang at the Auditorium Theatre before the Civic Opera House was opened in 1929.
>
> The book is sure to leave Miss Garden's real admirers in an unhappy state of mind, for frothy anecdotes and superficial platitudes are a poor substitute for a serious consideration of her art and a reasonably exhaustive and accurate factual account of her career.

Miss Garden owed it to us to strike a deeper and more important note. Mr Biancolli owed it to us to check her facts, if she was not sure of them, and to give a truer representation of the aura that surrounded her in her active years.

As one who has spent some of his childhood years three doors away from the house in which she had lived when she attended the Hyde Park High School and took her first voice lessons, and as one who passed many a dollar through the Auditorium Theatre ticket-window to sit in the second gallery and hear her in almost all her roles, I know all too painfully that very little of the real Mary Garden is to be discovered in this book.

Another lecture-tour followed in the winter of 1951. Speaking in Hollywood (where she stayed in Beverly Hills, as she had done on her previous tour, as the guest of Montemezzi), Mary revealed that she had had offers for her life-story from both English and American film producers – but she would not accept any of these until she knew who would play Mary Garden. During her lecture tour, she again planned to audition young singers for NAF scholarships.

Interviewed back in Aberdeen two months later by the *Los Angeles Examiner* (16 February 1952), Mary said she had had a difficult winter. She had slipped on Aberdeen's ice-covered cobbles while shopping, wrenching her leg and was ordered to bed. She was interviewed in her favourite sitting-room where deep carpets were overlaid with a magnificent leopard-skin rug. The key-note of the room was red (she favoured this colour and the clothes she wore always had a touch of it) – there were red silk coverings on period furniture, antique pieces from France and a brooding bust of Napoleon. Shortly, she said, she would be going to Paris to see about the French publication rights for her autobiography.

On 28 January 1952 her book was published in the United Kingdom by Michael Joseph. Maggie Teyte, reviewing the book for the *Sunday Times* (2 March 1952), was as disappointed as Cecil Smith had been:

With my memory still keenly alive to her superb and unsurpassed interpretations of the roles of the Jongleur, Thaïs, Mélisande, Monna Vanna and other heroines of opera, I am a little bewildered by *Mary Garden's Story* which recounts the life of that gifted Scottish soprano. Equally and justly famous in France and America. I cannot reconcile the wonderful illusions she gave us before the scenery with what, Miss Garden would have us believe, happened behind it. Her story seeks to give the impression that hard work had little to do with her performances, or that it consisted only in learning musical notation.

That August, Mary gave a lecture on Debussy at the Edinburgh Festival. Six months later, in February 1953, she spoke before the Chicago Association of Commerce. She told them that opera was good for business and would give Chicago prestige. She added that she had plans to return to America for another lecture tour and that she would act as a consultant on a script of a motion picture of her life.

Caroline Kaart was a young soprano who appreciated the advice Mary gave her during this period.

In 1953 as a member of the Wilson Barrett Repertory Company, I played Her Majesty's Theatre, Aberdeen and because I had now studied for five years with Beatrice Miranda [the Australian diva of the Carl Rosa Opera Company], I thought the time had come for a change and was considering which teacher to entrust my voice to – a very risky business! I had a Caird Scholarship and was itching to make a decision. So I summoned up all my courage one morning and phoned Madame Garden at her home. I was thrilled that she was willing to listen and we (or rather, she) made an appointment with me, to meet at a famous piano music shop in Aberdeen's prestigious main shopping street. She arrived, swathed in black furs – silver foxes around her neck and (what I always have remembered clearly) a very Parisian hat, perched on her head and it had a thick meshed veil. That threw me a bit as a young, naive lassie. I couldn't see her face properly, you see. I had asked the local cinema organist to accompany me – I remember only the 'Habanera' from *Carmen* and she was so enthusiastic. She at once told me about an Italian singing teacher in London. She'd read his books and was impressed: E. Herbert Caesari was his name. She ended up singing, (darting between the rows of pianos upstairs), for me: pieces from *Pelléas et Mélisande* ('Ne me quittez pas'). And the light, flirty tone was just right for *Carmen*. Without doubt her enthusiastic approbation of my talent gave me the impetus to ask for an audition at Glyndebourne the following year.[19]

Mary was back in New York in January 1954 after what she declared to be her fifty-first Atlantic crossing, still proclaiming: 'I am absolutely happy I never married. I had my career and I put all my life and love into it.'[20] She visited the Metropolitan Opera House, where she was greeted by the soprano Jean Fenn, one of the current Met personnel. Then she went to Chicago and paid a final call on the abandoned Auditorium. She stood for a few minutes on the stage; later she said that this was the one memory she would take back with her to Aberdeen.

Mary made her television début on the CBS Ed Sullivan Show, receiving a four-figure pay-cheque for her brief appearance. Seated at a table on a set simulating Manhattan's El Morocco night-club, she talked and she listened to younger opera stars. She had quite a bit to say to the men singers, who kissed her hand and told her they remembered her.

She was back in Los Angeles that October. 'Only in *Louise*,' she told the *Los Angeles Herald and Express* (21 October 1954), 'was I myself on stage, because she was so much like me.' Mary had nothing but praise for Mario Lanza: 'He has a wonderful voice – a gorgeous voice. If only he would go to Europe and study and then come back and sing at the Metropolitan. He could be truly a great singer'.

She heard Maria Callas in Chicago that November, making her American début in *Norma*. The accompanist Bill Browning was with her. 'She took hold of my arm and said "Listen carefully, son. There's not been anything like this since *I* was up there". And she was probably right. Then Garden said "You know, she is a great actress, she is a great singer, but she acts on impulse. That's very dangerous".'[21]

* * *

In 1955 Vincent Sheean accompanied Mary at the Met to see *Salome*. Bizarrely, she claimed that she had never seen or heard the opera before.[22]

By this time, Mary had moved from Albert Street in Aberdeen to a flat in Belgrave Terrace. Her solicitor Geoff Collie recalls that 'It was just like a reproduction of Versailles in miniature, very French.' She would visit her sister, Mrs Amy Bower, regularly. 'I remember Mary Garden one summer afternoon a few years ago strolling through the gardens of her sister Amy's home, Pitmurchie House, near Torphins. "I lived life to the full," she said with a laugh, "I have no regrets".'[23] And garage owner Forbes Philip recalled: 'I knew Mary for twenty-five years. I drove her about all the time. She adored stopping the car and walking through the fields and woods. When we went into Aberdeen she would stroll along the beach oblivious of time or inclement weather'[24], just as she had once loved to do so many years before at Deauville.

In August 1958 Mary signed an agreement with the NAF for a film and television series to be made of her life. She travelled to Paris to sign the agreement with Dr Carleton Smith, the director of the NAF. She also agreed to make another visit to America. But twelve months later, before she could do so, Mary had an accident in her home, in which she was overcome by gas-fumes; it was believed she became faint after turning on a gas-range and was unable to light it or turn it off. She crawled to a door and a neighbour heard her faint cries for help; she was taken to Pitmurchie. She was to have made an unannounced appearance at a performance of *Pelléas et Mélisande* by the Opera Association of Washington. But instead she announced that she could not travel to America after all.

In August 1961, the musician and broadcaster Madeau Stewart (alerted to the fact that the Debussy centenary year was imminent) came north to interview Mary for the BBC. She met Mary at Pitmurchie. Also in the house was her other sister, Helen (Hélène) Goetschel; all three sisters were now over eighty. Did Mary have any letters from Debussy, Madeau Stewart wanted to know? No, she said with a glint in her eye, she had burned them all. One letter was saved – addressed to 'Ma chère petite Mélisande'.[25]

In June 1962, Mary was admitted to an Aberdeen hospital to recover from a fall which had broken both her arms. Her fellow patients begged her to sing. At first she refused. Then she sang 'Annie Laurie' sitting in a chair in the ward; she reduced some of her audience to tears. Had she not been in hospital, she would have been a guest of honour at Scottish Opera's première of *Pelléas et Mélisande* at the King's Theatre, Glasgow. Maggie Teyte, another prestigious guest, had been looking forward to meeting her again.

Sadly, Mary celebrated her ninety-first birthday in the isolation of a Scottish country hospital, the House of Daviot, near Inverurie, which specialized in psycho-geriatric care. Mail arrived for her from all over the world. There she also received old friends, such as the ballet-dancer, Anton Dolin. But her final days were dreadful – the nursing staff could do nothing for her or with her. 'She was very, very difficult,' remembers the late Geoff Collie.[26] Mary's mind had now gone and she was living in the past, throwing herself about. Eventually, she had to be strapped to the bed. For her relatives and friends it was very sad. Mercifully, Mary passed away on Tuesday, 3 January 1967.

Mary had the most beautiful furniture, but the pearls that everyone thought were priceless turned out to be the next best thing to paste. Nobody ever knew what she had done with her money. Probably she had been far too generous. Her solicitor tried all the banks but could find no trace of her fortune. At her death, Mary had £34 beside her in the hospital and £2 in the bank. The value of her jewellery was £536 and that of her personal effects £1477. Her solicitor held £145 for her. As for the royalties from her recordings, the value of her estate abroad (namely royalties under contract to the American Phonograph Company dating from 1910) was a nominal £1. Her total worldly goods added up to just £2195.16.

Some fifty friends attended a ceremony at the Aberdeen Crematorium conducted by The Very Reverend Richard E. Kerrin, Dean of St John's Episcopal Church, Aberdeen. In a tribute to Mary, Dean Kerrin said: 'She was one to whom there had been entrusted the talent of a glorious voice.'

Although an injury had prevented Mary's sister Hélène from attending the cremation, she was staying at Pitmurchie some time later. When the BBC's Aberdeen manager Harry Hoggan heard that Hélène had arrived, he went straight away to Pitmurchie. 'The manager knew exactly what he wanted,' recalls Geoff Collie. 'As he was motoring up the drive at Pitmurchie, he saw smoke. It was a bonfire and there was Hélène, who had been unable to attend the cremation due to an injury she had received whilst staying at the Villa Antoinette nursing home at Peille near Monte Carlo. The home cared for her free of charge out of gratitude to her generous sister. Collie introduced himself. Hélène said to him "Och, these are a lot of letters of Mary's from Debussy. Nobody will be interested in them now. I've just burnt the lot". Hélène was a very odd person. There was no accounting for what she might do.' The solicitor adds: 'My wife always tells the tale that when they were tidying up in Pitmurchie, there was a bag and Hélène said "Och, it's just full of old rubbish". And they opened it and inside was the chinchilla fur which at one time was valued at £1000.'

In April 1982 a distant relative, the conductor and musical critic Neville Garden, placed a plaque on the house in Dee Street, Aberdeen. A year later, a Mary Garden Memorial Prize – instituted by Aberdeen District Council – was awarded to the mezzo, Yvonne Burnett.

Notes

1. Grace Moore (1947), *You're Only Human Once*, London: Latimer House, pp. 151–2.
2. Ibid.
3. Rowena Farrar (1982), *Grace Moore and Her Many Worlds*, New York: Cornwall Books, pp. 215–16.
4. Interview by author with Mario Goetschel, 1 July 1993.
5. Noël Coward (1986), *Autobiography*, London: Methuen, p. 437.
6. Gwen Morgan (c.1946), 'Mary Garden Says No to Crooning', journal unknown.
7. Beverley Sills and Lawrence Linderman (1987), *Beverley: An Autobiography*, New York: Bantam Books, p. 28.
8. *New York Times*, 23 October 1949.
9. *New York Times*, 14 September 1949.
10. *New York Times*, 29 September 1949.
11. *Washington Post*, 3 October 1949.
12. *Los Angeles Examiner*, 9 October 1949.
13. Geraldine Farrar (1991), *All Good Greetings*, ed. A.C. Truxall, Pittsburgh, p. 115.
14. Ibid., p. 117.
15. *New York Times*, 10 December 1949.
16. Garry O'Connor (1979), *The Pursuit of Perfection*, London: Gollancz, pp. 198–9.
17. Geraldine Farrar, op. cit., p. 128.
18. *Seattle Times*, 20 November 1950.
19. Caroline Kaart, letter to author, 26 July 1994.
20. *Los Angeles Examiner*, 18 January 1954.
21. Interview by author with Bill Browning, 1993.
22. Vincent Sheean (1956), *First and Last Love*, New York: Random House, p. 250.
23. Iain Parr, *Weekly Scotsman*, 19 January 1967.
24. Ibid.
25. Madeau Stewart, p1 43/4/MS/3 Oxfordshire Archives.
26. Telephone call to author, 23 July 1994.

Postscript

In spite of her protestations, Mary Garden was a highly accomplished concert singer; even when shorn of scenery, lighting and orchestra, she had enough vocal and physical resources to be truly effective on the concert stage. Her unique achievement was to integrate music and drama into a single living creation on the stage. She strove to go beyond what she saw as the immobile school of coloratura singing, as exemplified by Melba and Tetrazzini, both of whom she nevertheless greatly admired. But coloratura brilliance alone was not for her.

She did not like her own recordings and those of her contemporaries who have heard them have agreed, on the whole, that they do not do her justice. In any case, the experience of going to an opera with Mary Garden in it was as much visual as it was vocal. On the other hand, the only visual record we have of her acting (the 1918 silent films of *Thaïs*) shows that her stage technique was of the overstated variety which suited the vastness of an opera house but not the intimate scrutiny of the camera lens.

As a person, Mary Garden was larger than life. She was generous to a fault, supporting members of her family for many years. She loved to tease an audience of journalists, especially the American press, and they in turn loved her for the extraordinary stories she plucked out of the air. She had a wicked sense of humour. We would probably be safe in believing her when she (repeatedly) emphasized that she was faced with a choice between Marriage and Art, and chose Art. Art, in spite of the hard work and dedication involved, brought her immeasurable satisfaction. Though there seems to have been a persistent notion that she led a double-life of scandal and depravity, there is no evidence to suggest that such a lifestyle ever existed. She had one deep relationship – with J. Ogden Armour, but marriage was out of the question.

Bill Browning, the distinguished Chicago-based accompanist, emphasizes that Mary Garden was a superb musician. 'The conductor Giorgio Polacco once said Garden was the only singer he ever knew who was so musically secure she could stand at the back of the stage facing away from the orchestra and then turn around and say "Maestro, the flutes are playing a D flat. It should be D natural".'

'Her instinct for characterization was sure and direct,' continues Browning:

> In Paris once around 1950 she invited a young soprano she had been coaching in *Carmen* and myself down to Pigalle. She had found a place where the demi-mondaines (prostitutes) were frequenting and we sat at the bar just like any common citizens and nobody recognized Mary.
>
> She said 'Watch them. Watch the girls. Watch what they do. How they handle their breasts, touch themselves. Everything is there. They know the value of their sexuality.' It was a great lesson.
>
> Musically, she was always a great person. Regardless of all the anecdotes, it was a tremendous brain. I always remember I was about 12 and playing some Debussy. She came by. She would never normally get in the way. But this time she tapped me on the shoulder and said: 'Claude would not like that. It's too slow. Remember when Claude said "andantino" he meant "allegretto"'.

This volume has attempted to expose the perversity of some of the judgements made on the unique artist that was Mary Garden, such as that of the *New York Times* critic Richard Aldrich:

> Her personality was counted for more in her performances than her vocal art, which was defective, or her histrionic skill, which was limited and vitiated by many mannerisms.[1]

Mary Garden, as Claude Debussy well recognized, had the rare ability to move people in ways they could scarcely understand. That, in the final analysis, is what made her great.

Note

1. Richard Aldrich (1954), *Grove Dictionary of Music and Musicians*, 5th edition, edited by Eric Blom. London: Macmillan.

Appendix 1 Debuts

Listed chronologically (1,187 total career performances)

Composer	Opera & Role	Date	Location	Total performances
Charpentier	Louise (title role)	10 Apr 1900	Opéra-Comique	175
Lambert	La Marseillaise (Marie)	14 Jul 1900	Opéra-Comique	2
Pierné	La fille de Tabarin (Diane)	20 Feb 1901	Opéra-Comique	13
Massenet	Thaïs (title role)	25 Aug 1901	Aix-les-Bains	144
Massenet	Manon (title role)	21 Sept 1901	Opéra-Comique	72
Messager	Madame Chrysanthème (title role)	20 Dec 1901	Monte Carlo	5
Debussy	Pelléas et Mélisande (Mélisande)	30 Apr 1902	Opéra-Comique	106
Bunning	La Princesse Osra (title role)	14 Jul 1902	Covent Garden	2
Massenet	Grisélidis (title role)	7 Aug 1902	Aix-les-Bains	10
Debussy	La Demoiselle élue (title role)	21 Dec 1902	Paris (Colonne)	4
Verdi	La traviata (Violetta)	12 Feb 1903	Opéra-Comique	39
Gounod	Roméo et Juliette (Juliette)	6 Jun 1903	Covent Garden	6
Gounod	Faust (Marguerite)	15 Jul 1903	Covent Garden	25
Leroux	La Reine Fiammette (title role)	23 Dec 1903	Opéra-Comique	32
Saint-Saëns	Hélène (title role)	18 Jan 1905	Opéra-Comique	6
Massenet	Chérubin (title role)	14 Feb 1905	Monte Carlo	18
Erlanger	Aphrodite (Chrysis)	27 Mar 1906	Opéra-Comique	63
Thomas	Hamlet (Ophélie)	25 Sept 1908	Opéra de Paris	5
Massenet	Le jongleur de Notre-Dame (Jean)	27 Nov 1908	Manhattan	67
Strauss	Salome (title role)	28 Jan 1909	Manhattan	61
Février	Monna Vanna (title role)	7 Sept 1909	Opéra de Paris	36
Massenet	Sapho (Fanny)	17 Nov 1909	Manhattan	19
Herbert	Natoma (title role)	25 Feb 1911	Philadelphia	22
Bizet	Carmen (title role)	3 Jan 1911	Milwaukee	69
Massenet	Cendrillon (Prince)	6 Nov 1911	Philadelphia	10

204

Composer	Opera & Role	Date	Location	Total performances
Puccini	*Tosca* (title role)	28 Sept 1912	Opéra-Comique	39
Massenet	*Don Quichotte* (Dulcinée)	22 Nov 1913	Philadelphia	4
Février	*Gismonda* (title role)	14 Jan 1919	Chicago, Auditorium	5
Massenet	*Cléopâtre* (title role)	23 Jan 1919	Chicago, Auditorium	18
Montemezzi	*L'amore dei tre re* (Fiora)	9 Jan 1920	Chicago, Auditorium	34
Massenet	*Werther* (Charlotte)	28 Nov 1924	Chicago, Auditorium	6
Alfano	*Résurrection* (Katiusha)	3 Dec 1925	Gaîté-Lyrique, Paris	54
Honegger	*Judith* (title role)	27 Jan 1927	Chicago, Auditorium	6
Forrest	*Camille* (Marguerite)	10 Dec 1930	Chicago	6
Massenet	*La navarraise* (Anita)	24 Dec 1930	Chicago	4

Excluding her later lecture-recitals, Garden gave some 96 concerts between 1900 and the end of her stage career.

Appendix 2 Discography

by Jim McPherson and William R. Moran

In the Columbia and Victor sections, the notations (E) and (F) indicate 'sung in English' and 'sung in French' respectively. A bold-faced number indicates an issued take. An asterisk indicates a supplementary note at the end of the discography.

PATHÉ CYLINDERS (AND DISCS), LONDON, 1903 with piano (in English)

matrix	cylinder	disc	CD issues
1.*	Comin thro' the rye (Traditional Scots)		
	50088	8558	GEMM 9067
2.	Annie Laurie (William Douglas; Lady John Scott)		
	50089		
3.	'Twas within a mile o' Edinboro Town (James Hook)		
	50090	——	
4.*	Jock o' Hazeldean (Traditional Scots)		
	50091	8558	GEMM 9067
5.	Afton water (Robert Burns: *Sweet Afton*; Alexander Hume)		
	50092	——	
6.	Robin Adair (Lady Caroline Keppel; Traditional Scots)		
	50093		

BLACK G.&.T., PARIS, 1904, with piano (Claude Debussy) (in French)

matrix	catalogue	78 rpm reissues	LP issues	CD issues
7.*	Il pleure dans mon coeur (Paul Verlaine; Claude Debussy: *Ariettes oubliées No. 2*)			
3074F	33449	IRCC 107rr, 3048rr	LA 1203; Scala 829; OASI-584	Sym 1135
8.*	L'Ombre des arbres (Verlaine; Debussy: *Ariettes oubliées No. 3*)			
3076F	33450	IRCC 107rr, 3048rr	LA 1203; OASI-584	Sym 1136

9.* Green (Verlaine; Debussy: *Ariettes oubliées No. 5*)

catalogue number	78 rpm reissues	issues	CD issues
3077F	33451	IRCC 106rr, 3048rr	LA 1203; OASI-584	Sym 1135

10. PELLÉAS ET MÉLISANDE: Mes longs cheveux descendent jusqu'au seuil de la tour! (Act 3, Scene 1) (Debussy)

| 3078F | 33447 | IRCC 106rr, 3048rr | LA 1203; Scala 829; MCK 502; OASI-584 | Sym 1093 PH 5038 |

EDISON TWO-MINUTE CYLINDERS, PARIS, 1905 (in French)

catalogue number	78 rpm reissues	issues	CD issues

11.* CHÉRUBIN: Chanson du Duc (Massenet)
17020

12.* Chant Vénitien (Georges Roussel; Herman Bemberg) (pf)
17323   IRCC 3007rr, 3055 rr   IRCC L-7025

13.* THAÏS: L'amour est une vertu rare (Act 2, Scene 2) (Massenet) (orch)
17595   IRCC 3007rr, 3055rr   IRCC L-7025

COLUMBIA, NEW YORK, 1911–1912, with orchestra

matrix	date	U.S.s/f	d/f	U.K.d/f	LP issues	CD issues

14. trial recording, title unknown
16473   14 Mar. '11   —

15.* LA TRAVIATA: È strano! è strano! ... Ah, fors' è lui (Quel trouble ... Quel est donc ce trouble charmant) (Act 1) (Verdi) (F)

| 30695-1 | 14 Mar. '11 | — | | | | |
| -2 | 14 Mar. '11? | 30695 | A5284 | | | GEMM 9067; Sym 1136 |

16. LA TRAVIATA: Follie! Follie! ... Sempre libera (Folie, folie! ... Pour jamais ta destinée) (Act 1) (Verdi) (F)

| 30696-1 | 14 Mar. '11 | 30696 | A5284 | | Scala 829; Odyssey | GEMM 9067; Sym 1136 |

17. LE JONGLEUR DE NOTRE-DAME: Liberté! Liberté! C'est Elle que mon cœur pour maîtresse a choisie (Act 1, Scene 4) (Massenet) (F)

| 30699-1 | 21 Mar. '11 | 30699 | A5289 | — | Scala 829; Odyssey; T-306; EMI RLS 724 | GEMM 9067; Sym 1136 |

HÉRODIADE: Celui dont la parole... Il est doux, il est bon (Act 1) (Massenet) (F)

	matrix	date	U.S.s/f	d/f	U.K.d/f	LP issues	CD issues
18.*	30701-1	21 Mar. '11					GEMM 9067; Sym 1136
	-2	21 Mar. '11?	30701	A5289	—	Scala 829; Odyssey	GEMM 9067; Sym 1136
19.	19886-1	17 May '12		A1190	D9703; D1363	Odyssey	GEMM 9067
20.	19887-1	17 May '12	—	A1190 2021M	D9702; D1362	Odyssey	
21.	19888-1	17 May '12	—	A1191	—	Odyssey	GEMM 9067
22.	36385-1	17 May '12	—	A5440	—	Scala 829; Odyssey	GEMM 9067; Sym 1136
23.*	36386-1	17 May '12	—	—	—		
	-2	17 May '12?	—	A5440	—	Scala 829; Odyssey; ML 6099	GEMM 9067; Sym 1136
24.*	19890-1?	18 May '12			D9703; D1363	Odyssey	GEMM 9067
25.*	19891-1	18 May '12	—	A1191	—	Odyssey	GEMM 9067

Row 19: John Anderson, my jo (Robert Burns; Joseph Marais) (E)
Row 20: Comin thro' the rye (Traditional Scots) (E)
Row 21: Jock o' Hazeldean (Traditional Scots) (E)
Row 22: LOUISE: Depuis le jour (Act 3) (Charpentier) (F)
Row 23: THAÏS: C'est Éros! c'est l'amour!... L'amour est une vertu rare (Act 2, Scene 2) (Massenet) (F)
Row 24: Irish love song (Margaret Ruthven Lang, Op. 22) (E)
Row 25: The blue bell of Scotland (Mrs James Grant; Traditional Scots) (E)

VICTOR RED SEAL, CAMDEN & NEW YORK, 1926–1929

	matrix	date	U.S.	U.K.	issues	CD issues
26.	BVE-40733 -1, -2, -3	22 Nov. '27 Cam				Romo
	-4, -5	4 Nov. '29 NYC	1480	DA 1141	OASI-584	GEMM 9067; Romo
27.	BVE-36732 -1, -2	25 Oct. '26 Cam				
	-3, -4	3 Nov. '26 Cam	1480	DA 1141	OASI-584	GEMM 9067; Romo

Row 26: Afton water (Robert Burns: Sweet Afton; Alexander Hume) (E) (pf. Jean Dansereau)
Row 27: Annie Laurie (William Douglas; Lady John Scott) (E) (pf. Jean Dansereau)

Discography table:

No.	Title / Matrix	Date				
28.	At dawning (Nelle Richmond Eberhart; Charles Wakefield Cadman, Op. 29, No. 1) (E) (pf. Jean Dansereau)					
	BVE-36731 -1, -2	25 Oct. '26 Cam			OASI-584; NW 247	GEMM 9067; Romo
	-3, -4, -5	26 Oct '26 Cam	1216	DA 865		——
29.	At parting (Fred Peterson; James Hotchkiss Rogers) (E) (pf. Jean Dansereau)					
	BVE-37329 -1, -2, -3	24 Dec. '26 Cam	1216	DA 865	OASI-584	GEMM 9067; Romo
30.	Beau soir (Paul Bourget; Claude Debussy) (F) (pf. Dansereau)					
	BVE-57524 -1, -2	4 Nov. '29 NYC	1439	DA 1098	OASI-584	GEMM 9067; Romo
31.*	CARMEN: Voyons, que j'essaie à mon tour … En vain pour éviter les réponses amères (Card Song) (Act 3) (Bizet) (F) (or. Nathaniel Shilkret)					
	BVE-57526 -1, -2 -3	5 Nov. '29 NYC	1539	DA 1248; VA 18	OASI-584	GEMM 9067; Romo; Sym 1136
32.	Clair de lune (Paul Verlaine; Józef Szulc, Op. 83, No. 1) (F) (pf. Jean Dansereau)					
	BVE-57525 -1, -2, -3	4 Nov. '29 NYC	1439	DA 1098	OASI-584	GEMM 9067; Romo
	-4, -5	5 Nov. '29 NYC				
33.*	In the gloaming (Meta Orred; Annie Fortescu Harrison) (E) (organ: Alexander Russell)					
	CVE-48957 -1, -2	5 Nov. '29 Wan				Romo (both takes)
	-3, -4	7 Nov. '29 Wan	7254	DB 1447	OASI-584	Romo
34.*	Jock o' Hazeldean (Traditional Scots) (E) (organ: Alexander Russell)					
	CVE-56801 -1	7 Nov. '29 Wan				Romo
	-2	7 Nov. '29 Wan	7254	DB 1447	OASI-584	Romo
35.*	LOUISE: Depuis le jour (Act 3) (Charpentier) (F) (or. Rosario Bourdon)					
	CVE-36734 -1, -2	25 Oct. '26 Cam	——	——	——	Romo
	-3, -4, -5	3 Nov. '26 Cam	——	——	——	
	-6, -7, -8, -9	9 Dec. '26 Cam	——	——	——	
	-10, -11, -12					
	-13, -14, -15,					
	-16	24 Dec. '26 Cam	6623	AGSB 44	LCT-1; 17-0022 COLH-127	GEMM 9067; Romo; Sym 1136
36.	LOUISE: Depuis le jour (Act 3) (Charpentier) (F) (pf. Jean Dansereau)					
	CVE-40735 -1	23 Nov. '27 Cam	——	——		Romo
	-2	23 Nov. '27 Cam	——	——	VIC-1394	
	-3	23 Nov. '27 Cam	——	——		GEMM 9067

209

	matrix	date	U.S.	U.K.	issues	CD issues

37.* (a) My ship and I; (b) The swing (Robert Louis Stevenson: A *child's garden of verses*; Reynaldo Hahn) (E) (pf. Dansereau)

| | BVE-36753 -1, -2 | 3 Nov. '26 Cam | | | IRCC L-7025 | Romo |

38. O cease thy singing, maiden fair (Ne chante pas, ma belle enfant) (Alexander Pushkin; Sergei Rachmaninov, Op. 4, No. 4) (F) (pf. Jean Dansereau)

| | BVE-40734 -1, -2, -3 | 22 Nov. '27 Cam | | | — | — |

39. Over the steppe (Pleschcheev, tr. Kurt Schindler & Deems Taylor; Alexander Grechaninov, Op. 5, No. 1) (E) (pf. Jean Dansereau)

	BVE-36733 -1	25 Oct. '26 Cam			—	—
	-2, -3	26 Oct. '26 Cam			—	—
	-4	9 Dec. '26 Cam			—	—
	-5, -6, -7	24 Dec. '26 Cam			—	—
	-8, -9	22 Nov. '27 Cam			—	—
	-10, -11	5 Nov. '29 NYC	1539	DA 1248; VA 18	OASI-584	GEMM 9067; Sym 1136; Romo

40. RÉSURRECTION: Voici l'heure! et lui n'arrive pas! ... Dieu de grâce (RISURREZIONE: Giunge il treno ed ei non giunge ancor! ... Dio pietoso) (Act 2) (Alfano) (F) (or. Bourdon)

	CVE-36735 -1, -2, -3	26 Oct. '26 Cam			—	—
	-4	3 Nov. '26 Cam			EJS 397	Romo
	-5	3 Nov. '26 Cam		AGSB 44	LCT-1158; OASI-584	GEMM 9067; Romo; Sym 1136
	-6	3 Nov. '26 Cam	6623			

41.* Somewhere a voice is calling (Eileen Newton; Arthur F. Tate) (E) (pf. Jean Dansereau)

| | BVE-40735 -1, -2 | 22 Nov. '27 Cam | | | Voce 88 | Romo |
| | -3, -4 | 5 Nov. '29 NYC | | | EJS 452 | Romo |

The swing: see No. 37

KNOWN SURVIVING RADIO BROADCASTS

42.* From Hollywood, with host Cecil B. DeMille: plays a small role in *The Lux Radio Theatre* adaptation of the film *Tonight or never*, with Jeanette MacDonald and Melvyn Douglas; she is also interviewed between the acts by DeMille.

CBS

1936

43.* From Aberdeen, guest on New York-based programme marking 25th anniversary of Debussy's death.
OWI
14 Apr. '43

44.* From Aberdeen, with Chicago-based host Charles Collingwood (?); interview; sings part of *Ca' the yowes to the knowes* (This programme was part of the *Transatlantic Call* series).
BBC   LCD-139-1
1943

45.* From New York?, with host Mary Margaret McBride; guest on *The Mary Margaret McBride Program.*
EJS 247
LR 142-5
NBC   3 Nov. '50

46.* From New York?, with host Hedda Hopper; guest on *The Hedda Hopper Show.*
NBC   3 Dec. '50

47.* From New York, with host Ben Grauer; guest on *NBC Silver Jubilee Program.*
NBC   13 Oct. '51

48.* From New York, with John Gutman; interview in Metropolitan Opera broadcast intermission.
NBC   3 Apr. '54

49. From Pitmurchie House, Torphins, with Madeau Stewart; interview (recorded August 1961).
BBC   28 Dec. '61 (rebroadcast 23 Jan. '62)

LPs

Audio Archives LA 1203; contains the four Debussy recordings; no further details known.
Columbia ML 6099: *The Boston Opera Company 1909–1914*; contains 23.
EJS 247; *Potpourri No. 16*; contains 43.
EJS 397; *Geraldine Farrar/Mary Garden/ Lawrence Tibbett*; contains unpublished takes of 39 and 40.
EJS 452; *Potpourri No. 22*; contains an unpublished take of 41.
EMI RLS 724: *The Record Of Singing, Volume 1*; contains 17.
HMV COLH-127; *An Operatic Anthology By Eleven Famous Singers*; contains the published take of 35.
IRCC L-7025; *Souvenirs Of Opera And Song (Eighth Series)*; contains 12, 13 and an unpublished take of 37.
Legendary Recordings LR 142-5; contains 44.
MCA-U.K. MCK 502: *The Creators Of Grand Opera, Volume 3*; contains 10.
New World NW 247: *When I Have Sung My Songs: The American Art Song 1900–1940*; contains 28.
OASI-584; *Mary Garden (Soprano) (1874–1967)*; contains the four Debussy recordings and all published Victors.
Odyssey 32 16 0079: *The Great Mary Garden*; contains all published Columbias.
RCA Victor LCT-1: *Composers' Favorite Interpretations*; contains the published take of 35; also issued on 45 rpm as WCT-5.

RCA Victor LCT-1158: *Critic's Choice*; contains 40.
RCA Victrola VIC-1394: *Unforgettable Voices In Unforgettable Performances From The French Operatic Repertoire*; contains an unpublished take of 36.
Scala 829: *Mary Garden Sings*; contains 7, 10, 15, 16, 17, 18, 22, 23; reverse is *Emma Calvé Sings*.
TAP T-306: *Twenty Great Sopranos – Twenty Great Arias*; contains 17.
Voce-88: *Great Singers*; contains an unpublished take of 41.

CDs

Legato Classics LCD-139-1: *Legends Of Opera In Live Performance*; contains 44.
Nimbus NI 7812: *Great Singers, Volume Two, 1903–1939*; contains 40.
Pearl GEMM CD 9067: *Mary Garden, A Selection Of Her Finest Recordings*; contains 1, 4, the published takes of 26, 27, 28, 29, 30, 31, 32, 35, 39, 40, an unpublished take of 36, and all published Columbias.
Phonographe PH 5038: *Great British Singers*; contains 10.
Romophone 81008-2: *Mary Garden, The Complete Victor Recordings (1926–1929)*; contains all published Victors plus unpublished takes of 26, 33, 34, 35, 36, 37, 40, 41.
Symposium 1093: *The Harold Wayne Collection, Volume Seven*; contains 10.
Symposium 1135: *Yale University Library: From The Yale Collection, Volume One*; contains 7 and 9.
Symposium 1136: *Opera in Chicago, Volume One*; contains 8, 15, 16, 17, 18, 19, 22, 23, 31, 35, 39, 40; remainder of disc is devoted to Edith Mason.

NOTES TO THE DISCOGRAPHY

1, 4:   These appear to be the only titles in the series also issued as discs; both are announced by a male.
7, 8, 9:   Three of the six songs, all to poems by Paul Verlaine, comprising *Ariettes oubliées*. Originally published in 1888 as simply *Ariettes*, they were republished in 1903 as *Ariettes oubliées* and with a dedication to Garden. The English title of *Green* is Verlaine's own. According to the late Harold Barnes, additional titles in this Paris series have long been rumored, among them *C'est l'extase langoureuse* (*Ariettes oubliées No. 1*), *Chevaux de bois* (*Ariettes oubliées No. 4*) and, of all things, Arditi's *Se saran rose*. Certainly matrix 3075F (within the known series) and 3079F (immediately following it) are unaccounted for, as far as is known. The preceding block (3068F through 3073F) belong to the baritone Henri Weber; 3080F and 3081F belong to the bass Juste Nivette.

11: Harold Barnes suggested that this mysterious record (as far as is known, no copy has ever turned up) might be of Chérubin's Act 1 aria *Je suis gris! je suis ivre!*, because it's sung *to* the Duke. But, until a copy comes to light, we can't be sure what it is; consequently, it is not designated here as a 'creator's record'. Further food for thought: Bill Moran reports that he owns an Edison cylinder by the bass Joachim Cerdan and that the box, while correctly listing the catalogue number and title, misidentifies the singer as Garden – an obvious Edison clerical error. Bill wonders if, perhaps, a similar error at the source has resulted in decades of speculation about a cylinder which, in fact, never existed.

12, 13: Both are announced, in French, by a woman – presumably Garden herself. Bill Moran reports that the reissues on IRCC 3055, made to correct the speeds, are vastly inferior to the original issues on 3007.

15, 18, 23: In each case, we know the date of Take 1 but cannot be sure that Take 2 was made the same day.

24: This title was issued only in the U.K., but U.K. pressings show no take number.

25: According to *The Great Song Thesaurus* by Roger Lax and Frederick Smith (Oxford University Press 1989), the correct title of this song – invariably rendered *The blue bells of Scotland*, or *Bluebells of Scotland* – is *The blue bell of Scotland*.

31: Ever the individualist, Garden sings, not 'Voyons, que j'essaie à mon tour', but 'Allons, que j'essaie à mon tour'.

33, 34: These titles were recorded during evening sessions at the Wanamaker Auditorium in New York.

35: Garden sings the aria transposed to the Key of F. Takes 6 through 16 include harp by Francis J. Lapitino. 17-0022 is a 45 rpm disc (reverse is Lotte Lehmann's *Da geht er hin* from the abridged *Rosenkavalier* set), issued in 1951 in album WCT-5, *Composers' Favorite Interpretations*, part of RCA Victor's *Treasury Of Immortal Performances* series. LP release of the same album is LCT-1.

37: *My ship and I* is listed first in the Victor recording books. IRCC L-7025 reverses the songs (as does the Romophone issue), gives the titles as *How do you like to go up in a swing?* and *Oh, it's I that am the captain of a tidy little ship*, and identifies them as transcriptions from a 1928 radio broadcast. Bill Moran reports that the late IRCC founder, William H. Seltsam, told him he had deliberately reversed the songs and fudged their origin because (in Bill's words) 'he was afraid that RCA would raise hell if they thought he had used a test.' The Take used by Seltsam is unknown, but Romophone claims to use Take 1.

41: Bill Moran reports that, on Take 1, the final two notes are the same (B natural), but, on Take 4, the final two notes are B natural and E natural above.

42: Copy known to be held in a private collection.

43, 45, 46, 47: Copies held by the Motion Picture, Broadcasting And Recorded Sound Division, Library of Congress, Washington, D.C.

44: Burns made two versions of the old ballad beginning *Ca' the yowes to the knowes*. On this broadcast, Garden sings (unaccompanied) the chorus and first verse of the second (1794) version. Both the EJS and LCD issues misidentify the song as *My bonnie Jeannie*.

48: Rebroadcast as a memorial on the Metropolitan Opera broadcast of 4 February 1967. A short portion was used yet again on the Metropolitan Opera broadcast of 1 April 1995.

213

Appendix 3   Stage Technique

The Mary Garden Course (1935), Chicago Musical College. Edited extracts from the notebooks of Janet Fairbank, by courtesy of The Newberry Library, Chicago.

1.   CARMEN (*Carmen*) general comments:

Very *zigane* – when smoking, holds cigarette in first two fingers – when you sing put wrist on back of hip – [keep from getting burned, keep smoke away from throat] – other fingers free. When something pleases Carmen that's OK [that's the whole part]. Carmen is a proud gypsy. All men come to her – she goes to none – loose hips; walk with a little loose bounce in hips *zigane* – feel music in walk; never stiff. She never has to fuss over men and throw herself at them. She has class – proud Spanish gypsy. Carmen walks with high heels – it's a quick heely walk – long steps – energy. Top of body always up. Bend from waist.

'L'amour' [spin the word]. Walk springing in hips; legs swing loose from hips. When you walk around chair in the 'Seguidilla' – never put tail out towards audience, keep legs straight, torso in when back is to audience.

'Si tu ne m'aimes pas' – the triolet (triplet) at the end is completely unimportant. The 'Toi' is the word that matters. Don't move head or shake head. Bring hand out shoulder height in front and on 'toi' bring it down decidedly, knuckles pointing to ground. Shoot it straight out to house.

Inn scene ('tra, la, la') Clasp hands low down during dance. Don't snap out 'amoureux' – messieurs nos amoureux'. Get it in exact time. No 64th notes! Exit up back of table to left.

2.   MARGUERITE (*Faust*) – Act III sc 3 'Le Roi de Thulé' (1)

Enter centre with prayer book down in both hands – turn to shut gate – go slowly 'with eyes down' to middle of stage; then raise eyes and say to audience – 'Je voudrais bien savoir quel était ce jeune homme' – feet together

– 'Si c'est un grand seigneur'. Cross to right – put prayer book on chair –
pick up spinning wheel – sit on chair and begin 'Il était un Roi de Thulé' (get
recitative <u>very</u> legato).

'Roi de Thulé' part: expressionless looking at words 'Il avait bonne grâce'
looking at audience – 'à ce qu'il me semble' [coy]. After first stanza put
wheel away during interlude – cross to flower bed – kneel and pick a couple
of flowers looking at them lovingly. 'Je ne savais que dire' [clasp flower to
breast] – 'Et j'ai rougi d'abord' – Then go on picking flowers – standing for
last phrase.

At chord at the end – look up at audience – one hand up thinking of Faust
– first resolute, then turning to 'douceur'. Then turn a little to think of
Valentine. Make it all daintily innocent, light, very simple. Only smile when
thinking of him. 'Allons, n'y pensions plus!' – (petite fille). 'Cher Valentin!'
warm and big. 'Me voilà toute seule'. Turn to go to gate. See flowers
('Pauvre garçon!' oh, poor child, smiling a little, condescendingly). Don't
pick up flowers until after 'Pauvre garçon'. Then stoop to pick them up.

Faust Act III sc 3 – 'Le Roi de Thulé' (2)

(aim for top notes in 'Ah' runs) 'Je voudrais bien savoir': stand perfectly still
as in a dream with dreaming tone (only one verse of 'Thulé' is sung in
America). Then stand. Start to move spinning wheel. Rest it a minute and
look up: 'Si c'est un grand seigneur'. Then go on. Put wheel back where it
was. 'Cher Valentin' from side of stage, crossing a little towards centre.
Then to audience: 'Me voilà, toute seule. Un bouquet! C'est de Siebel, sans
doute' – all to audience.

Faust Act III sc 3 – 'Le Roi de Thulé' (3)

When Mephistopheles exits ('Je voudrais bien savoir') keep eyes out on
house, just about at back of floor. Start 'Thulé' as you are about to sit. 'Les
grands seigneurs': hands clasped high on bosom. No retards on 'Réponds-
moi'. Don't drag.

Faust Act III sc 3 – 'The Jewel Song' (1)

See the box as you are smelling flowers; look over them. Let flowers dribble
to floor, forgotten! Don't touch box until chord where lid is thrown back.
Fling lid back and pick up jewel afterwards in childish confusion and
pleasure, kneeling. Rise on trill. Run forward on the 'Ah'. Run with mirror

in right hand extended above head. At 'Non, non, ce n'est plus toi' nestle mirror and look over it. Then act 'fille d'un roi'. Cross and run so as to be at box transported with pleasure at 'Achevons la métamorphose'. Put on necklace (at 'collier') first. 'Dieu! c'est comme une main' is a brief note of impending tragedy quickly forgotten on trill. At end of aria rush back to box again.

Faust Act III sc 3 – 'The Jewel Song' (2)

When you see the box, you see it while you stand back three paces, smelling bouquet. Stand back there during debate about whether to open it. On the three chords, advance and throw lid back (have elastic on earrings to go over ears). 'Pourquoi? Je ne fais, en l'ouvrant': gay, young, innocent. Take flowers gently, right hand and arm coming around them in a caressing gesture.

When you open jewel box, pick up first one thing; drop it, pick up something else in a frenzy. Sing to audience all the recitative. 'Ah, s'il était ici' clutching mirror to breast. Then, after 'il me trouverait belle' rush over to jewel case again. Be sure to move hands fast to show excitement when looking at jewels.

'Non! C'est la fille' (at end). Raise hand in gesture of command (going up with arm straight, finger pointed during whole word, ending with it above head: 'Au passage' (breath before 'a - a - ge' to end with).

To finish the aria, sing it for all you are worth. Come out strong (*bel canto*). Then run to jewel box again: 'ah, je ris de me voir si belle en ce miroir! Ah (breath) je ris' etc. Convert 'mirroir' and 'Ah' into a laugh of joy.

Faust Act IV sc 2 – Church Scene

Devil is hidden in a huge stone column which lights up and audiences sees him but you don't. Come in sad and very solemn: 'De s'agenouiller'. Everyone has turned against you. You are ultimately and absolutely alone. You come in timidly: 'humble servante'. Walk in to centre and walk down centre-stage. Walk steadily; hands are down in front of you. Raise eyes to God. Stand still. Cover voice. Breathe before 'devant vous' ('votre humble': say as 'vo - trum - ble').

When you first hear Devil, show it with eyes. Look at audience: 'What's that?' – 'Qui m'appelle?' to yourself. Don't turn to look for anyone. 'Je chancelle': stagger just a little. Then put hands up in air in front of you, elbows bent. 'Est-ce déjà l'heure?': hands down (dramatic), palms parallel to floor. 'Quel voile sombre [breath] sur moi [breath] descend?' (very dark – start with hands up and bring them down and out slowly).

Then timidly kneel on outside of crowd at chapel, praying at right wall. You kneel almost stage centre. You can't pray. You reach up but, baffled, bring hands down. Try again (clasped hands being wrung). Then 'Ah! ce chant m'étouffe et m'oppresse'. Stand up. Gesture with both hands for 'un cercle de fer'. Then go to back of column. On 'Seigneur' make a gorgeous walk down to centre front. Sing whole supplication to house. Then you hear him and turn and see him. He has come out of column. Scream and fall head-first toward right wall parallel to footlights. Just fall straight down. A few villagers hang around you and help you up and lead you out centre.

3. LOUISE (*Louise*) Act III sc 1 – A little garden in Montmartre. 'Depuis le jour' (1)

Opening of soul to love. It is not a vocalise but full of the awakening of love. Julien is sitting in chair at centre. You come down and stand behind him, one hand on chair. Take his hands after 'premier baiser!' and 'Quelle belle vie!'. My goodness, what a gorgeous life!

Stay back of chair, think it all; never go ahead of him. Drop hands on 'Quelle belle vie!' The whole end is soft. In final 'je suis heureuse!' do a regular tenor move, turning to look at whole house to build it up – 'et je tremble': 'et je' is parenthetic leading up to 'tremble' which must not be dramatic, but poignant with warmth and quiet, overpowering, relaxed and satisfied emotion. Then every syllable in 'délicieusement' must be brought out particularly.

Watch 'e' sounds in 'trop heureuse' and 'délicieusement'. Just before this, you know it can't last. And it doesn't. The Mother is coming. Bring hand down in a presentiment of disaster. This rest is a real note of tragedy – just 'this can't last' idea.

Sing 'au souvenir charmant' with a slight pause after the Air. 'Du premier jour': melt into 'jour' with no accent on 'j'. Spin the tone – keep it soft and full of overtones.

Louise Act III sc 1 – 'Depuis le jour' (2)

Come out on steps registering 'amour libre'. Then come down – arms up, look out at Paris. Turn very quietly and walk to left side of Julien's chair – a little back of it. 'Donnée' important word. Bring out both 'n's and the 'é---e'.

'Mon rêve n'était pas un rêve!' *pianissimo*. First long 'heureuse' – eu – eu – eu – exultant *forte* – bring arms up. When you do your *piano*, go out further and higher to the audience.

Practice on 'délicieusement' to get same tonal value up to the F# on different scale levels. 'Trop heureuse': 'r' forward on 'trop'. 'Souvenir charmant': think of word; throw the '-mant' forward; sing it with the lips; 'du premier jour' – audible breath – take your time on 'd'amour'.

Louise Act IV sc 2 – A working man's tenement

All through first time on knee. Pick a light and look at it and mad mad. Twiddle fingers a little: 'c'est où' – furtive look but don't move.

'L'enfant serait sage' – mad self, contained compressed anger. Pick up tempo a little on 'si son père'. Turn a little, use hands a little. During Father's part hold still. 'La belle image' to audience. Pick a light. Turn to him. Rise on the rest before 'c'est' (break) 'de n'être plus'; 'est pire que la mort' – stamp and point down; say it to audience. Then turn to Father, mad: 'Mon rêve de folie'. Turn to audience and sing it. 'Vous voulez', turn back to Father; 'et que je mente' to audience, beating chest. 'Comme vous mentites' (accent 'mentites'). Make a sudden lunge and point at Mother, who is to left of table.

'Ô! elle sera libre maintenant': turn to house halfway then. 'Ce que nous demandons': to audience. 'Car nous l'aimons': hand to heart until Mother. 'Elle nouse aimait avant de vous connaître' – this much to Mother, then fling wild loose right arm back.

'Le droit de vous marier' – turn away from them on 'Comment!' Wheel on them, lunging with same foot on second 'comment'. 'De me laisser libre?': bring out the 'libre'. During Father's reply turn with arms crossed. As he finishes, wheel around (to left) and go to room. Father catches you and pulls you back on knee on chair by my door. 'Les parents': bring out 'parent' – bring out 'volonté'.

'Pourquoi serais-je belle': (turn a little to him). The word 'belle' has made you think of Julien again. End 'belle' to audience and go *swooooop* down to footlights in a breath, ending with hands: 'pour être aimée'. Stand holding exalted look on face. Wheel – 'Vous prenez la mienne' – then turn to audience, arms crossed; then bring other right foot point to floor in front of you (it is said to Father who is at right end of table, a little back). Turn back away from them. When he says 'commander!' turn, head back as though he'd hit you and confront him. Then turn gradually bringing up right hand, remembering Julien's words. Bring out 'droit', 'libre', 'devoir'. Stand perfectly still, except for arms.

By the time the Father is half way through next bit, you have arms crossed and look mad. On first 'jolie' (you alone hear the calls), eyes right up. On the second, become transfigured with joy. Hands move jerkily down to side. On the third, fling arms up and half rush, half stagger in. Turn to left and to window.

Don't begin really going over to side until waltz changes 'de thème'. 'Ô . . . musique': back all the way around the balcony. On the 'Paris, Paris' begin to work forward.

Say first 'Paris' to audience. 'Paris m'appelle' out of window. 'Des hymnes d'allégresse': arms up on long high note and snap them down with a stamp. Hold pose and rest for seven beats.

On 'Encore un jour d'amour', step on two bars before the first one, but not the second one. Then go right to wall and get a good rest, leaning against it (left wall). At the end go back off towards left corner. Try to run for door at back of table. But Father is there and catches you on: 'Ah, ah! ah! toutes les filles sont là' and drags you down by both hands to front of table. Break away from him and run to right wall on 'On rit à pleurer'. Lean back against wall on: 'allons, va!' Begin to edge to door. 'Ou je te jette à la porte': run out before 'porte'. Start edging from wall to door when he starts to tell you to go out. Get quite near door and run out just before 'à la porte'. On last 'Ô Paris': run forward, arms to audience.

4. MANON (*Manon*) Act II – Rue Vivienne: the apartments of Manon and Des Grieux

'Adieu, notre petite table'. Begin sitting on chair front right. Stand on 'Non, non!'. Then you hear his voice back left. Look where you hear his voice, don't look. 'Fragilité' – raise over hand thumb and first finger. Make circle, other fingers out in fan 'fragilité' gesture.

Then the intermediate part: you get to one side of chair between table and chair. On 'Adieu', turn to table and slowly cross to it. Walk back of it. Don't bend over it. 'Si grande pour nous' and you are right behind. Look up with clasped hands for a bit. Look down and 'Adieu' again. Then cross to left side of table. Reach for glass. Hold it out with both hands and then reach over, crying, one arm out long. Put glass down. Other hand up to head. Elbow [drawing] then fall with head on table. From time you put glass down, you are crying.

Manon Act III sc 2 – The seminary of St Sulpice

Enter. Ask warder. Don't enter further than centre stage. Work down stage. Turn around, looking [at] books on prie-dieu. Point towards back stage right: 'Ô, je voudrais prier!'. Beat breast, then see statue of Jesus. A very slow cross to prie-dieu. Put hand on top of it and kneel on one knee, pretending to sing to Jesus, but really to audience. Only on high note, turn to Jesus.

You haven't been in a church for so long that you don't know what to do. When you pray, keep shoulders well parallel to feet, even though your arms may be across your chest. At end of prayer, put head down on prie-dieu.

5.   MÉLISANDE (*Pelléas et Mélisande*) Act I sc 3 – In front of the castle

Walk in somewhat before triplet measure, giving audience a profile of your walk. Then when triplets start, you are looking up at trees ahead of you (stage right). Look up over head, letting it turn you so that when you say 'Il fait sombre' you are turned to Geneviève in profile.

'Vous aurez la clarté de la mer' is when you run upstage. Hold garland limp at entrance; back of hands to audience (garland held by rings). When you turn to look at Pelléas, turn your torso.

'Le navire' – dotted crochet with crescendo hairpin over it – same on 'voiles'. 'C'est le navire' slow like the sea. Bend well down as he leads you out. Straighten up and look at him when you sing: 'Oh! pourquoi partez-vous?'

Pelléas et Mélisande Act II sc 1 – A well in the park

'Elle n'ouvre plus les yeux des aveugles?' While he answers, let your eyes wander to tree tops; slowly turn head a little away from him – don't drag on 'n'entend rein' – just a simple remark.

'C'est au bord d'une fontaine aussi?' Sit with profile to audience. 'Nous n'en trouverons pas d'autres non plus'. 'Loin' almost like 'Luhan'. Don't end it with an 'in' nasal sound.

Pelléas et Mélisande Act II sc 2 – A room in the castle

'Je l'ai sentie glisser' – not too close to finger; draw hand back and up – step off platform at same time. Cross on 'Je n'ose pas – je n'ose pas aller seule.'

6.   JULIETTE (*Roméo et Juliette*) Act I (1)

Come in with Father and be led around, bowing to guests. Keep chest high and steady. Bow from waist. Get led all around till you get led to centre. Then walk down centre on 'Écoutez'. On bows, when Father leads you around, with one foot a couple of inches forward, draw weight back – almost like a man's gavotte bow, only much slighter with hands at side, very dignified. On 's'envole', on top of run, fling arms up.

When Father leads you around, be gracious, but don't smile. On the dramatic runs, reach out to house as you go up and draw back as you come down.

Roméo et Juliette Act I – 'Waltz Song'

Let the 'je' drop from your lips as you finish: 'Je veux VIVRE!'. When you cross on 'Ah, je n'ai pu m'en défendre', just step in front of him, hardly past him.

Roméo et Juliette Act I – 'Ange adorable'

During aria move a little back and forth across front. 'Mais à sa bouche, la main qui touche': don't look at hand, look at him. When he kisses your hand, it's your first kiss. 'Ah!': step in front of him, thrilled at first being kissed. 'No, no, I won't give it back'. Delighted. Sweet angel. Nothing sad. Just step past him, so he isn't covered. Almost cuddle the kiss to yourself. Stand still at end until music changes. Then you step back a little to the far right wall.

Roméo et Juliette Act I - 'Finale'

'C'est mon cousin Tybalt'. Go down step on 'C'est'. You are delighted to see who it is. Very charming, like a child. Simple; delighted. <u>Not</u> 'la fille du seigneur' – just quick and natural. 'La fille' du seigneur ('That's who I am'). Look after Roméo as he goes out up right. Step forward when you say: 'Roméo'. The child drops off in a quarter of a second. Weight on front foot. 'Est le berceau' [breath] de cet amour fatal!'

7.   THAÏS (*Thaïs*) Act II sc 2 – In the house of Thaïs

Hold entrance a second, touch Venus (your only god), then bring hands to your own face to transmit beauty – 'ces hommes ... Les femmes méchantes'. Enter centre arms akimbo – 'Ah, je suis seule, seule <u>enfin</u>!' [key word]; 'tous ces hommes' – cross to Venus at right put three fingers on the mouth then bring hand to own mouth – cross to centre – raise arm on 'brutalité ... pesantes': give a yawn. 'Brutalité' (advance on audience with sweep of one hand). Convey 'Les femmes ... méchantes' with head. Make a little start when you see the mirror, then cross to couch and pick up mirror having eased over with a sort of courtesan series of stretching gestures. Keep sinuous lines. Stand looking in mirror – make gestures with long straight arms and chest way back.

Never bend forward – stand up high. Handle lips and hair as you look in mirror taking Tanagra* poses for 'Un jour, ainsi, Thaïs ne serait plus Thaïs' to audience. Just before that, raise both hands and mirror above head – reach over and, reaching out and over, put mirror down. Then, stay rooted to the spot until you turn to Venus.

'J'ai l'âme vide' ('vide' is the key word): drag hands up (begin with shoulders) along body and up. When you look in mirror wheedle it to tell you what you know is not true. 'Où trouver le repos?' One hand to audience; three-quarters of the way up and out. 'Et comment fixer le bonheur?' Bring out every syllable.

Then, clutching mirror: 'Ah! Tais-toi'. Cross and drop mirror. 'Thaïs, tu vieilliras': all in one line of crescendo of emotion straight at the audience, very steady and dramatic. In 'Thaïs ne serait plus Thaïs', she knows she's getting old, so she sings it with increasing but restrained honour. Then 'Non! Non!' – change mood. Step back on as though seeing a spectre, then cross to Venus, both arms out. Invocation to Venus ('Toi, Vénus') is as in a dream-like chant in church, reaching higher and higher, looking in sky for Venus – towards sky and audience, all as if enchanted. Sing very softly with slur down to 'Dis-moi que je suis belle. Éternellement!': climax (remember you are a <u>dancer</u>!). Arms out. Bring out every syllable.

During the Interlude, make a Tanagran* dancing pose with hands on head. Hand with mirror up towards Venus. Then turn (on feet) looking in mirror which is above head. Very theatrical.

---

* Tanagra – Greek city 12 miles east of Thebes where pottery funerary figurines in dramatic poses (inspired by the plays of Menander) have been found dating from the period 330–200 BC.

8.   TOSCA (*Tosca*) Act I – The Church of Sant' Andrea della Valle

Beat on door at third 'Mario!' Make the 'Mario's' sound like calls! Hold the third 'Mario!' He opens the door. Come in like a flash, mad and jealous. Pay no attention to him. Cross toward picture, then to chapel, look for the dame. Agitated and jealous – long steps – foot down flat, knees bent. Tosca is a woman jealous with rage. Turn and face him (he is at easel) angrily in 'Perchè chiuso?' Keep after him, give him hell!

Bring out rustle of dress ('un <u>fruscìo</u> di vesti'), an important word. After 'la Madonna' he takes stick from her. 'Not before the Madonna' (to audience) bring one hand down in a slow gesture of stopping him, slow as he tries to kiss her – on interlude turn completely round and go to altar – cross yourself. As the music stops you are facing the altar. Bend one knee in obeisance, leg under you, not back – it always makes a bad line to see a leg sticking out when the back is turned. Music stops – cross towards him. He is sitting on the easel ladder. 'Stassera canto' – matter of fact. Stand at the back of his shoulder. Cross gradually, conversationally, making up a little to him. Don't be coy however. He is thinking about how to get rid of Angelotti. Tosca perceives his preoccupation and gets in a pique as any woman would. 'Lo dici male'. Then, wheedling him: 'Lo dici male!'

The whole first act is one long jealous scene with occasional beautiful singing. Stand after first part of aria, cross gradually. Cross to centre with Cavaradossi at the end of the aria. He brings the stick. Tosca starts to go out – tenderly. Suddenly she sees the picture. Cross towards the picture trying to remember. Sing phrase before 'per le silenzio' lightly, in one swoop.

'Me discacci?' draw self up step back, look a long, sure again there is someone – then be reassured and go towards door. Then you still feel there is a woman – look around to see if you can't see some belonging of hers – then see the picture – all turns. Then act in quick, mad turns. When you point to the picture use swift full arm and forefingers in gesture.

'Aspetta': hand towards picture while you try to remember – not fingers together. Second 'Aspetta', hand to chin, turn to audience, trying to think. Then, just with face and eyes 'É l'Attavanti!'.

At 'A me, a me!' cross to put her eyes out with stick. Cavaradossi stops her. 'Ah, quegli occhi!', sadly, almost pathetically. Then you are nicer again.

9. VIOLETTA (*La traviata*) Act I – 'Drinking Song' (1)

In France there are trays of champagne passed instead of the large banquet table used in America. In France Violetta sings 'Tra voi' as a drinking song. Hold glass up, changing hands. Look at Alfredo for a second once in a while. He is trying to waltz her all through the song; she, the leading courtesan of Paris, to persuade her to give herself free to anyone. At every advance, just get younger and laugh it off, until the very end when you part. Behind your back, without looking at him, you give him a rose. Then the tragedy begins. Violetta realises that she has fallen in love.

During the drinking song, don't clink glasses in bourgeois fashion; just a wave of the looks and glasses. So far he is just a gay acquaintance. Don't be sentimental. After the fainting scene, during the duet, you are trying to keep him from knowing what you are thinking. Perform business with fan.

'Sto meglio'. 'Oh, thank you. I'm better'. Gay self again. Fan yourself with a slow, languished motion with elbow out, moving from shoulder, the whole forearm in the motion. In France, Violetta sits on a sofa and looks into a hand mirror which she puts down between them when Alfredo sits down.

During his aria, you stand looking away from him to house. You are liking to hear what he says. When you answer you are very coquette. Give him flowers. Then you are very gay, rustling him off. Then stand looking after him.

La traviata Act I – 'Drinking Song' [2]

Don't flirt coquettishly with him during drinking song. Almost sing with back to him, giving song punch and gaiety to audience. He is crazy after you, but you are turning your back to real love, chic and gay, averting a real heart affair.

Violetta is dying of tuberculosis and the gay world that is hers always rushes off without her to parties. That's why she makes light of her ailment. When Alfredo comes back, she is looking at mirror. She is used to having people who do not really care. Then he sings that he loves her ('Un dì felice') and she is really touched. It's the first time someone has been really interested in her without wanting something; the first time she hasn't been paid.

La traviata Act I – 'È strano' – 'Ah, fors' è lui'

Walk in to back of stage then down to footlights. During the recitative, fan in hand, hold it out with both hands in front, at about face level. On chord interlude, put head down, then hands again up to him. Stand in thought. Very quietly bowed in thought. Then begin aria. Stand still. This must be done with great finesse, with almost no gesture. Begin aria. Leave hands clasped to breast. Just lift head and begin to sing.

Long pause after orchestra, before you begin 'È strano'. Take steps on chords between phrases in recitative. On 'all'amor' (two *lunga pausas* indicated on 'a' and 'o'), play it way up. Hold. Get the effect.

Then when you sing 'Follie!' hand up laughing. 'Follie' – Say it to audience. Do it all with chic! 'Gioir' and echo: don't listen to yourself. Bend forward to audience for the echo. Take a large breath before the high C, then hold it and come down and begin next part all in one breath.

He begins to sing and in the music you are stamping your foot. A great scene to learn how long to hold high notes. Run back at laughing part and get a carnival doll and run forward to continue laughing.

La traviata Act II

As Violetta takes letter back from Giorgio Germont, sing to audience 'O come dolce' and to him. Cross to down right. Stand at down stage end after 'Di due figlie'. He draws up chair and sings – look at him and out to audience.

'What do you want me to do?' – arms back and out as taking a suitcase – then 'Nol credera' crossing – turn fast for 'seguirammi' – have him kiss forehead then rush sobbing to desk, hurl arms and head on desk sobbing.

Then on 'Generosa' it's dramatic – head to audience – keep moving. When he sings, put head down on desk. Then up to sing about sacrifices. Stand for part where you begin to sing 'Cognosca il sacrifizio'. Grand climax, then sink on chair without looking at him. Someone is coming: 'Adio' – 'I have made my sacrifice ... I shall never see him again'. Don't look at him – look dramatic at audience – right hand simple straight arm gesture, palm down.

GENERAL ADVICE

- Stage Kiss (where your back is to audience): if you come at tenor from right side, you put your right arm under his left one as you turn; your right leg bends with sole of foot up, weight on toe and left foot. You can now lean way back, your arms are under tenor's and you cling to his shoulders.
- The bigger the house, the bigger the gesture must be in order to assure success.
- The more you stand still, the more the audience is taken in, the more articulation is demanded. The character of a woman shows in the <u>thighs</u>.
- Make the things you handle on a stage – chairs, mirrors, books, letters etc. – live!!
- Always pick a light in the house to sing to – not too high – at about the front of the balcony.

Bibliography

The main reference and research materials on Mary Garden are to be found at:

Chicago Historical Society (clippings and photographs); Newberry Library, Chicago (Miscellaneous Manuscript Collection, The Janet Fairbank notebooks); New York Public Library (Billy Rose Theatre Collection – Robinson Locke Collection of Dramatic Scrapbooks 1856–1920 Vols 224–236, Series 1; The Fine and Performing Arts Library – six miscellaneous scrapbooks (Ref. *ZB – 2210 Reel 1); Boston Public Library (Music Department: Special Scrapbooks Vols 1–2 **ML46. G37R4 – Mary G. Reed: Mary Garden, 1907–26); Royal College of Music, London (Department of Portraits and Performance History – photographic scrapbooks and memorabilia); City of Aberdeen Central Library, Aberdeen, Scotland.

M. Armitage (1944), *Accent on America*, New York: E. Weyhe.
——— (1965), *Accent on Life*, Ames: The Iowa State University Press.
Barnes, H. M. Jr (1947) 'Historical records: The recordings of Mary Garden', *Hobbies*, 52/7 pp. 29–30.
——— (1947), 'Mary Garden on Records', The Holcombe-Blanton Printery, San Angelo, Texas.
——— (1979), 'Mary Garden (1874–1967): discography', *Recorded Sound*, No. 76, pp. 113–16.
Berg, A. (1989), *S. Goldwyn: A Biography*, New York: Alfred A. Knopf.
Boyer, P. S. and James, E. T. (1971, supplement 1980), in *Notable American Women* edited by J. W. James, Cambridge, Massachusetts.
Brubaker, R. L. (1979), '130 Years of Opera in Chicago', *Chicago History*, Vol. III, Chicago Historical Society, pp. 156–69.
Bulliett, C. J. (1930), *How Grand Opera Came to Chicago*, printed and published privately.

Celletti, R. (1964), *Le grandi voci*, Istituto per la collaborazione culturale, Rome, pp. 320–21.

Collings, R. (Summer 1935), 'Mary Garden on Record', *International Discophile*, pp. 26, 31.

Davies, R. J. (1966), *Opera in Chicago*, New York: Appleton-Century.

—— (1965), *A History of Opera in the American West*, New Jersey: Prentice-Hall.

Dizikes, J. (1993), *Opera in America: A Cultural History*, New Haven and London: Yale University Press.

Fassett, S. (1947), 'Historical records: Garden recordings', *Hobbies*, 52/8, p. 34.

Fletcher, R. D. (1954), 'The Mary Garden of Record', *Saturday Review*, 27 February, p. 47.

—— (1963), 'The Short, Mad Reign of Mary the First', *Panorama*, 7 September.

—— (1972), 'Our Own Mary Garden', *Chicago History*, Vol. II, Chicago Historical Society, p. 34.

Garden, Mary and Biancolli, Louis (1951), *Mary Garden's Story*, New York: Simon and Schuster.

Garden, Mary (1962), *Souvenirs de Mélisande*, Liège: Editions Dynamo.

Garden, Neville (1967), 'Mary Garden', *Scottish Opera Magazine*, Spring, pp. 4–11.

Gardner, V. and Rutherford, S. (1992), *The New Woman and Her Sisters: Feminism and Theatre 1850–1914*, Harvester Wheatsheaf.

Glackens, I. (1963), *Yankee Diva*, New York: Coleridge Press.

Goldwyn, S. (1923), *Behind the Screen*, New York: George H. Doran Company.

Heap, J. (1953), 'Mary Garden' in *The Little Review Anthology*, New York: Hermitage House Inc.

Huneker, J. (1920), *Bedouins*, London: T. Werner Laurie, pp. 3–44.

Insull, S. (1992), *The Memoirs of Samuel Insull*, Polo, Transportation Trails.

Irvine, D. (1994), *Massenet: A chronicle of his life and times*, Portland: Amadeus Press.

Kahn, O. C. (1926), *Of Many Things*, London: Jonathan Cape.

McDonald, F. (1962), *Insull*, Chicago: The University of Chicago Press.

Marbury, E. (1923), *My Crystal Ball*, New York: Boni and Liveright.

Moore, E. C. (1930), *Forty Years of Opera in Chicago*, New York: Horace Liveright.

O'Connor, G. (1979), *The Pursuit of Perfection*, London: Victor Gollancz Ltd.

Pearson, Edward (1995), 'The Other Traviata: Hamilton Forrest's *Camille*', *Opera Quarterly*, Vol. II, No. 2, pp. 17–38.

Pleasants, H. (1966), 'Mary Garden', *The Great Singers*, New York, p. 308.

Robinson-Duff, S. (1919), *Simple Truths Used by Great Singers*, Boston: Oliver Ditson Co.

Sheean, Vincent (1967), 'The Great Mary Garden', *Opera News*, New York: February.

Stevenson, F. (1968), 'Arias in Gangland', *Opera News*, No. 21, 23 March, pp. 8–13.

Thompson, O. (1937), 'Mary Garden', in *The American Singer: A Hundred Years of Success in Opera*, New York: Dial Press.

Wagenknecht, E. C. (1964), *Seven Daughters of the Theatre*, University of Oklahoma Press.

Whelan, G. (1952), 'The Recorded Art of Mary Garden', *The Gramophone*, xxix, p. 367.

Williams, C. (1964), 'Mary Garden', *Le Grand Voci*, edited by R. Celletti, Rome, pp. 318–21.

Van Vechten, C. (1917), *Interpreters and Interpretations*, New York: Alfred A. Knopf.

Index of Names

Ackté, Aino 51
Adelaide, Mina 70
Alda, Frances 117, 125, 145, 184
Alexandra, Queen 46
Alfano, Franco 155, 162
Altchevsky, Ivan 61
Armitage, Merle 52, 138, 142, 150, 178
Armour, J Ogden 140, 144, 146, 168
Armstrong, William 85
Astor, Mrs Vincent 134
Atwell, Ben H 144, 163

Baklanov, George 145
Ballin, Hugo 128, 131
Bancroft, Charles 87
Banès, Antoine 137
Bardac, Emma (Mme Debussy) 32
Barélli, Marie 161
Barnes, Harold 173
Barry, John 111
Barthelémy, Richard 142, 165
Beecham, Sir Thomas 51
Beethoven, Ludwig van 71
Bel Geddes, Norman 159
Benchley, Robert 187
Bennett, James Gordon 133
Benoist, André 93
Bentonelli, Joseph 186
Bernhardt, Sarah 18, 42, 43, 89, 136
Bertin, Émile 16
Bertoni, Marc 81
Bey, James 82
Beyle, Léon 21, 35
Biancolli, Louis 1, 35, 51, 62, 141, 195, 197

Bing, Rudolf 196
Blanchi, Louis 162
Borowski, Felix 114
Bouhy, Jacques 10
Boulanger, Nadia 149
Bourdin, Honoré 101
Bourdon, Rosario 166
Bouyer, Raymond 41
Bower, George 1
Bower, James Anderson 1
Bowes, Major Edward 187
Brenon, Herbert 125
Bréval, Lucienne 71, 80
Briand, Aristide 50
Brockway, Howard 88
Browning, Bill 198
Bruneau, Alfred 28
Brussel, Robert 60
Bunning, Herbert 35
Buonaparte, Napoleon 51, 162, 197
Burnett, Yvonne 200
Burns, Robert 3
Burrian, Carl 51

Cadman, Charles Wakefield 75, 166, 186
Caesari, E Herbert 198
Callas, Maria 198
Calvé, Emma 11, 40, 45, 55, 94
Cameron, Basil 180
Campanini, Cleofonte 56, 69, 76, 94, 98, 110, 117, 131, 135, 138, 140
Campbell, Mrs Patrick 42, 58, 183
Canterbury, Archbishop of 46
Caplet, André 103, 104

Carelli, Emma 146
Carnegie, Andrew 64
Carré, Albert 14, 17, 18, 19, 20, 22, 25, 26, 27, 30, 31, 34, 37, 47, 49, 165
Carré, Marguerite 45, 47, 48, 49, 51, 60, 71
Caruso, Enrico 101, 111, 117, 125, 131, 135, 194
Casini, Gutia 142
Castle, Irene 158
Cather, Willa 142, 143
Cavalieri, Lina 45, 66, 67, 71, 92, 102, 116
Chabrier, Emmanuel 60
Chaigneau, Ferdinand 12
Chaliapin, Feodor 57
Charpentier, Gustave 17, 24, 26, 34, 58, 93, 109, 154
Chasles, Mme 63
Chauncey, William F 89, 92, 95, 161, 162, 168
Chenal, Marthe 124
Chevalier, Jules 13
Churchill, Viscount 46
Claribel (Mrs Barnard) 4
Clayton, John 176
Clément, Edmond 30
Cochran, Alexander Smith 144
Cocteau, Jean 165
Collie, Geoff 2, 199, 200
Collver, Burton 108
Conkling, Richard 128
Conried, Heinrich 55, 64
Coquelin, Benoît 43, 136
Coué, Emile 157, 160
Courtney, Inez 188
Coward, Noël 165, 183, 191
Craig, Edward Gordon 135
Crane, Frank 129
Cuénod, Hugues 44, 88, 99, 165

d'Alvarez, Dina 162
d'Alvarez, Marguerite 184
D'Annunzio, Gabriele 46, 113
Dalmorès, Charles 57, 80, 81, 184
Daly, Arnold 81
Damrosch, Walter 122
Dansereau, Jean 166
David, Léon 124
Davis, Jessie Bartlett 6
Davis, William 5, 6

De Casseres, Benjamin 147
de Castellane, Marquis de 50
de Cisneros, Eleonora 105
De Courcey, Florence 104
de Hidalgo, Elvira 161
de Koven, Reginald 58, 64
de Lesseps, Fernand 82
De Reszke, Edouard 9
De Reszke, Jean 7, 9, 164
De Rieux, Max 192
de Sabata, Amedeo 177
de Trabadelo, Ange-Pierre 11, 13, 29, 30, 73, 90, 103, 154, 170
de Weerth, Ernest 62, 128
de Wolfe, Elsie 56, 118, 125, 158
Debussy, Claude 29, 30, 31, 32, 33, 34, 35, 36, 39, 42, 43, 44, 46, 49, 50, 58, 101, 103, 109, 141, 161, 176, 177, 180, 183, 184, 187, 193, 197, 199
Debussy, Lily 32
Défrère, Desiré 163
Delius, Frederick 123
Destinn, Emmy 61
Dippel, Andreas 80, 83, 92, 105, 111, 117
Dolin, Anton 200
Donnadieu, Françoise 191, 193
Downes, Olin 173
Draper, Muriel 149
Dreyfus, Camille 192
Duff Gordon, Lady 136
Dufranne, Hector 72, 80, 127
Duncan, Mrs Jean 4
Duse, Eleanora 46, 136

Eames, Emma 6, 10, 11, 18, 81
Eames, Hayden 6
Eames, Mrs 10
Eastman, George 167
Eddy, Nelson 187
Edvina, Louise 196
Edward VII, King 46
Eekhoud, Georges 49
Eells, George 187
Eichberg, Julius 6
Elman, Mischa 135
Erlanger, Camille 47

Farrar, Geraldine 30, 62, 71, 111, 125, 129, 143, 152, 154, 170, 184, 194, 195

Farwel, Arthur Burrage 83
Fauré, Gabriel 45
Faye, Stanley K 126
Fenn, Jean 198
Ferrier, Paul 162
Février, Henri 73, 123, 134
Fielden, Lionel 162
Fitzmaurice, George 187
Flagstad, Kirsten 193
Fletcher, Richard D 39, 43, 44, 53, 87, 99, 166, 172
Forbes-Robertson, Johnston 35
Forrest, Hamilton 171, 196
Fox, William 125
France, Anatole 86, 129
Fremstad, Olive 51, 61, 66, 143
Froelich, Bianca 66
Fugère, Lucien 13, 14, 15, 25, 30, 35, 45

Galli, Rosina 184
Galli-Curci, Amelita 134, 138, 145, 147
Gallieni, General Joseph Simon 119
Gandrey-Rety, Jean 161
Ganz, Rudolph 167, 187
Garden, Agnes 1
Garden, Amy (Mrs Edward Walsh; Mrs George Bower) 1, 56, 149, 199
Garden, Helen (Mrs Hélène Goetschel) 184, 199
Garden, Mrs Mary (Joss) 1, 3
Garden, Neville 200
Garden, Robert Davidson 1, 3, 6, 7, 55, 123, 159
Garrigue, Mme 116
Gatti-Casazza, Giulio 27, 64, 131
Gauthier-Villars, Henry 79, 80
Gay, Maria 94
George of Greece, King 36, 46, 62
Gerville-Réache, Jeanne 95
Gest, Morris 159
Gheusi, P B 136
Gibbon, Margot 174, 185
Gieseking, Walter 173
Gilbert, Sir William 4
Giordano, Umberto 81
Glasser, Alfred 172
Gluck, Alma 154
Goetschel, Mario 184, 191
Goldwyn (Goldfish), Samuel 32, 128, 129, 132, 141

Goossens, Eugene 123, 167
Grehier, Léon 15, 70
Grovlez, Gabriel 150, 151, 152
Gugenheimer, Untermayer & Marshall 117
Guilbert, Yvette 136
Gunn, Glenn Dillard 114
Gunsbourg, Raoul 177

Hackett, Carleton 75, 126, 145
Hackett, Charles 174
Hahn, Reynaldo 188
Hale, Philip 104
Halévy, Fromental 12
Halévy, Ludovic 12
Hammerstein, Mrs 148
Hammerstein, Oscar 48, 49, 50, 51, 55, 59, 66, 67, 72, 74, 75, 76, 77, 80, 93, 102, 128, 134, 135, 146
Hanau, César 162
Handler, Louis 80
Hansen, Jack Winsor 48, 49, 69
Harlow, Jean 188
Hedley, Charles 167
Hempel, Frieda 115, 116
Herbert, Victor 76, 87, 196
Herman, Edward 158
Hertz, Alfred 51
Heugel, Henri Georges 26, 27
Hill, Barre 36, 173, 174
Hiller, Paul 61
Hirsch, Max 89, 90
Hogan, Agnes Gordon 113
Honegger, Arthur 165
Horan, Harold 169
Horgan, Paul 184
Howe, Gene 171, 173
Hubbard, W L 137
Huneker, James 69, 135, 136, 142, 143

Ince, Tom 123
Insull, Samuel 151, 152, 153, 163, 176, 180, 181, 182, 196

Jardon, Dorothy 143, 144, 147
Jehin, Léon 29
Jepson, Helen 186
Jeritza, Maria 168
Johnstone, Robert E 108, 123, 124
Jolson, Al 187
Judson, Arthur 180

Kaart, Caroline 197
Kahn, Otto 75, 152
Kaiser, Horst 185, 186
Kardux, Earl 160
Kellogg, Clara Louise 10
Kemp, Robert 136
Kerrin, Very Rev. Richard E 200
Kiepura, Jan 187
Koussevitsky, Sergei 179
Krehbiel, Henry 95
Kuznetsova, Maria 91, 134

Lambert, Lucien 25
Landry, Louis 31, 33
Lane, Katherine 141
Langtry, Lily 162
Lanza, Mario 198
Lauder, Harry 108
Lauri-Volpi, Giacomo 161
Le Flem, Paul 182
Leblanc, Georgette 30, 32, 33, 71
Lebrun, President Albert 180
Leoncavallo, Ruggiero 114
Leroux, Xavier 41
Leslie, Amy 68, 69
Liebling, Estelle 192
Lindberg, Charles 168
Lombardi, Vincenzo 71
Long, Robert 185
Longone, Paolo 161
Loti, Pierre 30
Louÿs, Pierre 47, 182

MacDonald, Jeanette 187
Mackay, Mrs Clarence (Anna Case) 195
Macomber, King 161
Maeterlinck, Maurice 30, 32, 33, 42, 49, 61, 71, 73, 141, 162
Mahler, Gustav 81
Malone, Dudley Field 158
Manners, Lady Diana 159
Mapleson, Col. James 15
Marbury, Bessie 118, 125
Marchesi, Mathilde 10, 11, 12, 26
Marinuzzi, Gino 143, 144, 196
Markus, Herr 81
Marnold, Jean 50
Martin, Linton 171
Martinelli, Giovanni 113
Mascagni, Pietro 26
Mason, Dr 178

Massenet, Jules 12, 14, 16, 28, 37, 45, 65, 69, 71, 102, 109, 115, 160
Masson, Louis 165
Mastio, Catherine 19
Maudru, Pierre 164
Mavrocordato, Prince 63, 70, 71, 72
Maxwell, Elsa 154
Mayer, David 7, 16, 49, 68, 69, 71, 143
Mayer, Ed 15, 70
Mayer, Louis 187, 188
Mayer, Margaret 188
Mayer, Mrs Florence 6, 7, 9, 13, 15, 59, 68, 69, 70, 71, 143
Mayo, Margaret 129
McCay, Neil 14
McCormack, John 77, 81, 117, 133
McCormic, Mary 157, 164
McCormick, Harold F 75, 84, 144, 146, 148, 150, 153
McCormick, Mrs Edith Rockefeller 150, 151, 153, 196
Melba, Dame Nellie 7, 40, 44, 46, 47, 59, 60, 68, 69, 131
Meltzer, Charles Henry 95, 99, 114
Merimée, Prosper 86, 98
Merola, Gaetano 180
Messager, André 20, 21, 22, 26, 27, 28, 29, 30, 31, 35, 36, 56, 60, 63, 79, 92, 93
Meyer-Helmund, Erik 5
Miranda, Beatrice 198
Mocchi, Walter 146
Montagne, François 158
Montemezzi, Italo 160, 161, 197
Moore, Edward H 82, 158, 160, 162, 163, 167, 168, 185
Moore, Grace 154, 158, 164, 170, 177, 184, 185, 187, 190
Moore, Val 190
Morgan, Gwen 192
Morgan, Anne 118
Morlay, Madeleine (Mrs Vanni Marcoux) 116
Morner, Stanley 188
Morris, Chief of Police 151
Morris, Clara 4
Mozart, Wolfgang Amadeus 44, 52
Muratore, Lucien 91, 92, 115, 116, 131, 145, 152, 154
Murkland, Mrs 3

Mussolini, Benito 162
Muzio, Claudia 168, 176

Namara, Marguerite 152
Napoleon III 184
Newby, Helen 109
Newby, John 109
Nijinsky, Vaslav 127
Norbeck, Senator 178
Nordica, Lillian 9, 81, 89, 101, 102,
   143

Paderewski, Ignacy 55
Paget, Lady 122
Parratt, Sir Walter 47
Parsons, Louella 131, 133
Pavlova, Anna 146
Payen, Louis 137
Peeler, Clare 99
Pierné, Gabriel 26, 50
Plançon, Pol 9, 39
Platy, Fernand 45
Plessis, Pierre 169
Polacco, Giorgio 151, 152, 167
Pons, Lily 192
Poor, Henry W 143
Pope, Col. George 4, 5
Porter, Cole 157, 187, 195
Porter, Linda 157, 187
Potter, Howard E 149, 163
Primoli, Count Giuseppe 46
Prokofiev, Sergei 150, 154
Puccini, Giacomo 30, 103
Pugno, Raoul 149

Quin, Jeremiah 84

Rabaud, Henri 92
Rabinoff, Max 123
Raisa, Rosa 138, 148, 161
Raney, Bill 191
Rascoe, Burton 143
Ravel, Maurice 50
Ravelle, Hamilton 129, 131
Rawling, Sylvester 95, 132
Reardon, Billy 158
Reed, Fanny 102
Reinhardt, Max 159
Renaud, Maurice 10, 45, 57, 63, 72, 80,
   100, 136
Ricordi, Tito 83

Ricou, Georges 165
Rioton, Marthe 19, 20, 25
Robinson-Duff, Mrs 5, 7, 9, 10, 11, 12,
   60
Rockefeller, John D 177
Rogers, George 87
Rolland, Romain 50
Rollot, Jean 182
Ronald, Landon 46
Roof, Katherine M 64
Roosevelt, Colonel Theodore 79, 91,
   125
Roosevelt, Theodore jr 134
Rosenfeld, Maurice 134
Roze, Marie 2, 15
Rubinstein, Artur 135
Ruffo, Titta 114, 145, 148
Russell, Henry 52, 104

Sabin, Stewart 169
Sahara-Dejeli 80
Saint-Saëns, Camille 10, 37, 44
Saint-Gaudens, Augustus 143
Sammarco, Mario 88, 105, 107
Sanborn, Pitts 147
Sanderson, Sibyl 9, 12, 17, 19, 20, 22,
   28, 30, 36, 37, 42, 49, 60, 68, 69, 81,
   143
Sard, Frederick N 146
Sardou, Victorien 27, 43
Sbriglia, Giovanni 9, 10, 13
Schaffer, John C 75
Schirmer, Gustave 50
Schlippenbach, Baron 82
Schmuck, Justice 178
Schwab, Arnold T 143
Scotti, Antonio 117, 122
Sébastian, Georges 192
Sembrich, Marcella 59
Shawe-Taylor, Desmond 44, 88, 99,
   166
Sheean, Vincent 199
Sheldon, Edward 196
Sills, Beverly 187, 192
Singher, Martial 194, 195
Skelton, Mrs Nellie 6
Skinner, Mr and Mrs Otis 122
Smallens, Alexander 196
Smith, Cecil 196
Smith, J Carleton 194, 199
Smith, Moses 179

Smith, Walter 4
Spangler, George M 146
Speyer, Lord and Lady 50
Steward, Leroy T 83
Stewart, Madeau 3, 199
Stichel, Mme 79
Stinson, Eugene 196
Stone, Bentley 174
Stotesbury, E T 117
Strauss, Richard 42, 50, 51, 52, 61, 62, 79, 119, 125
Stuart, Paul 79
Sullivan, Ed 198
Sullivan, Sir Arthur 4
Sunday, Billy 89
Supervia, Conchita 176
Swarthout, Gladys 187, 195
Swindall, Bart 163, 172
Sylva, Marguerite 24, 91, 94

Taft, President William H 76
Talma, François 43
Telva, Marion 184
Tempest, Marie 122
Temple, Hope (Mrs André Messager) 26, 31
Tennyson, Jean 186, 192
Ternina, Milka 56
Terry, Antonio 13, 17
Tetrazzini, Luisa 59, 60, 66, 67, 72, 75, 110, 111
Teyte, Maggie 47, 48, 49, 61, 95, 105, 184, 195, 197, 199
Thomas, Ambroise 5, 13
Thompson, Fanchon 5, 15
Tibaldi, Arturo 88
Tilden, Ben 168
Tolstoi, Count Paul 37
Toscanini, Arturo 117, 134
Tosti, Francesco Paolo 47
Truman, President Harry S 194

Ulrich, Bernard 140

Van Dresser, Marcia 5
van Dyck, Ernest 39
Van Grove, Isaac 142
Van Studdiford, Grace 5
Van Vechten, Carl 36, 63, 70, 84, 191, 195
Vanderbilt, Mrs W K 134
Vanni-Marcoux 104, 105, 107, 108, 112, 113, 114, 116, 161, 173, 174
Venturini, Emilio 113
Verlaine, Paul 43
Villa, Pancho 149
Villiani, Luisa 196
von Hofmannsthal, Hugo 62
von Kraft, Herr 82
von Schuch, Ernst 51
von Suppé, Franz 178
Vuillemin, L 61, 73, 81

Wagner, Charles L 52, 138, 145, 146, 153, 176, 177, 178, 180
Wagner, Richard 61, 113, 118
Wallenborn, Robert 186, 187
Walska, Ganna 144, 147, 184
Walter, Bruno 196
Wayne, Frances 90
White, Carolina 105
Whitehill, Clarence 14
Wiesner, Chief 159
Wilde, Oscar 42, 50, 67
Wittich, Marie 50
Woodward, Stanley 194

Youssoupoff, Prince Felix 162
Ysaÿe, Eugène 103

Zenatello, Giovanni 46, 66
Zendt, Marie 185